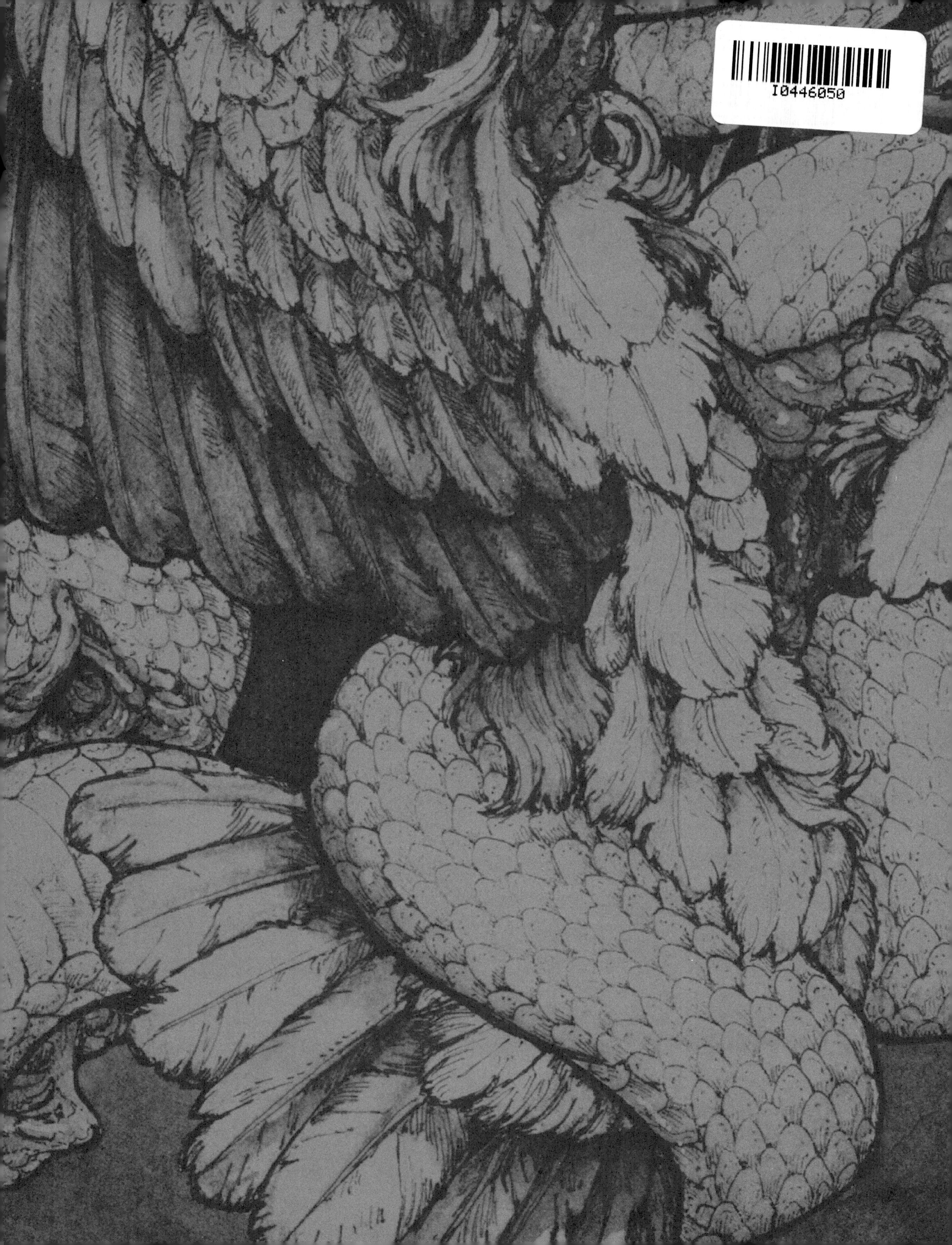

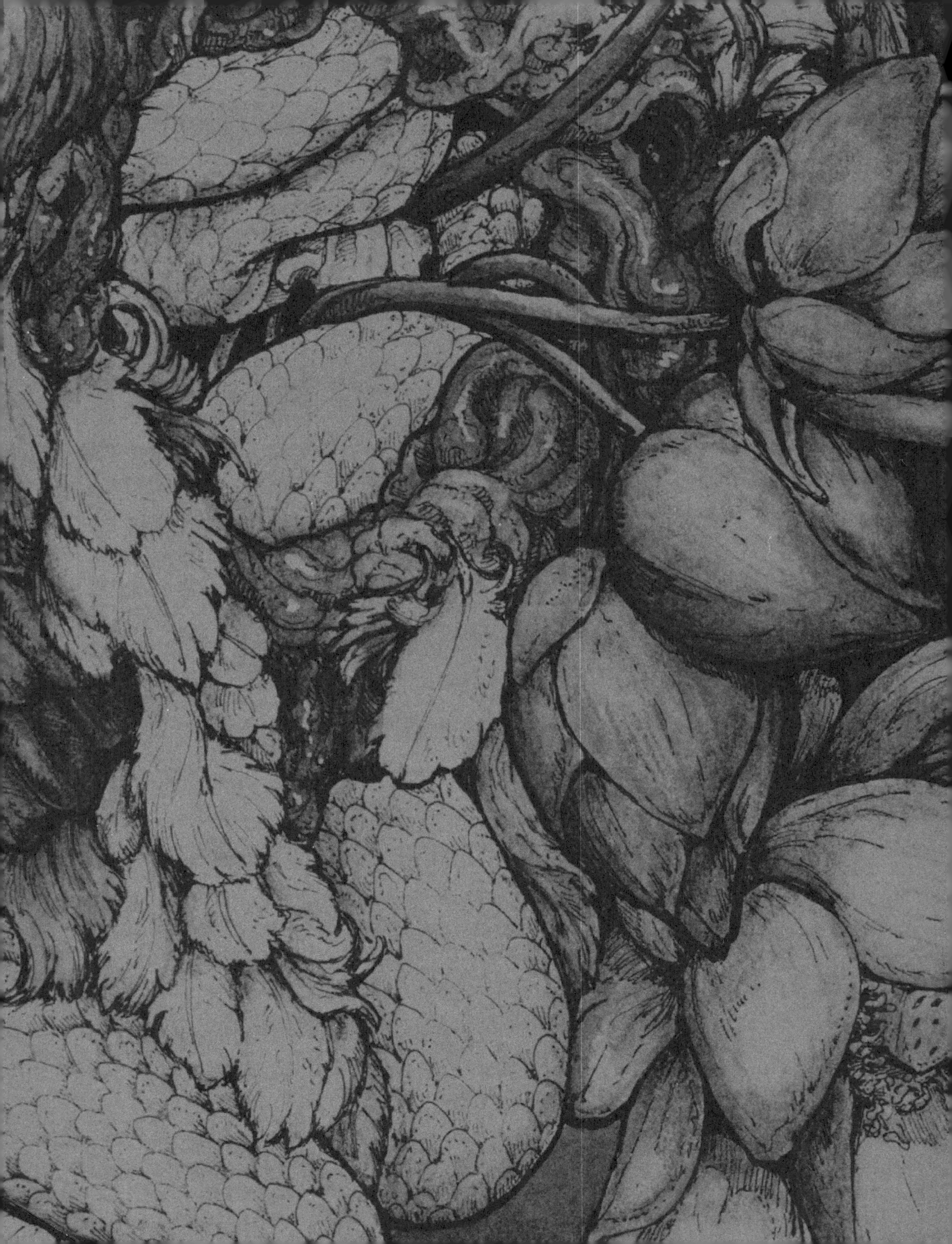

SACRED DECAY

THE ART OF LAUREN MARX™

SECOND EDITION

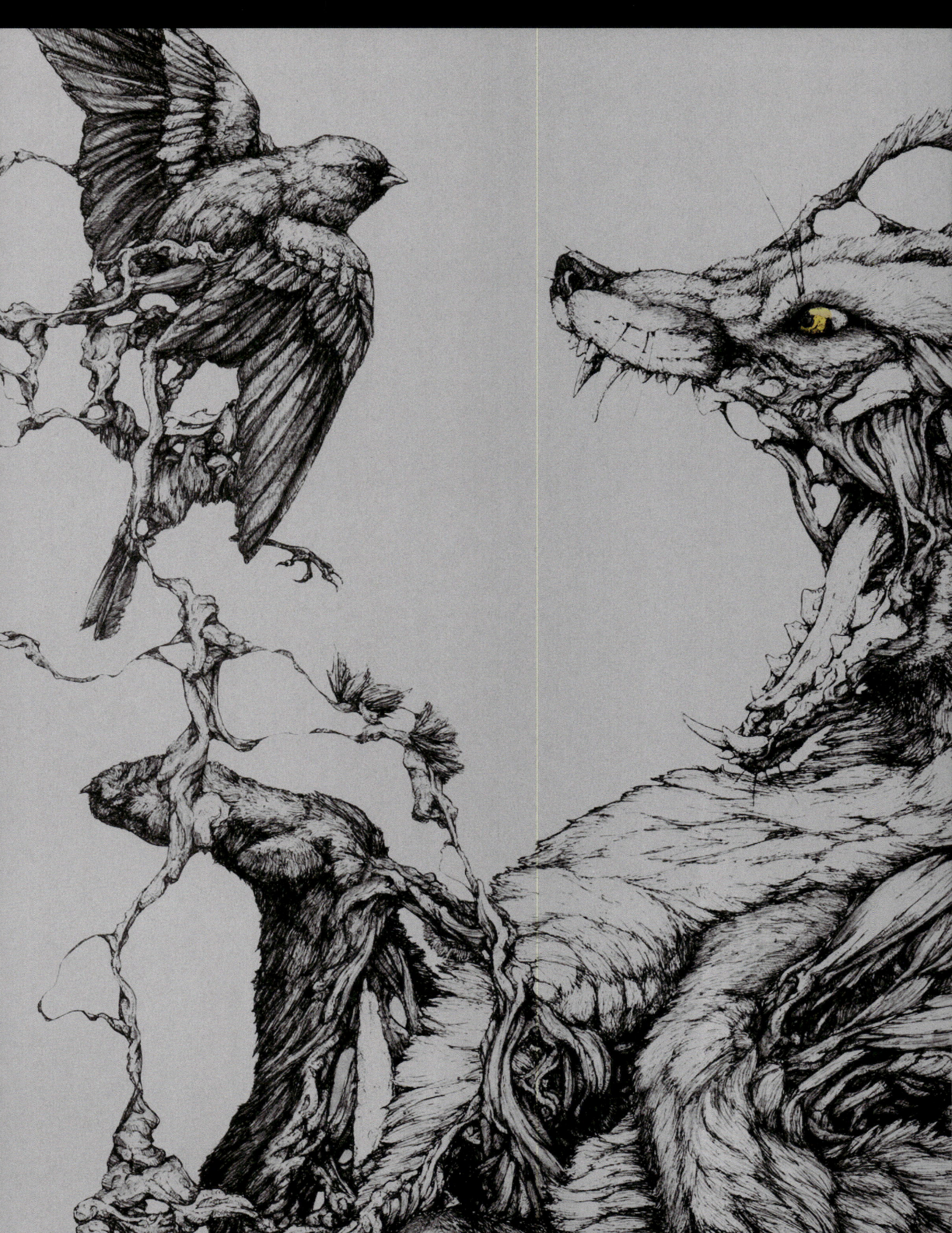

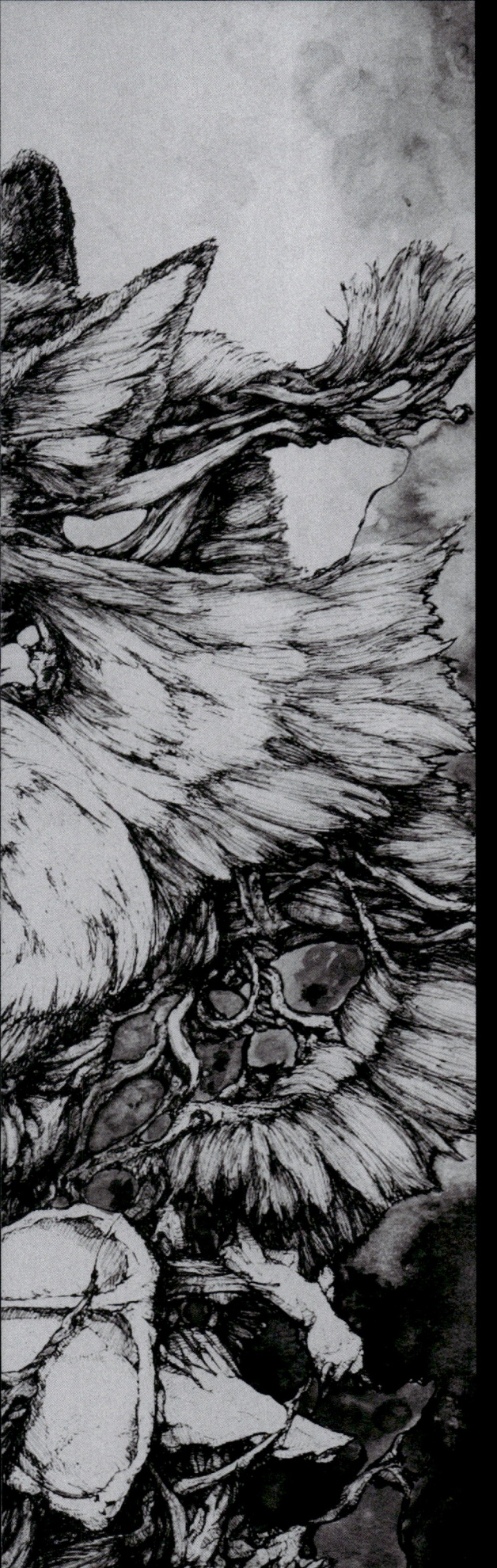

SACRED

THE ART O

Foreword
Introdu

DEDICATION

This book is dedicated to my mom, MARTHA, who has supported me with endless inspiration and love.

President and Publisher MIKE RICHARDSON

Editor JENNY BINGHAM-BLENK

Assistant Editor MISHA GEHR

Designers CINDY CACEREZ-SPRAGUE & KRISTOFER McRAE

Digital Art Technician CHRIS HORN

PrePress Technician RIKKI MIDNIGHT

Special thanks to RACHEL ROBERTS AND KONNER KNUDSEN.

SACRED DECAY: THE ART OF LAUREN MARX™
Second Edition © 2025 Lauren Marx. All rights reserved. All other material, unless otherwise specified, is © 2025 Dark Horse Comics LLC. Dark Horse Books® and the Dark Horse logo are registered trademarks of Dark Horse Comics LLC. All rights reserved. Dark Horse is part of Embracer Group. No portion of this publication may be reproduced or transmitted, in any form or by any means, without the express written permission of the copyright holders.

Dark Horse Books
A division of Dark Horse Comics LLC
10956 S.E. Main Street
Milwaukie OR 97222

Represented in the EU by
Authorised Rep Compliance Ltd.
Ground Floor, 71 Lower Baggot Street
Dublin, D02 P593, Ireland
ARCCompliance.com

DarkHorse.com | LaurenMarx.com

Printed in China. | Second edition: July 2025
Ebook ISBN 978-1-50674-942-6
Hardcover ISBN 978-1-50674-937-2
10 9 8 7 6 5 4 3 2 1

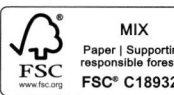
MIX
Paper | Supporting responsible forestry
FSC® C189328

PAUL SCHWAKE Chief Operations Officer
TOM WEDDLE Chief Financial Officer
DALE LaFOUNTAIN Chief Information Officer
TIM WIESCH Vice President of Licensing
VANESSA TODD-HOLMES Vice President of Production and Scheduling
MARK BERNARDI Vice President of Book Trade and Digital Sales
RANDY LAHRMAN Vice President of Product Development and Sales
CARA O'NEIL Vice President of Marketing
DAVE MARSHALL Editor in Chief
MELISSA TEEMAN Controller

Library of Congress Cataloging-in-Publication Data

Names: Marx, Lauren, 1991- artist, writer of introduction.
Title: Sacred decay : the art of Lauren Marx / foreword by Daniel W. Wright ; introduction by Lauren Marx.
Description: Second edition. | Milwaukie, OR : Dark Horse Books, [2025] | Summary: "A Stunning Depiction of Visceral Truth Fungus blooms and dies, bones weather, and moths form halos around dismembered animals in this darkly exquisite collection from acclaimed artist Lauren Marx, now celebrated in a second edition! With an impressive eye for detail, Marx brings her. Uncanny subjects to life-or death-with awe-inspiring texture and intensity. Birds, beasts, fish, plants, and more unfurl radiantly on the page in their cycle of birth and destruction. This second edition of the celebrated collection features new cover art, an expanded sketchbook section, and an all-new introduction from the artist herself"-- Provided by publisher.
Identifiers: LCCN 2024060611 (print) | LCCN 2024060612 (ebook) | ISBN 9781506749372 (hardcover) | ISBN 9781506749426 (ebook)
Subjects: LCSH: Marx, Lauren, 1991---Themes, motives.
Classification: LCC N6537.M39355 A4 2025 (print) | LCC N6537.M39355 (ebook) | DDC 759.13--dc23/eng/20250205
LC record available at https://lccn.loc.gov/2024060611
LC ebook record available at https://lccn.loc.gov/2024060612

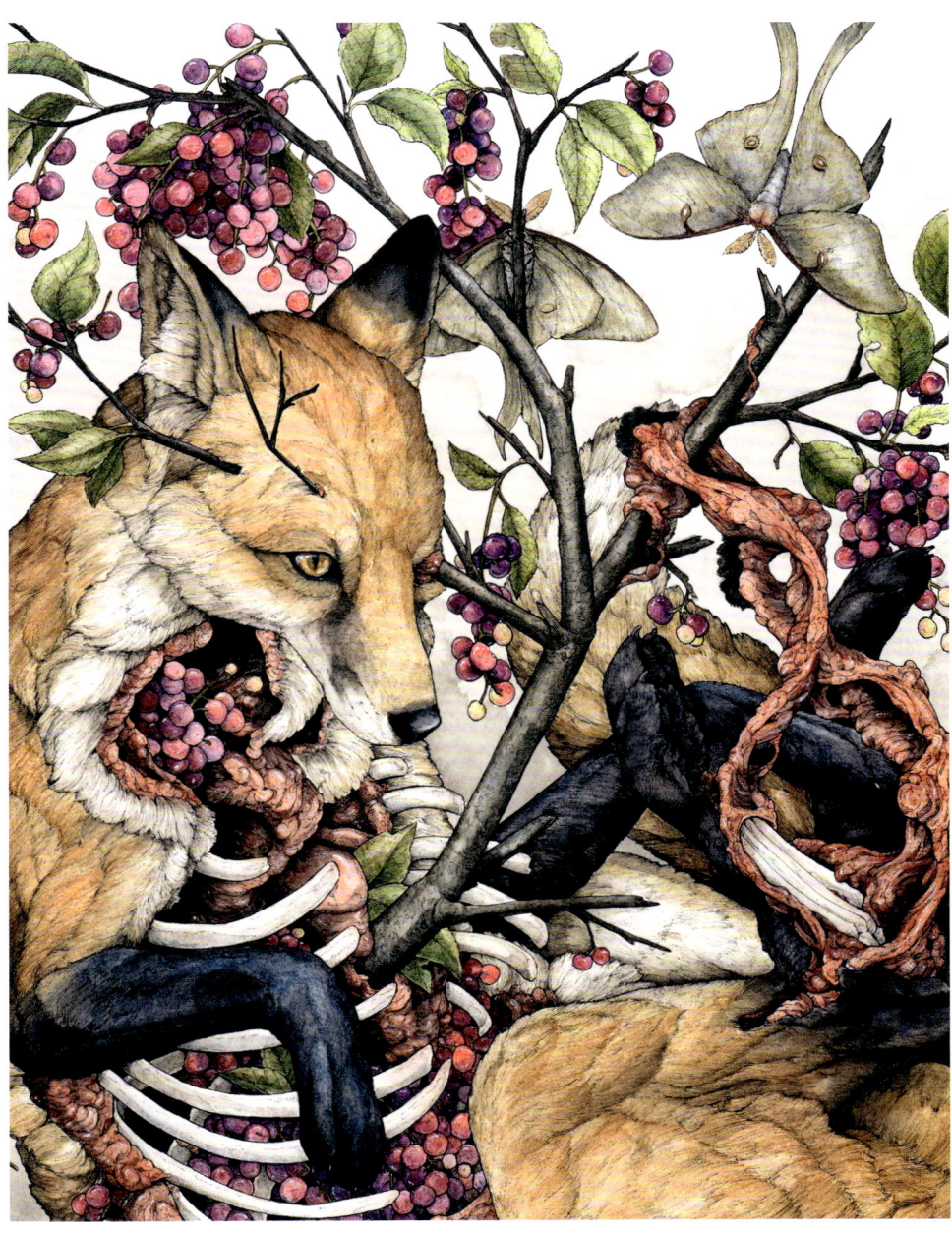

I've had the pleasure of knowing Lauren Marx for many years. When she and I first met, we were just two young artists spending time at a bar, working on our art during the day, talking about whatever we were working on at the moment and what was inspiring us.

Lauren's art spoke to me then as it does now. Her work is dark and mythic. Earthy yet majestic. Its demonstration of death is alive, makes you flash a devil's grin. It's the little things that always make me go back to Lauren's art. Her use of color is one of the best and, at times, mesmerizes. From a crown of moths to the regal positioning of an animal displaying its insides, her work speaks for those afraid of what may be hidden inside of them, a call to arms for the beauty of the human heart.

Sacred Decay is a perfect title for this book. It's an examination of the consequences of action and inaction, and peers into the notion that our insanities only confirm us to be the animals that we pretend not to be. Lauren's work shows nature for what it is—letting you see the decay of all things in such a way that it makes you appreciate life all the more.

Though it is human nature to run from death, acceptance of it that brings an extra light into life, a further appreciation for the temporary because all good things must pass. In the end, we are all just meat hoping to not spoil, because there are no do-overs. It's great art, like Lauren's, that inspires one to try and get it right the first time.

—**Daniel W. Wright,**
author of *Rodeo of the Soul*

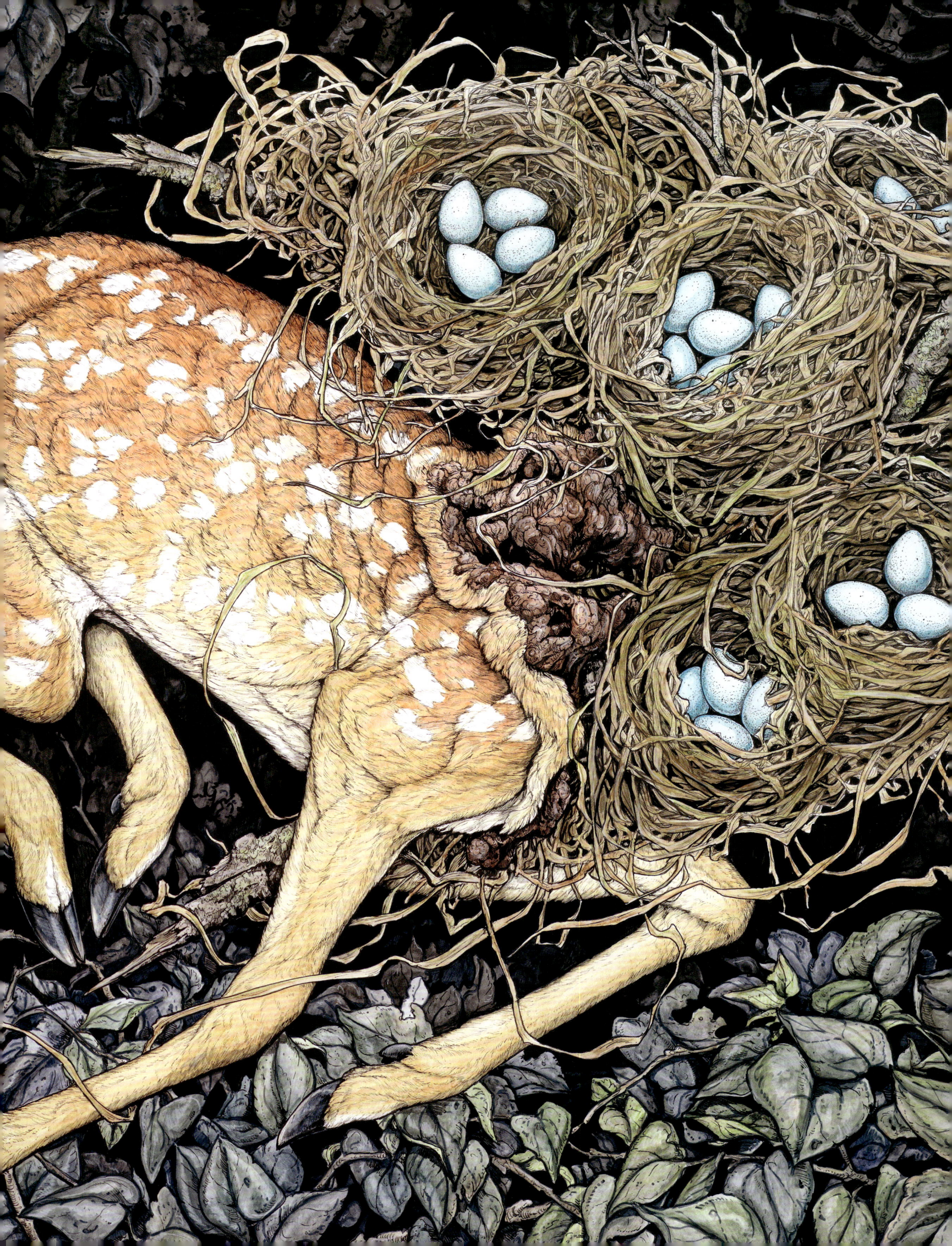

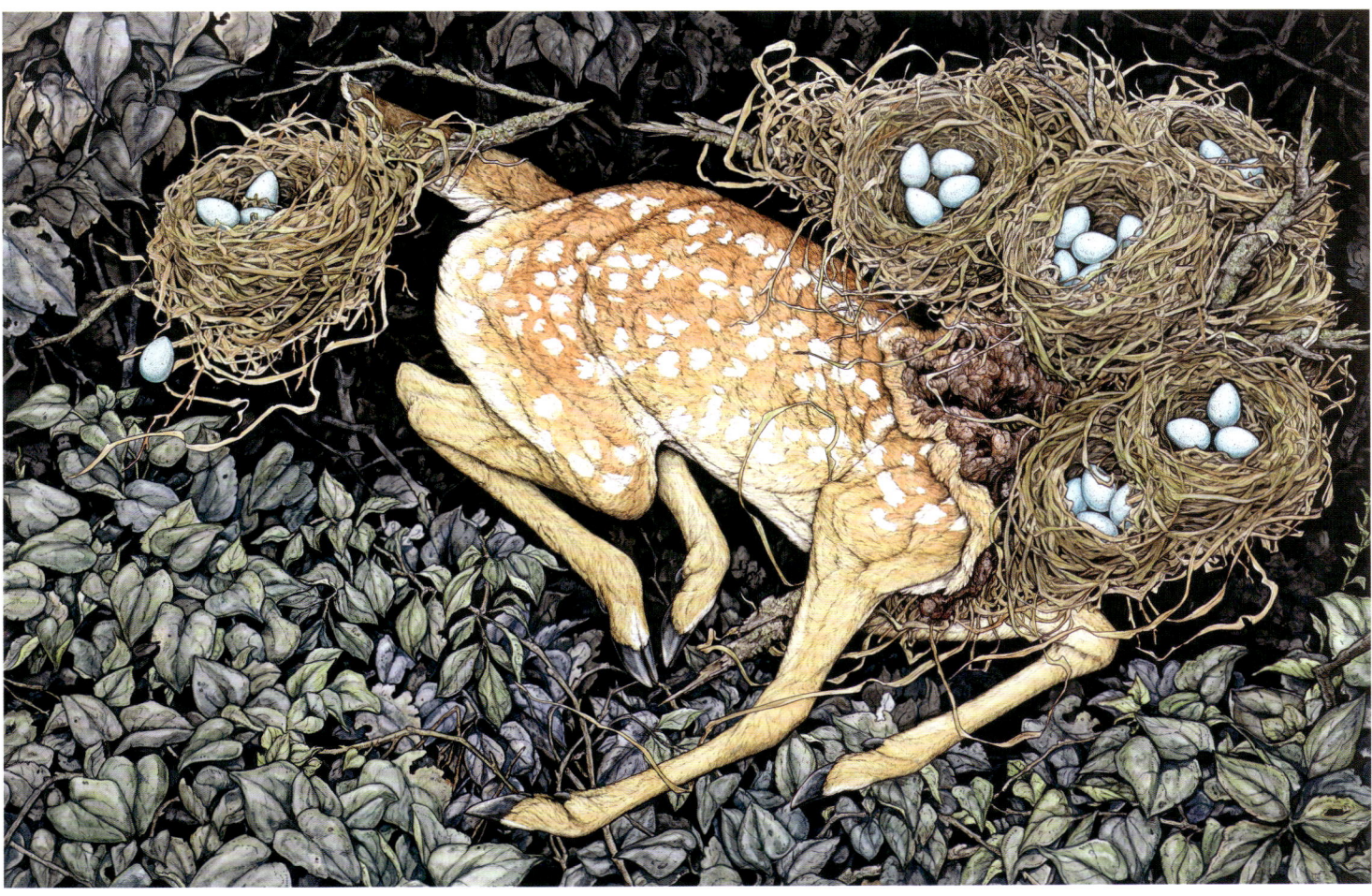

Hello, and thank you so much for picking up this book!

I am very excited to share with all of you the updated second edition of *Sacred Decay*, an artwork collection showcasing my personal favorite pieces chronologically from 2012 through 2019. This isn't the full body of my work, but these pieces have deep therapeutic meaning to me and are dear to my heart.

This book follows the evolution of the illustrative representations of my hopes, fears, struggles with mental illness, my past, interpersonal relationships, and my deep fear of the unknown of life after death. I use flora and fauna as my visual subjects, with the goal of confronting and healing myself on my ongoing quest to find what happiness and peace mean to me.

When editor Jenny Bingham-Blenk of Dark Horse Comics first reached out to me in 2016 with the proposal to make an art book, I was over the moon and still am. After three years of planning, *Sacred Decay* was officially completed in the winter of 2019. This beautiful book's reception led to multiple printings and now a shiny new second edition. It went above and beyond anything I could've ever imagined.

In this book you will see the evolution of my obsessively detailed watercolor and pen-focused mixed-media paintings as I have embraced more vibrant colors and complicated compositions, to better express my inner thoughts and feelings during the years of personal journey depicted within these pages. I hope you'll resonate with my love for undulating serpents, blooming plants, dancing moths, floating fawns, torn flesh, religious symbolism, folklore, and scientific illustrations.

I came from a family of artists who were very supportive of my dreams to pursue creating art, for which I am forever grateful. I am spoiled by the gorgeous natural world within driving distance of my home—the Saint Louis Zoo only a few miles away, the beautiful forested Midwestern nature reserves, and the hiking trails leading the way to the densely wooded hills of the Ozarks just south of St. Louis City. These places have always been a huge inspiration for my work.

Thank you so much for your support for not one, but two editions of this volume, and I hope you enjoy this beautiful book and all the artwork within.

—**Lauren Marx**

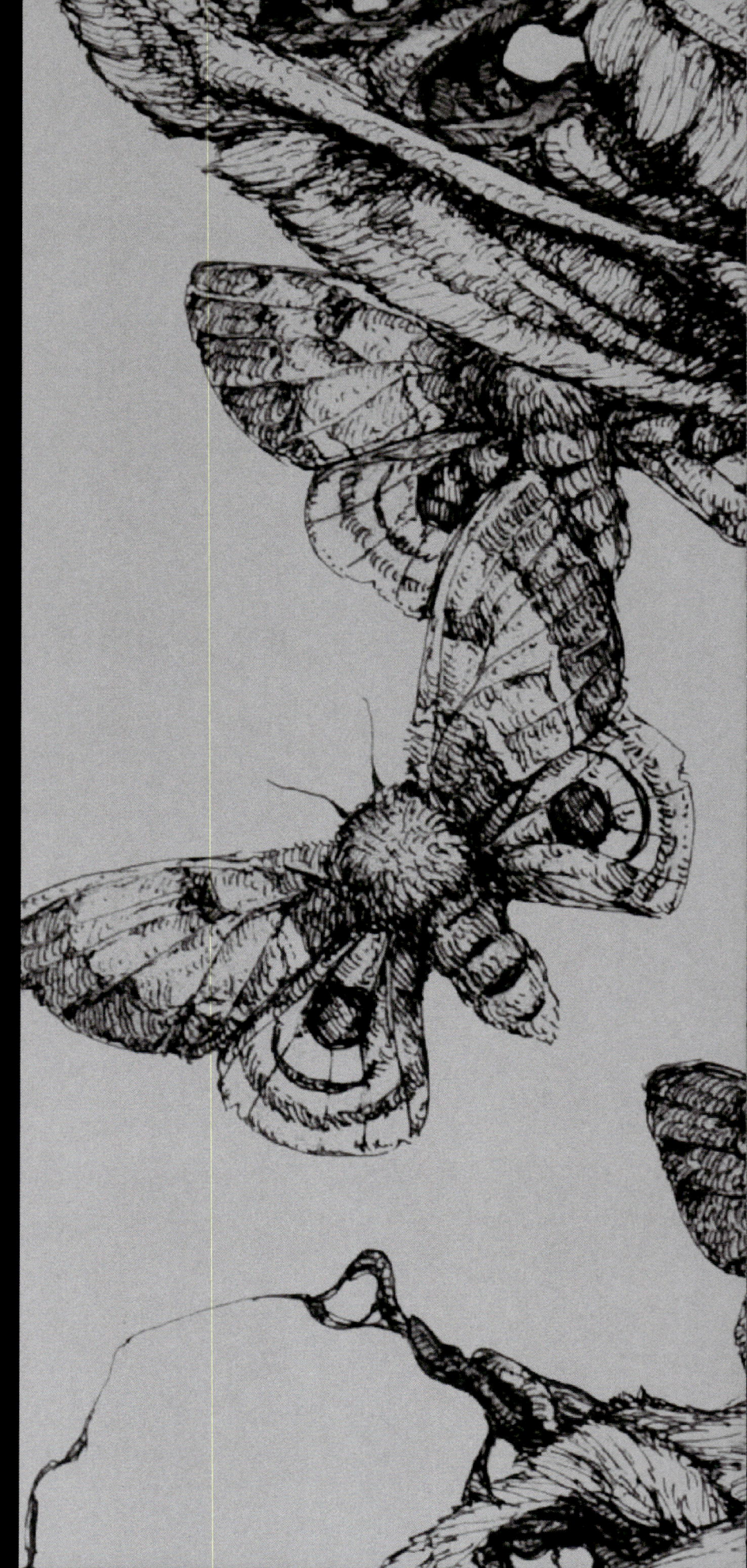

SACRED DECAY

2012–2014

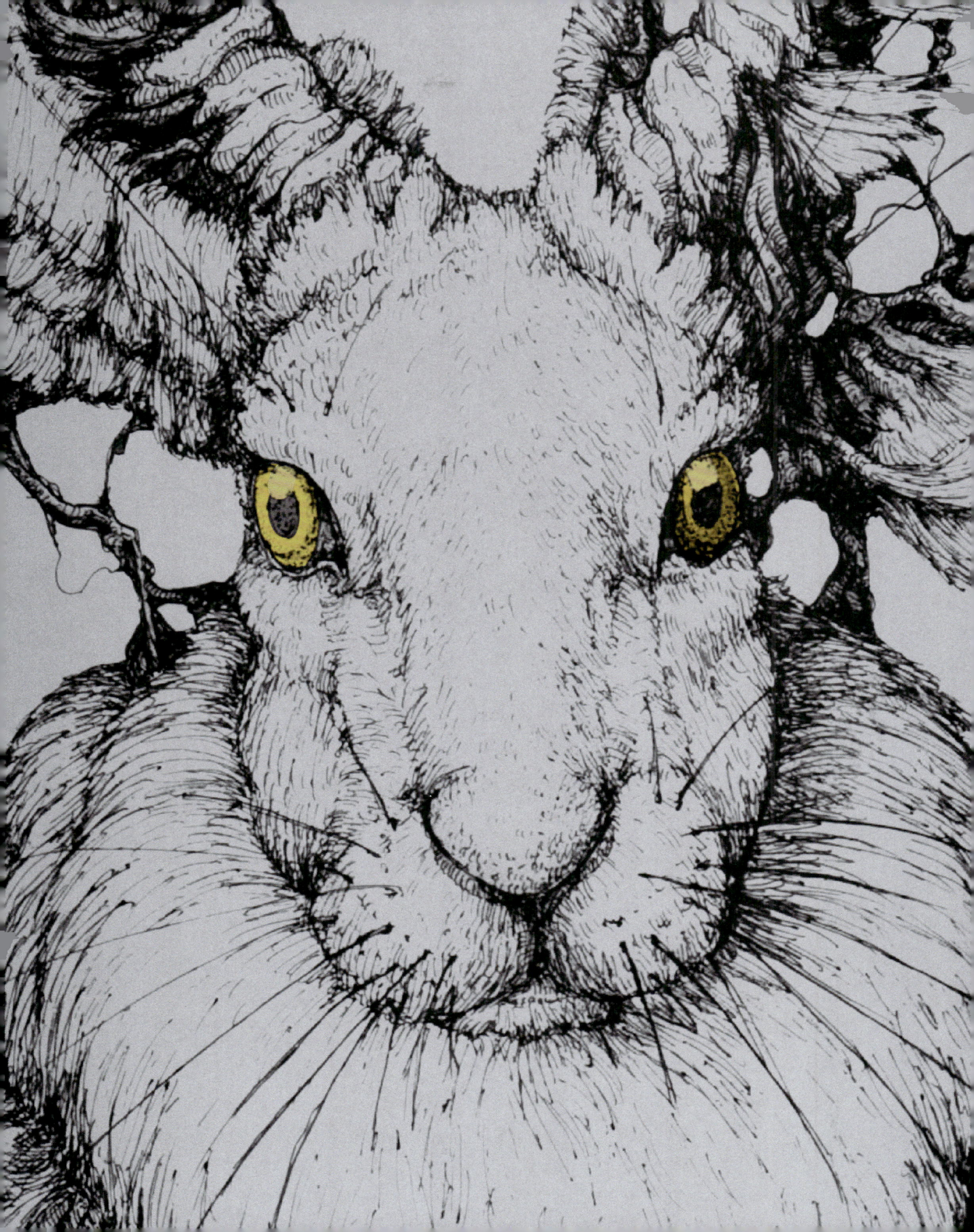

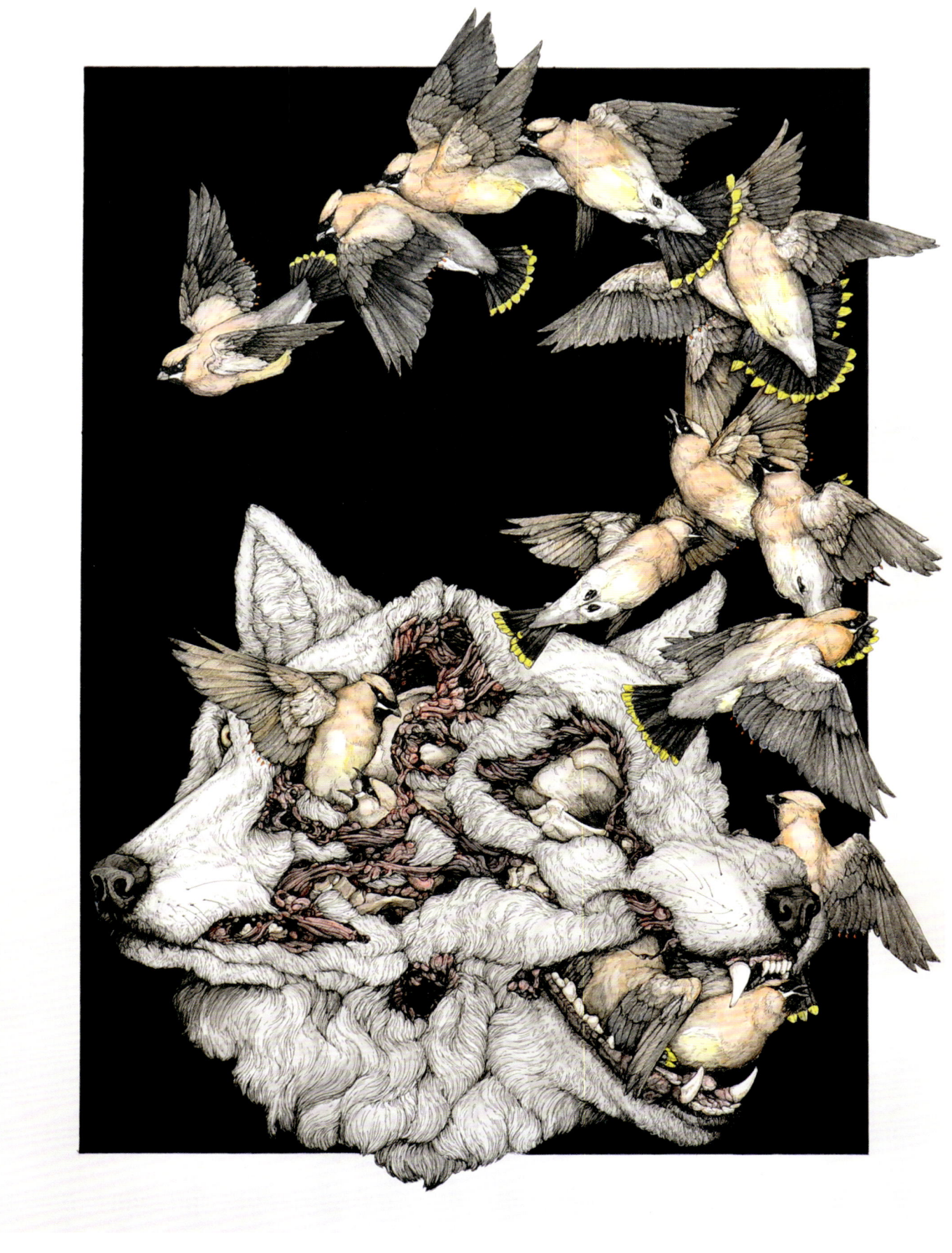

FIRE-BREATHER

18″ x 24″

Pen, ink, and colored pencil on paper

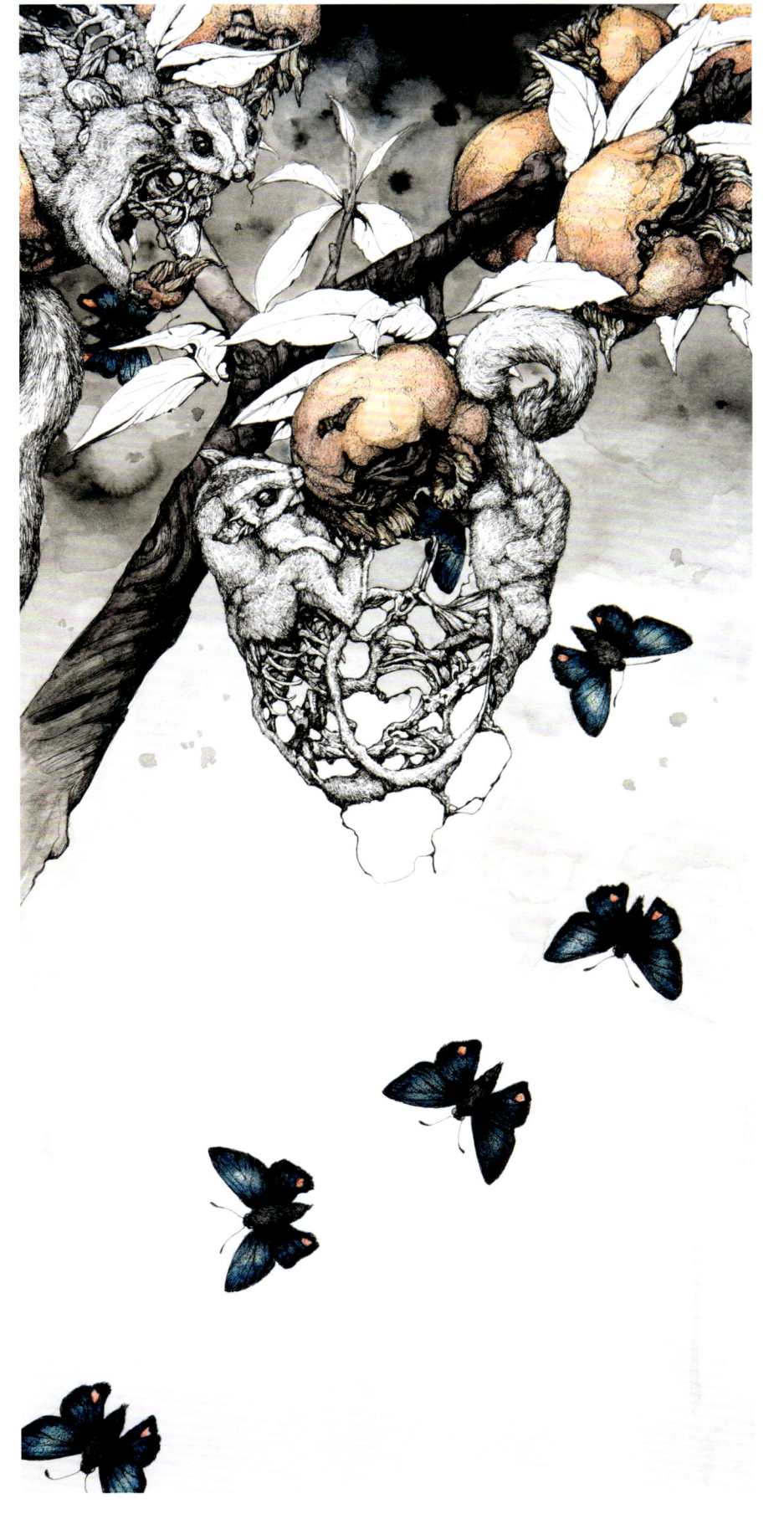

SUGAR GLIDERS

10" x 24"

Pen, ink, colored pencil, and gel pen on paper

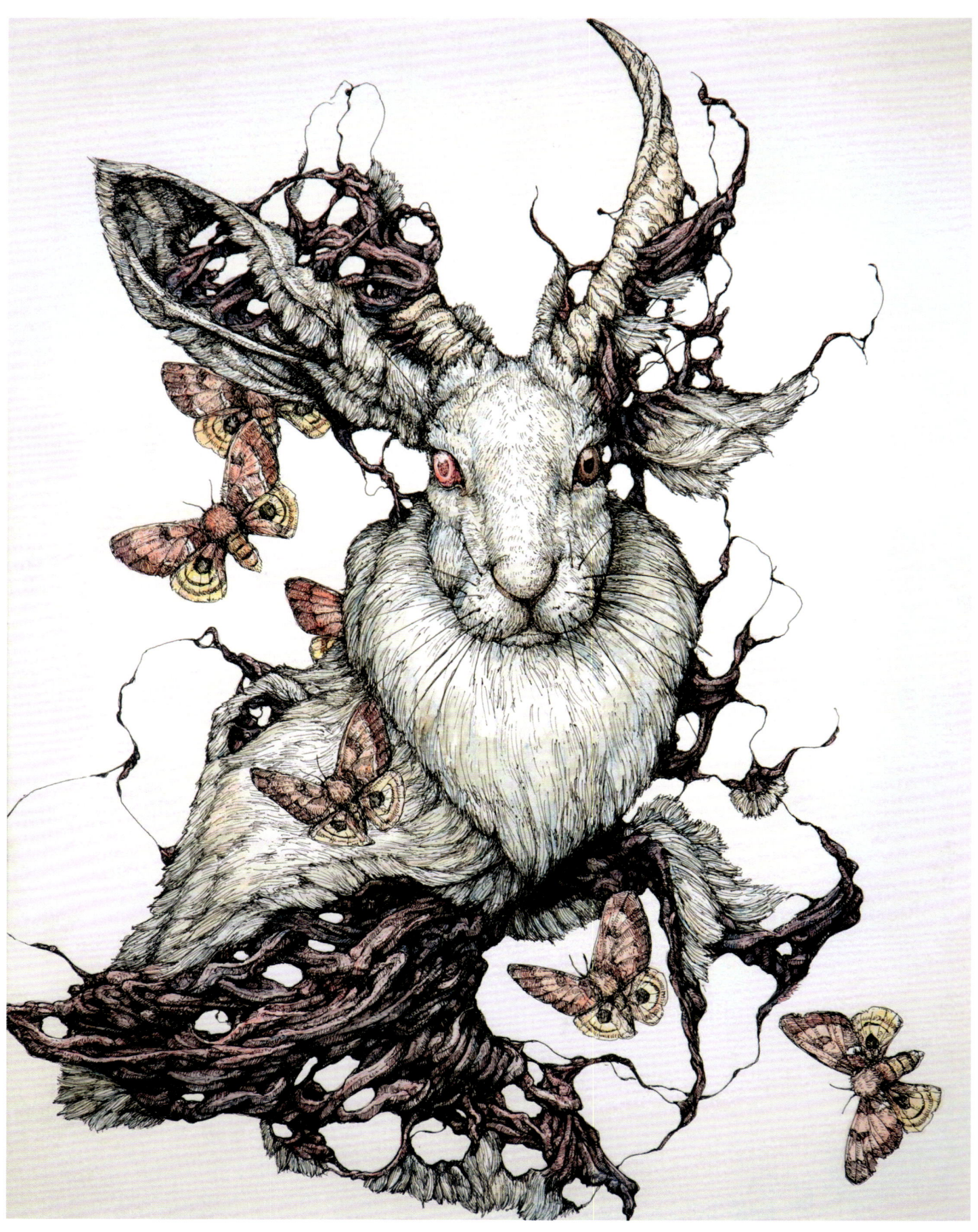

ALBINO JACKALOPE

11" x 14"

Pen and ink on paper

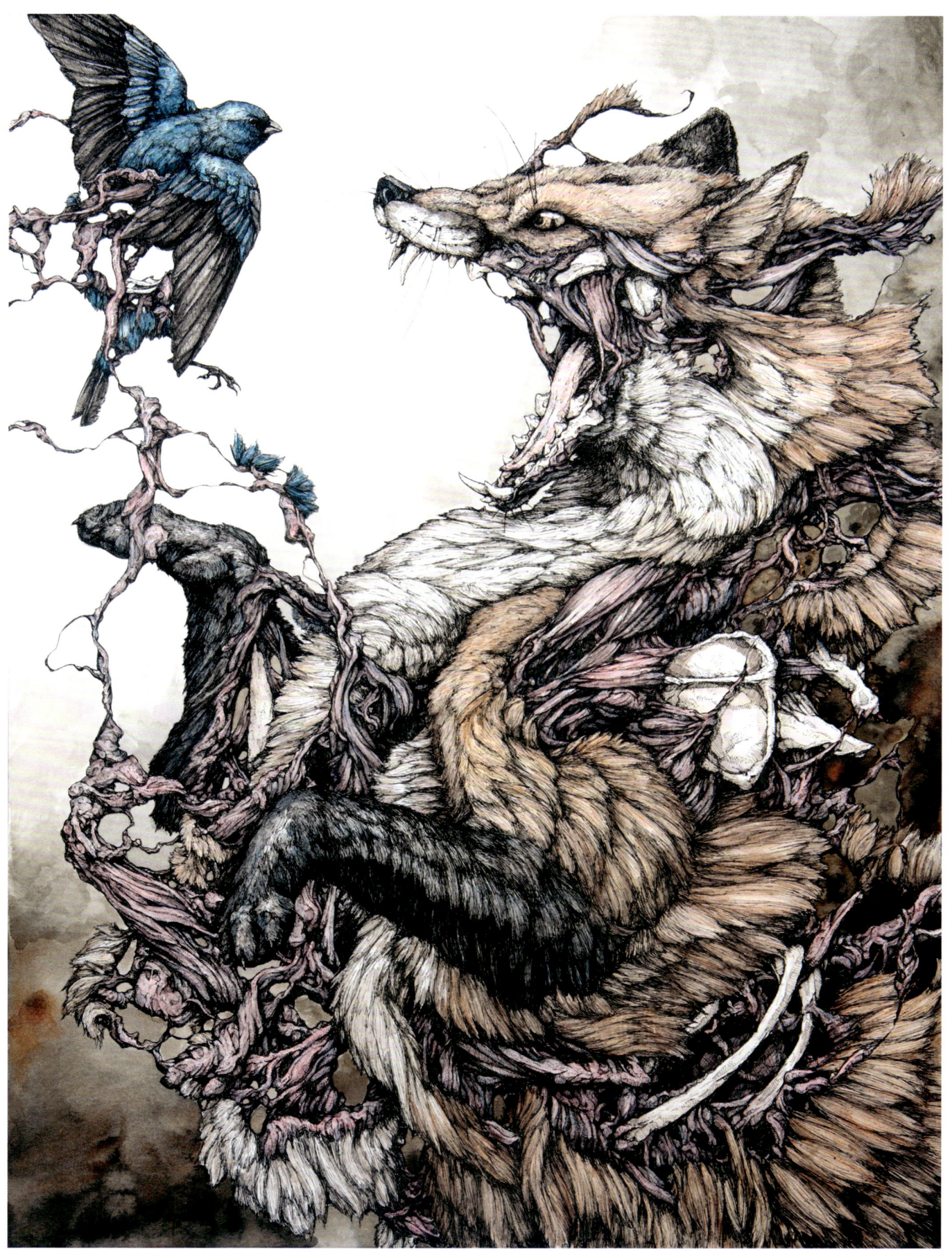

RED FOX AND INDIGO BUNTING

18" x 24"

Pen, ink, and gel pen on paper

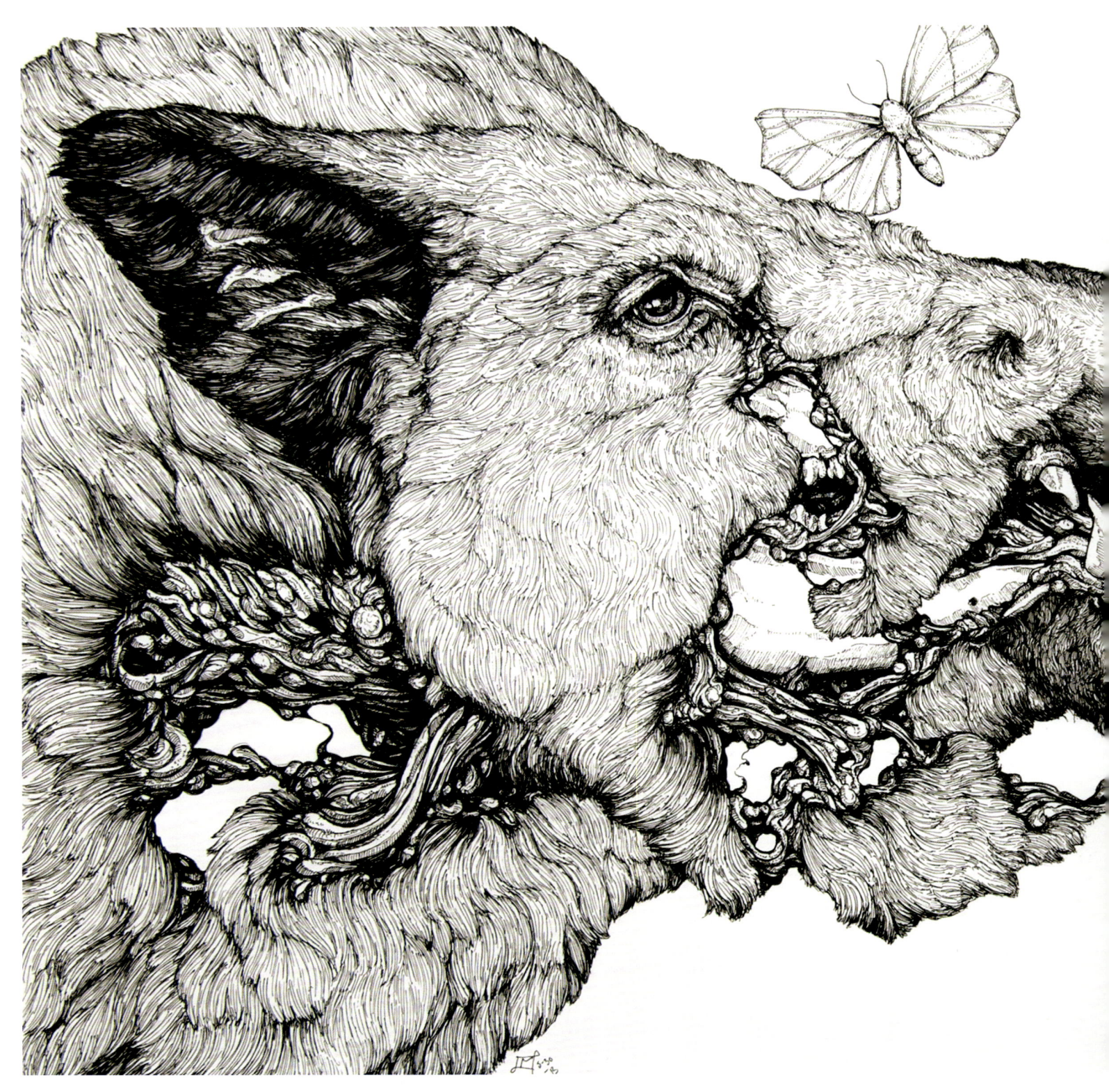

CHURNING UP THE STARS

23.75″ x 11.25″

Pen on paper

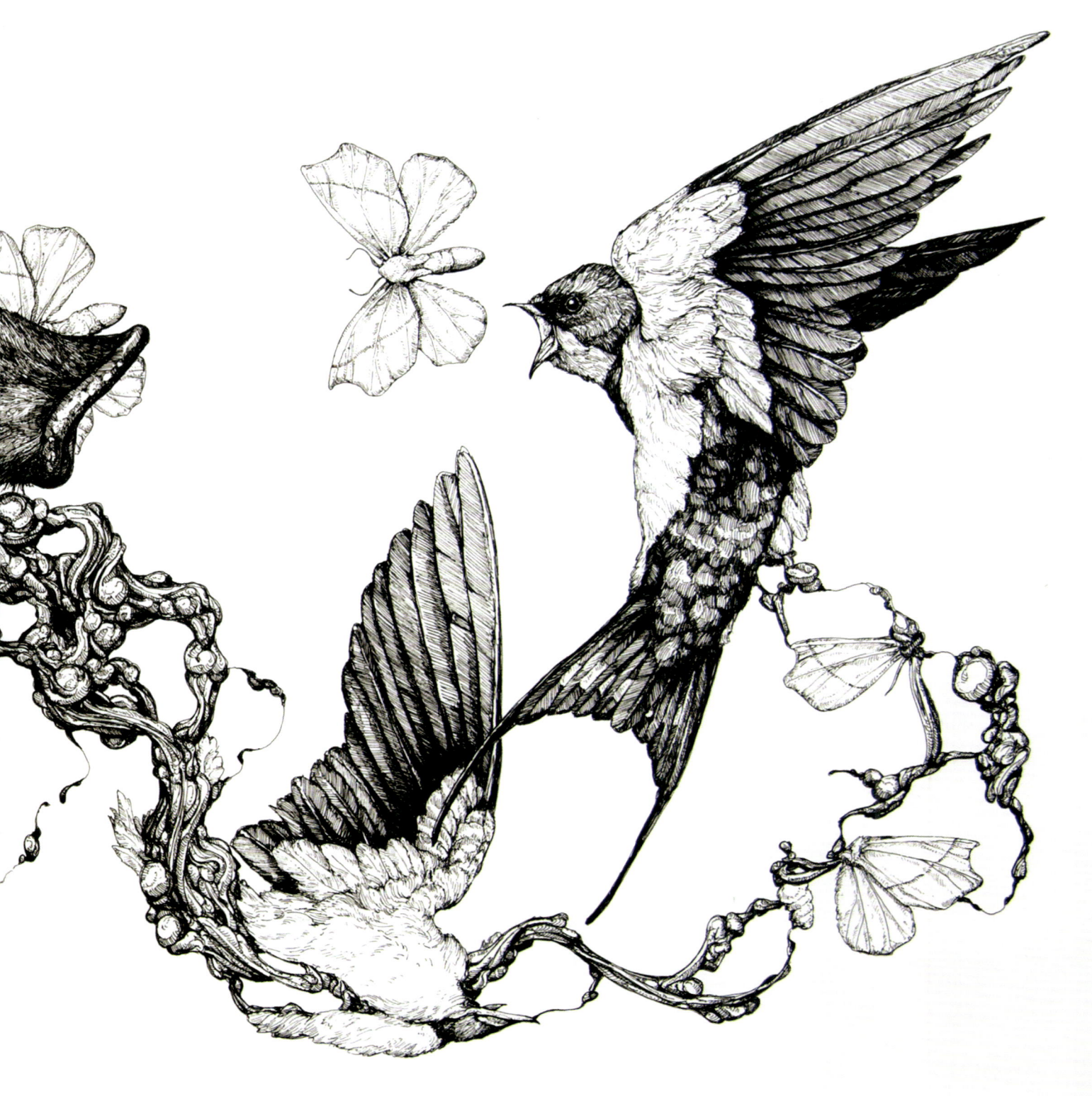

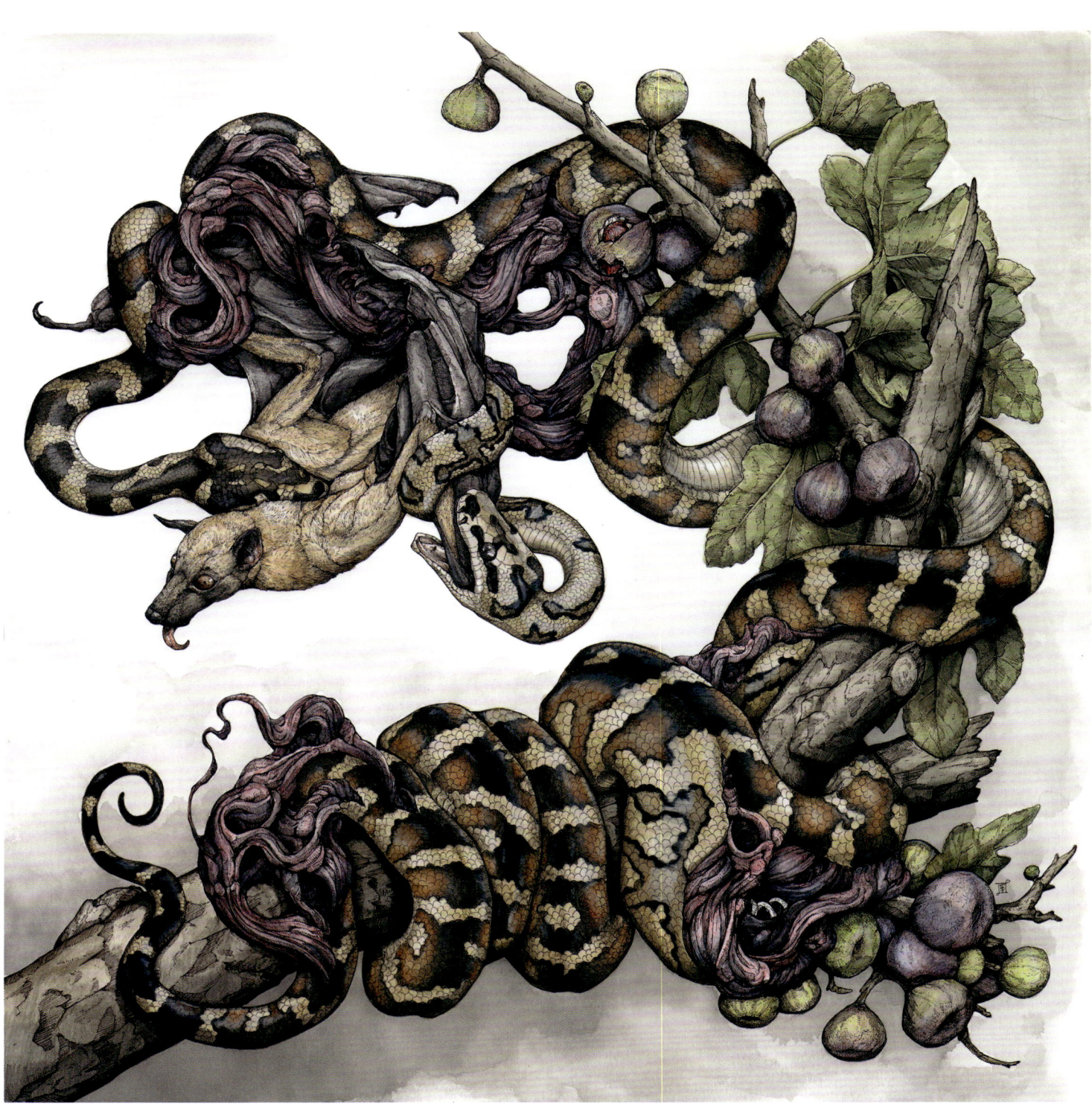

UNTITLED: COMMISSION

24" x 24"

Pen, ink, and colored pencil on paper

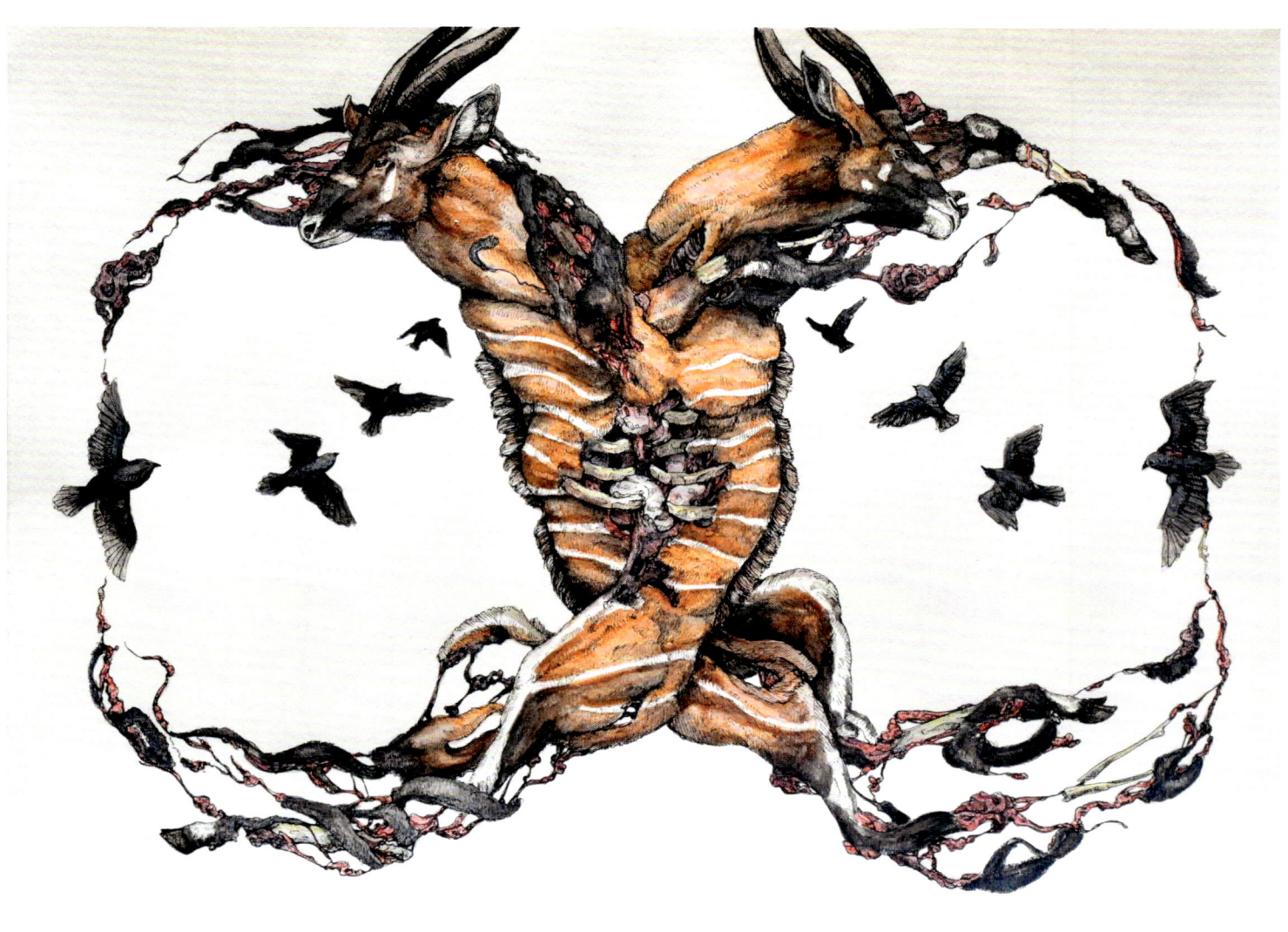

BOW TIE NEBULA

18″ x 12″

Pen and ink on paper

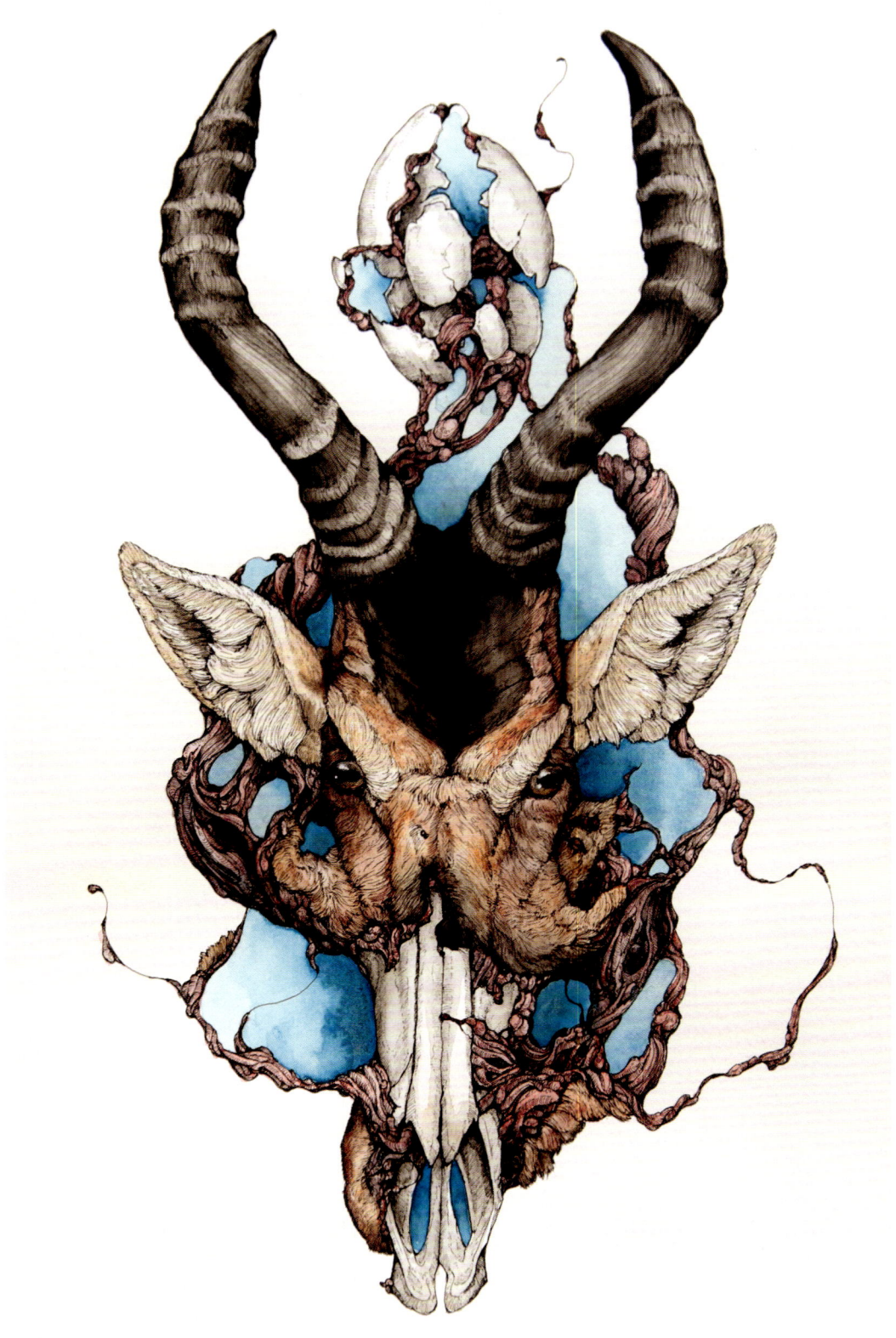

MOTHER'S GHOST

12″ x 21″

Pen, ink, colored pencil, and gel pen on paper

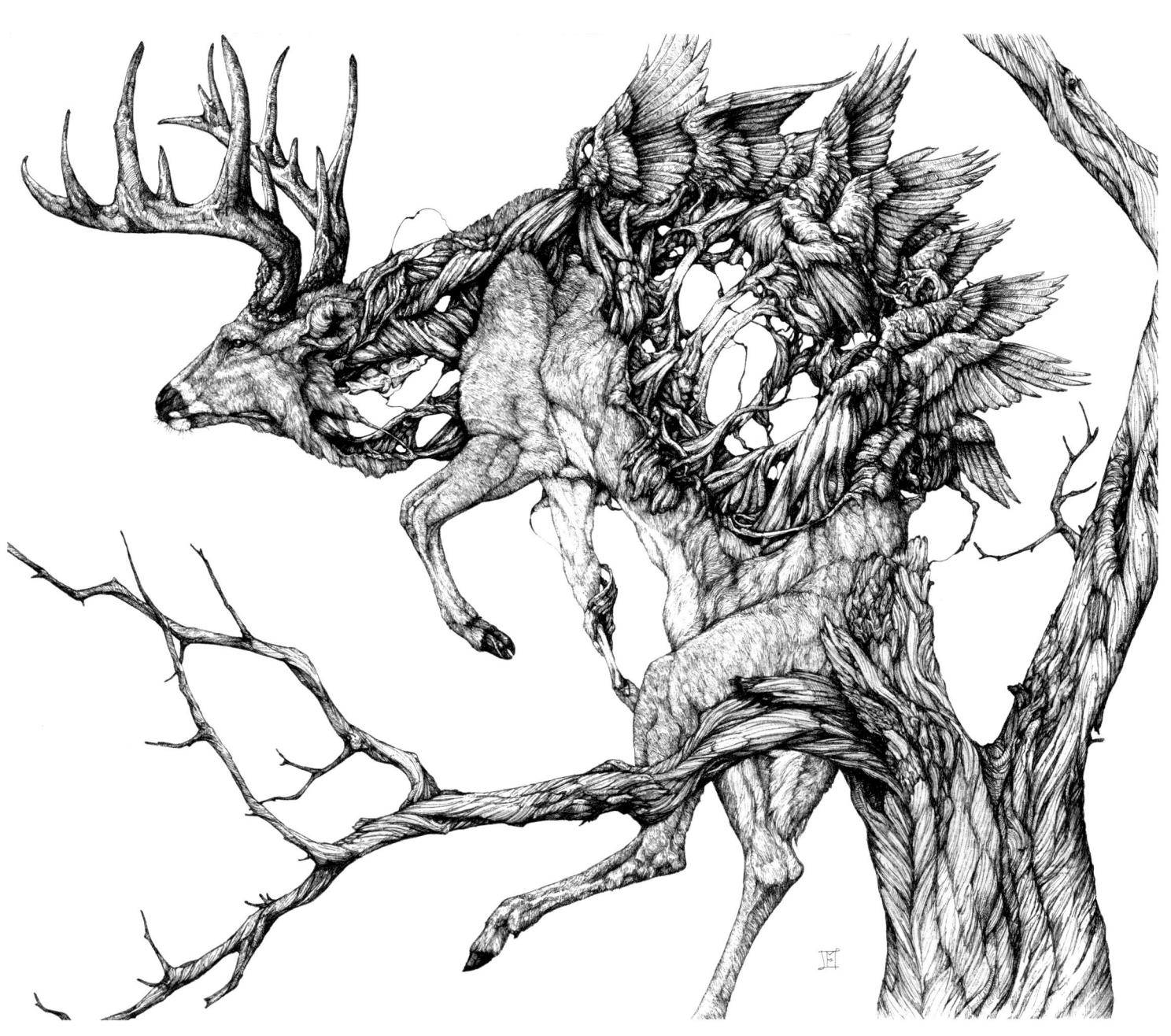

PERYTON

28" x 22"

Pen and ink on paper

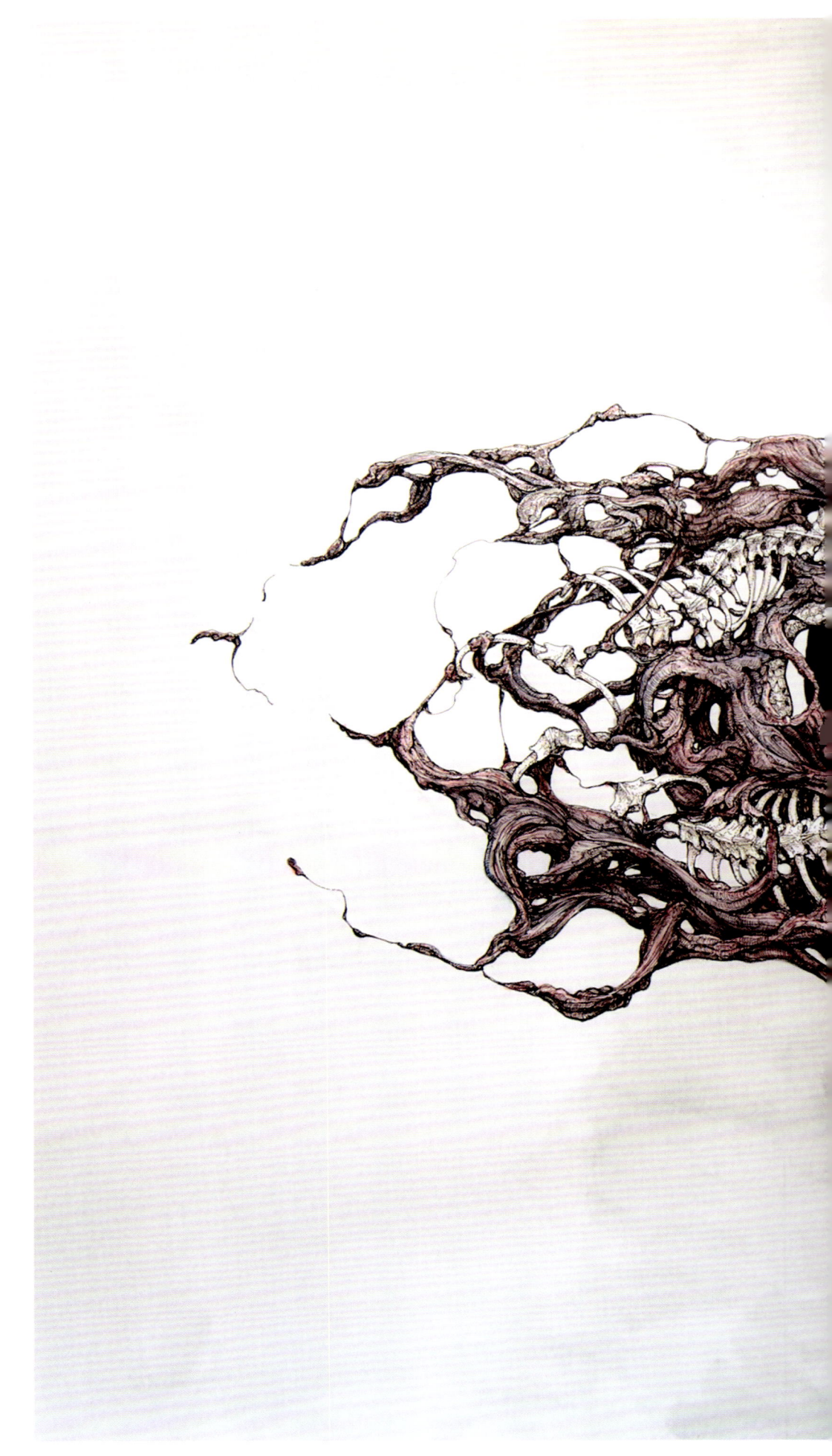

OUROBOROS

24" x 18"

Pen, ink, gel pen, and colored pencil on paper

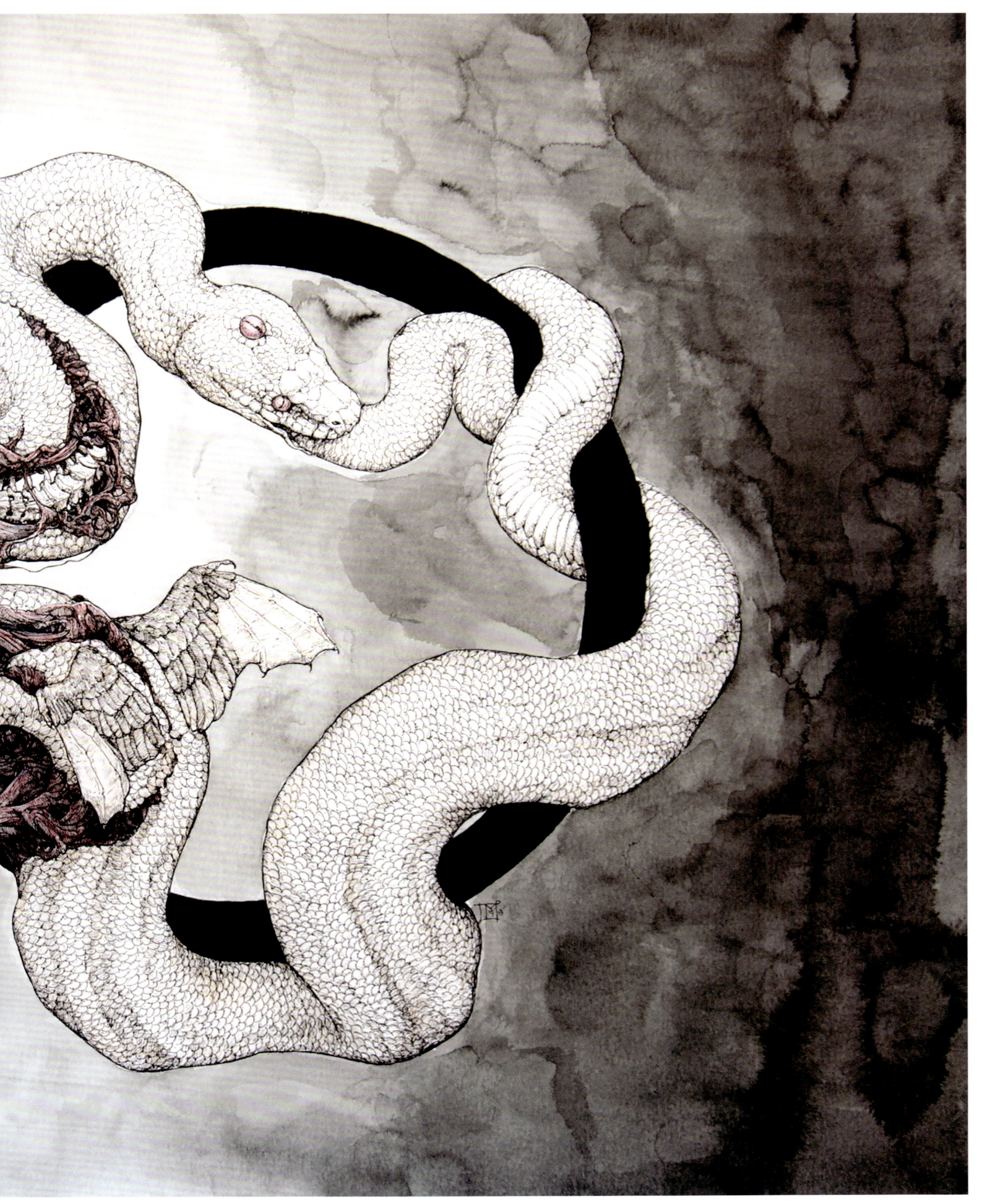

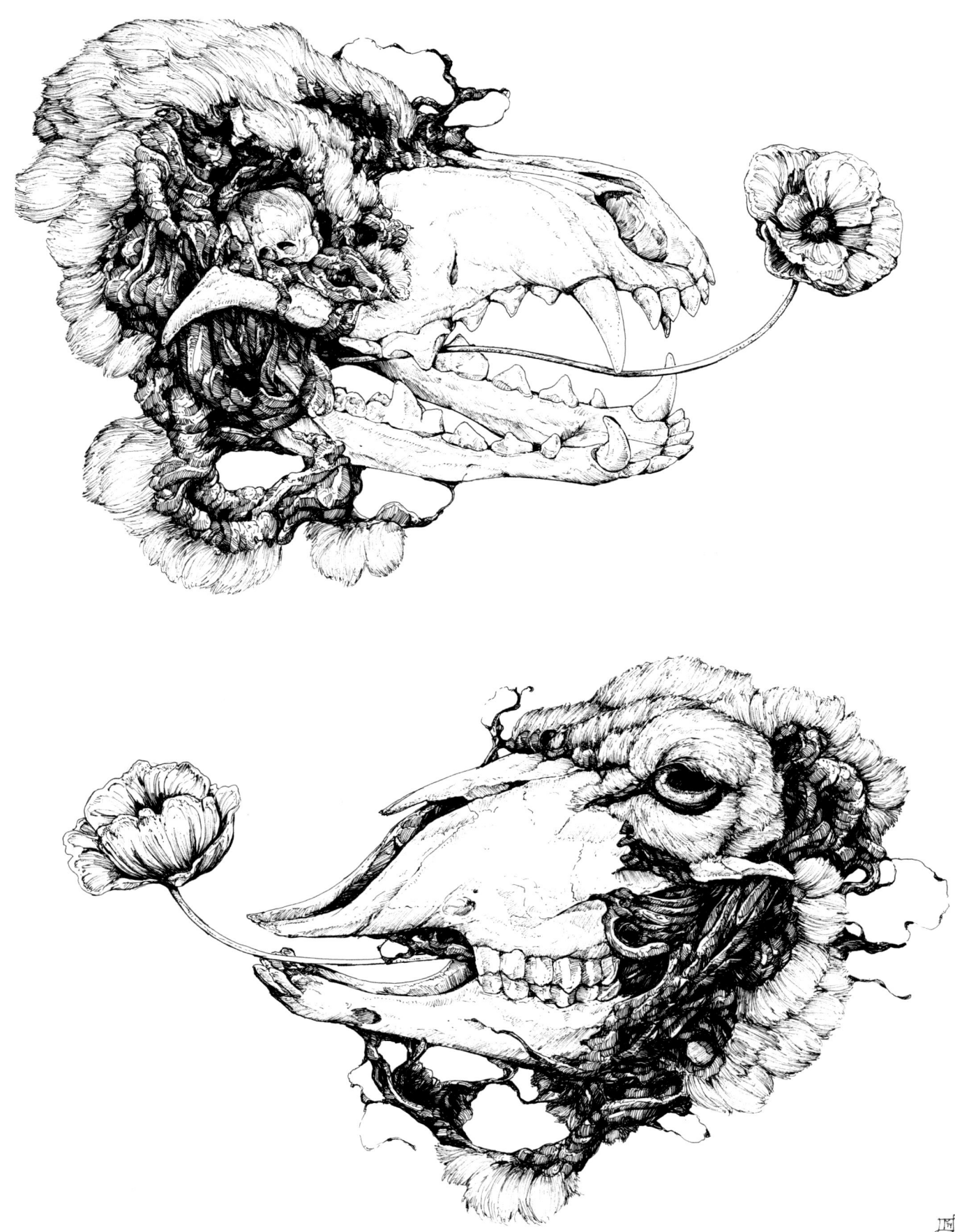

FLOWER CHILD AND FLOWER POWER

11″ × 7″

Pen on paper

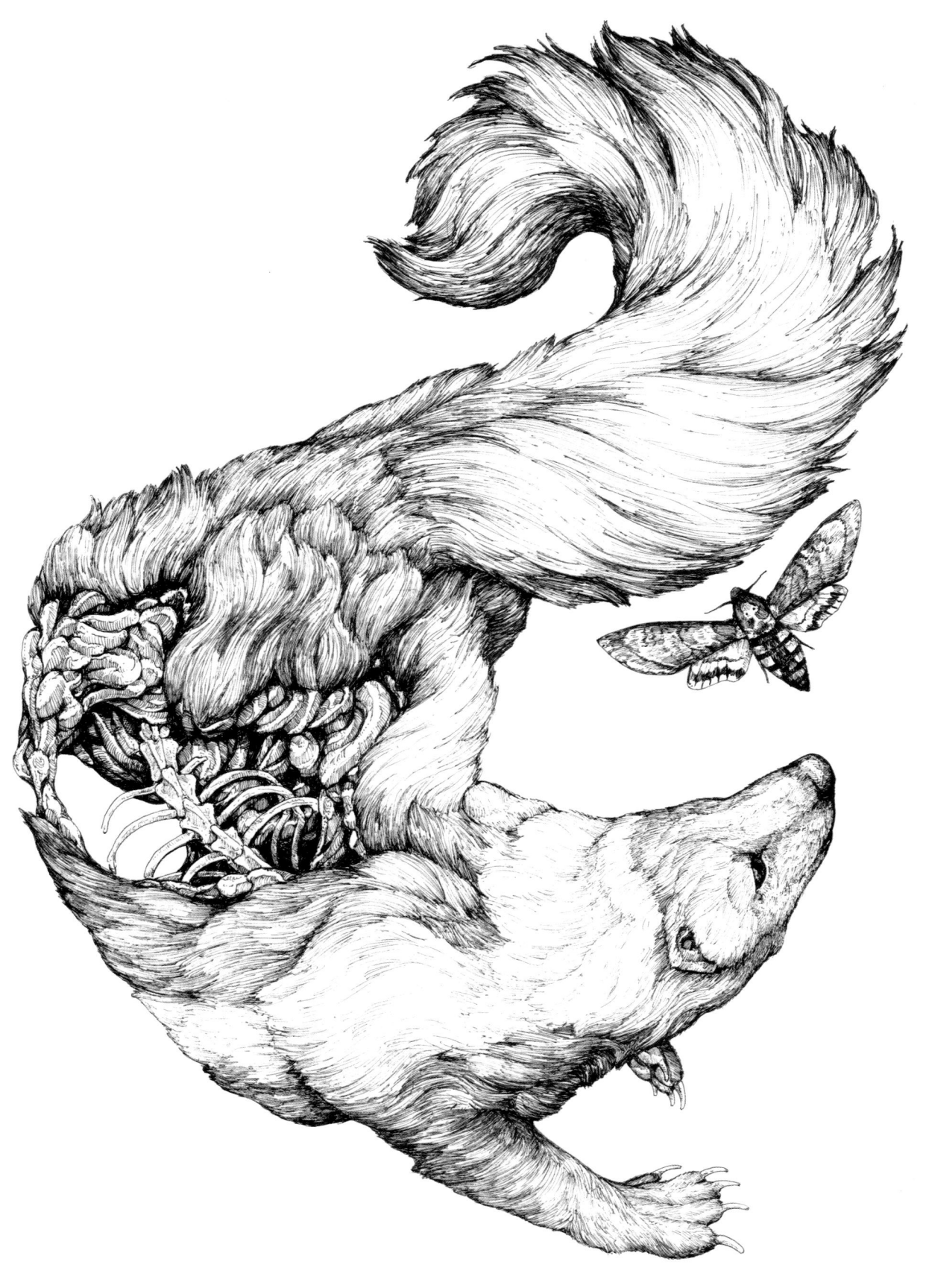

DEATH'S HEAD

10.5″ x 14″

Pen on paper

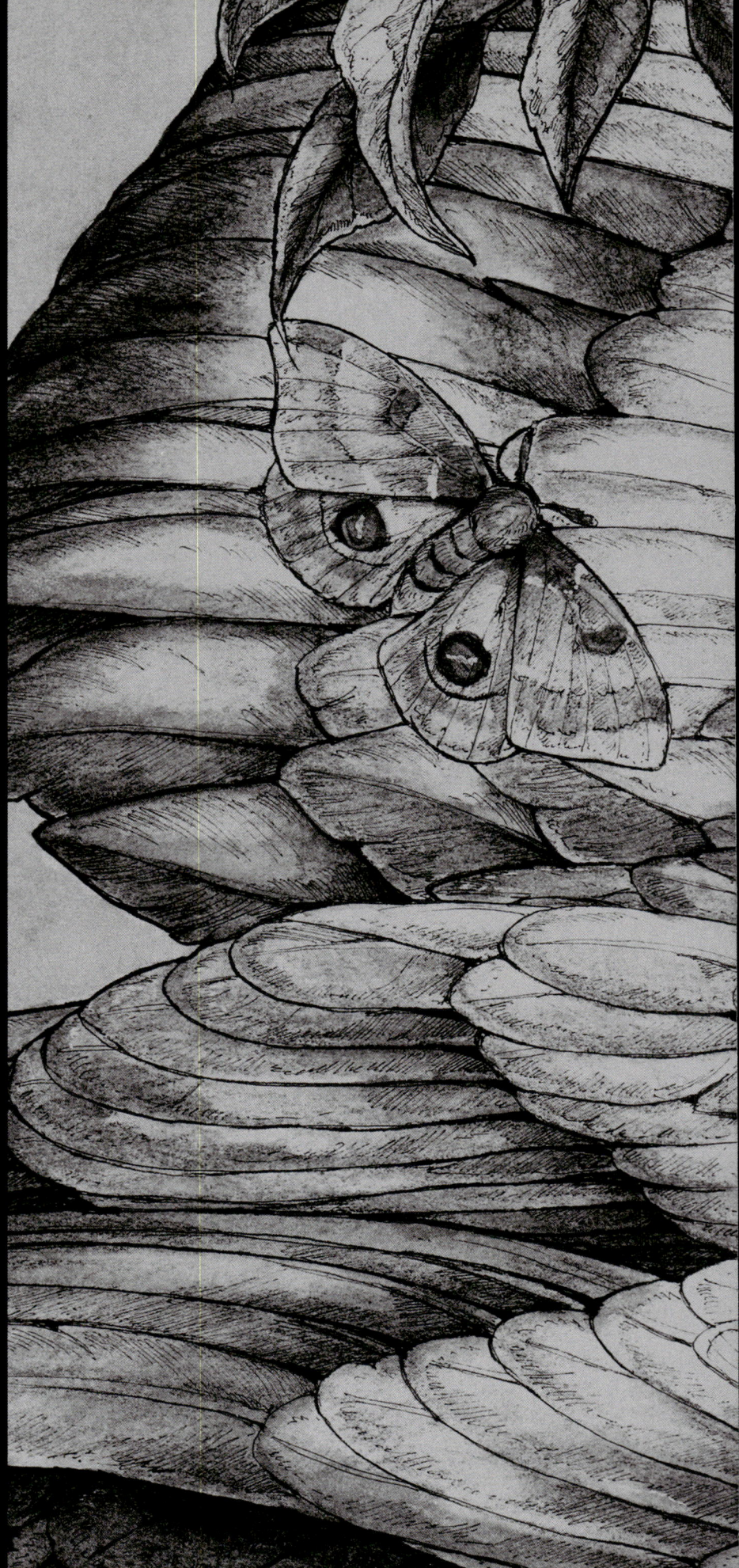

SACRED DECAY

2015

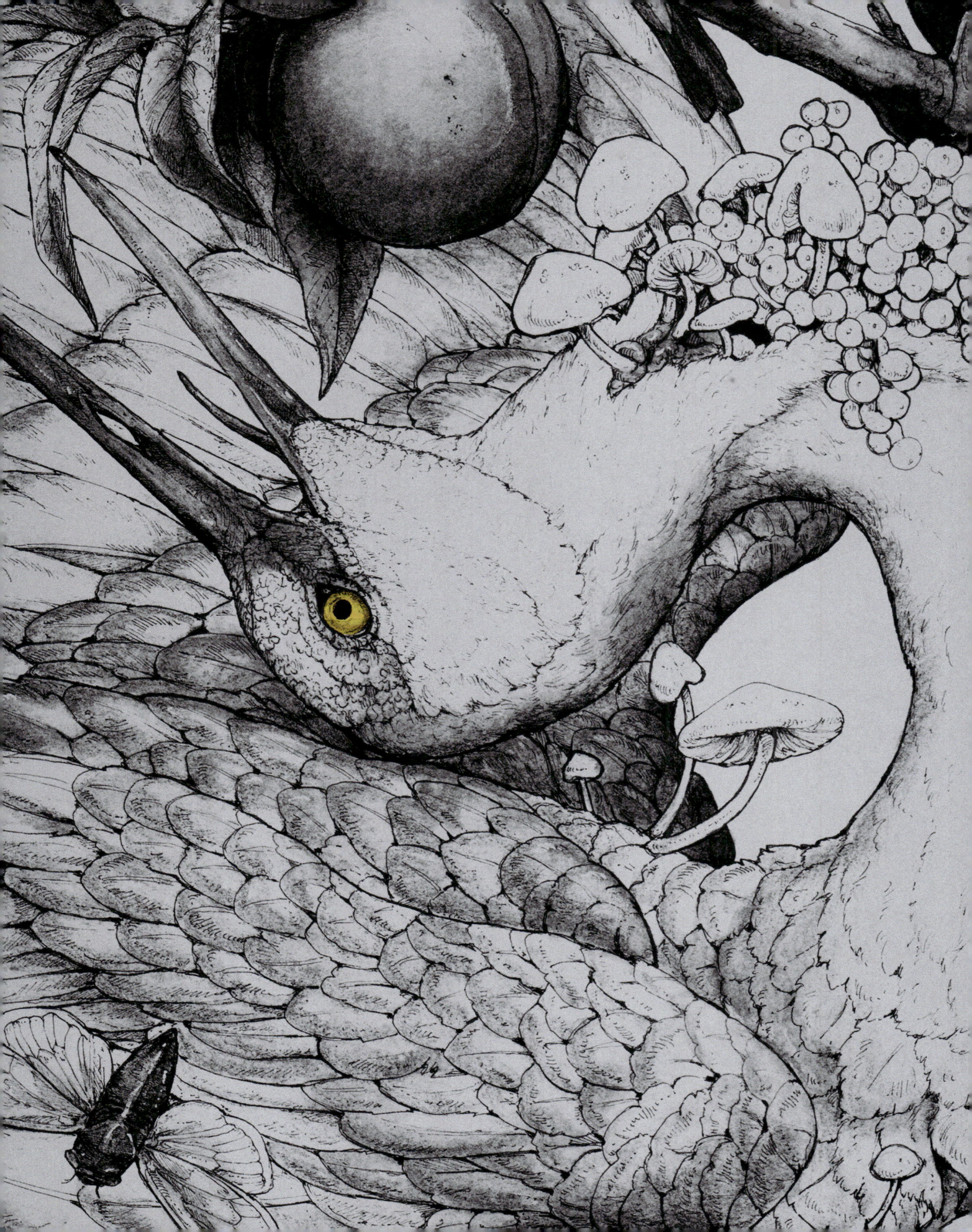

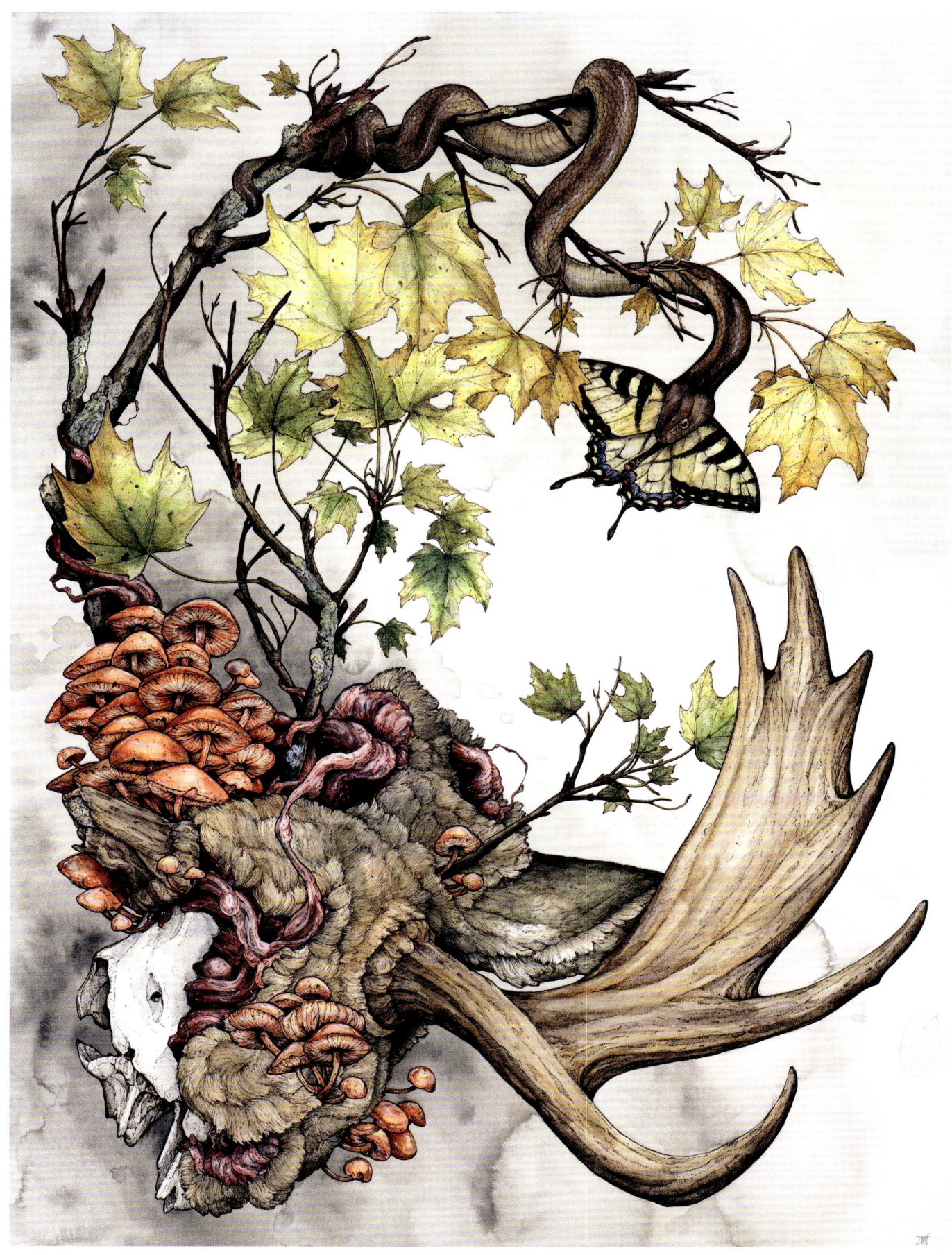

ALCES ALCES

18.25″ x 24″

Pen, ink, colored pencil, graphite, and gel pen on paper

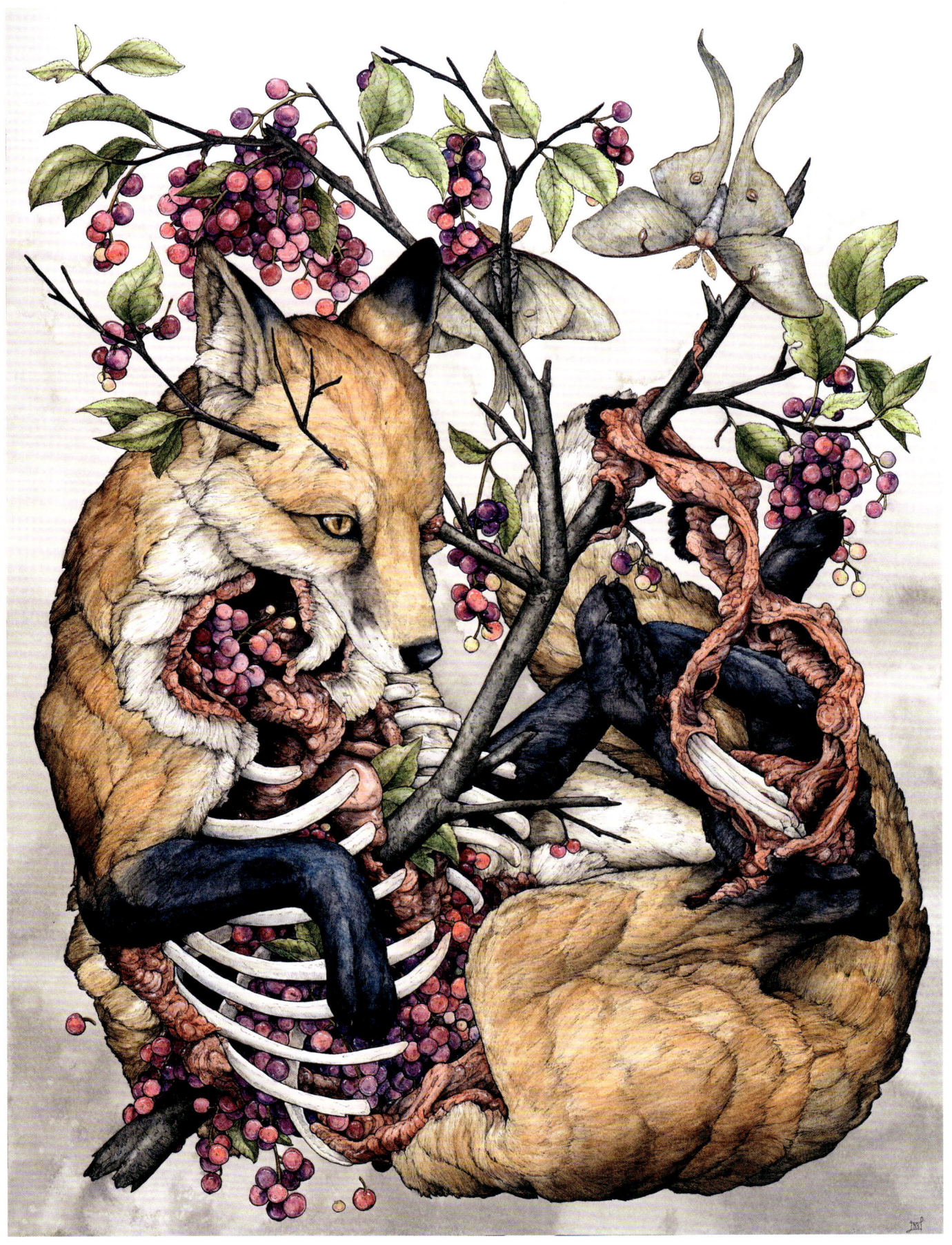

VULPES VULPES

18.25" × 24"

Pen, ink, colored pencil, graphite, and gel pen on paper

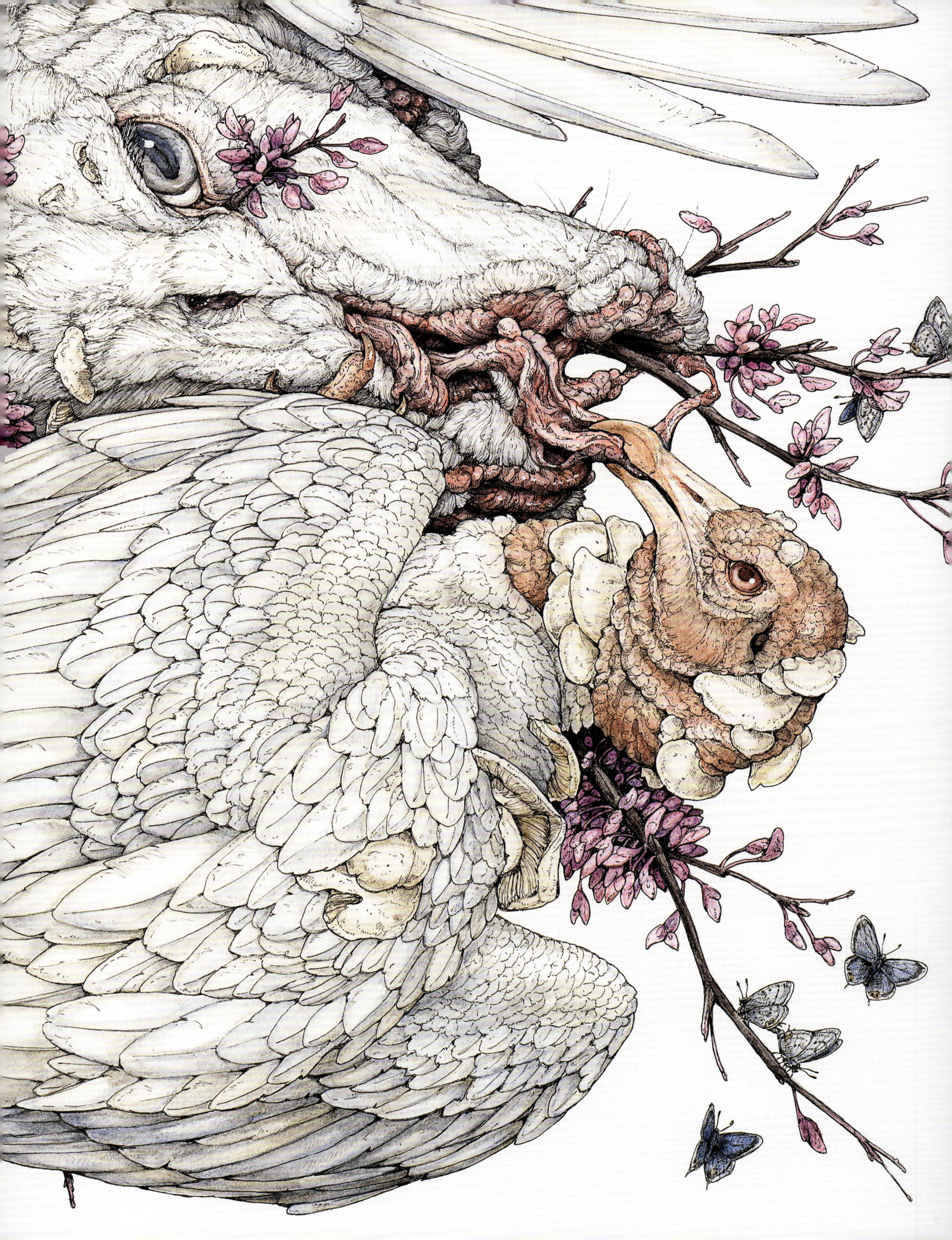

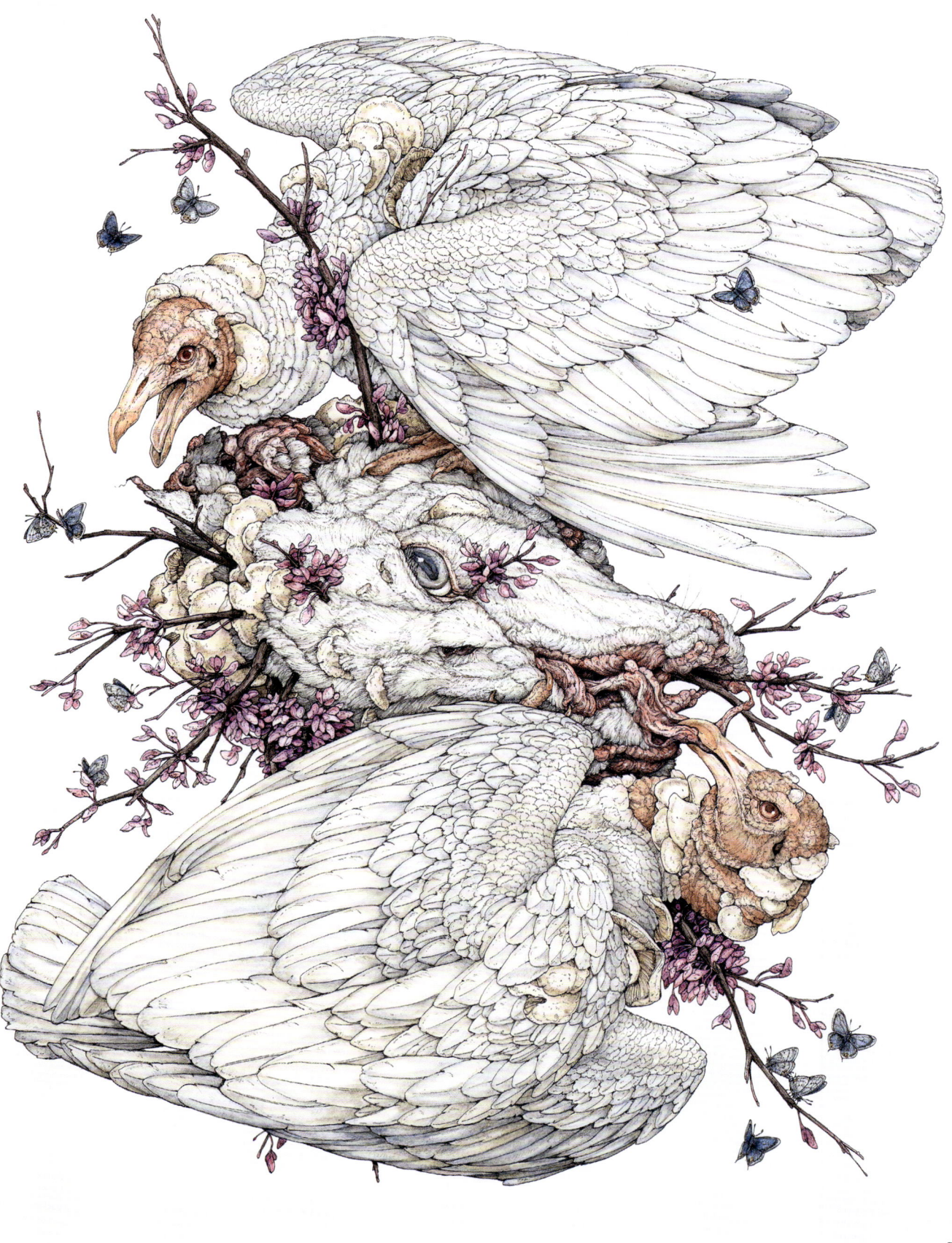

CORAGYPS ATRATUS

18.25" x 24"

Pen, ink, colored pencil, graphite, and gel pen on paper

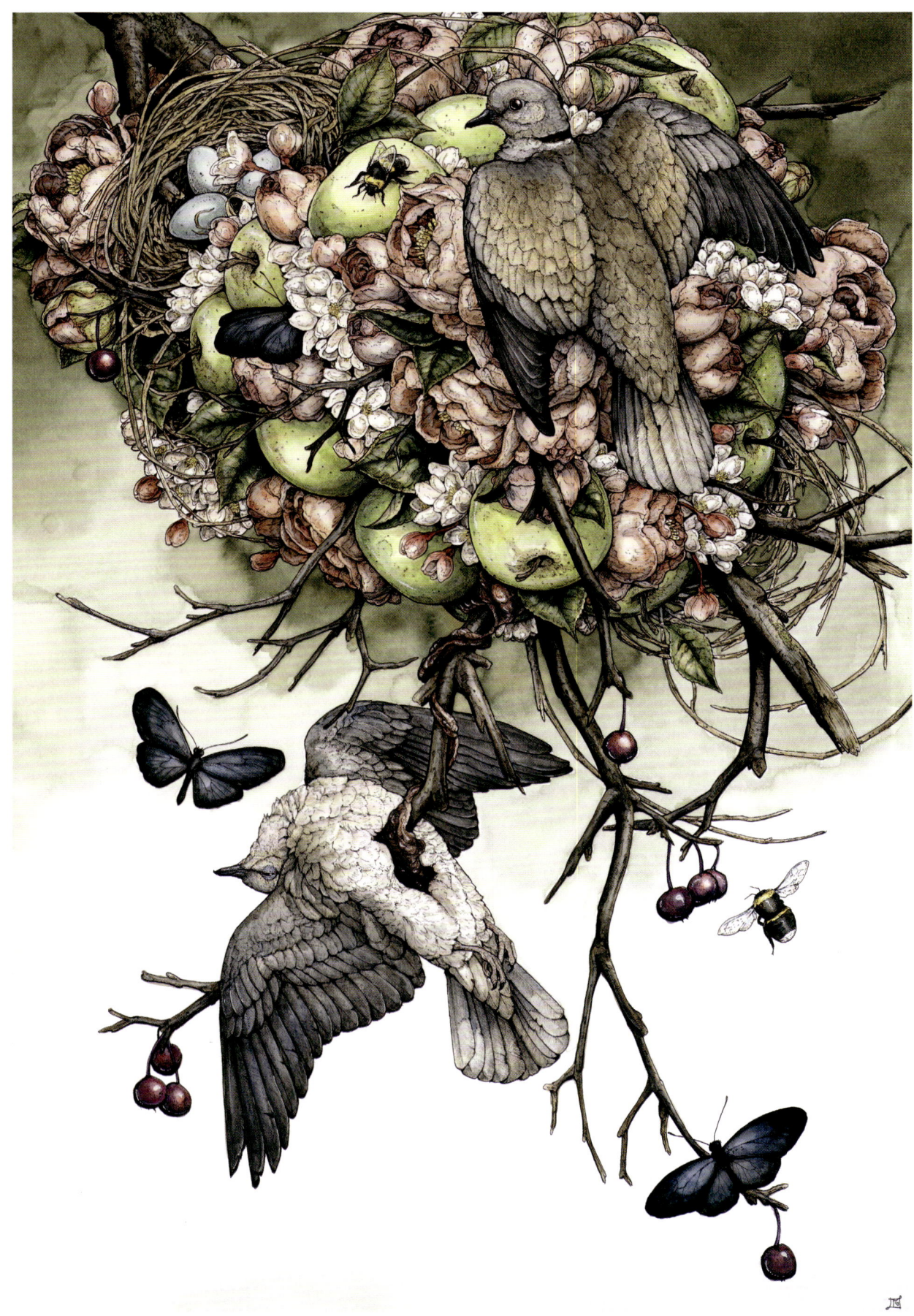

COLLARED DOVES

15.75" x 22.75"

Pen, ink, colored pencil, graphite, and gel pen on paper

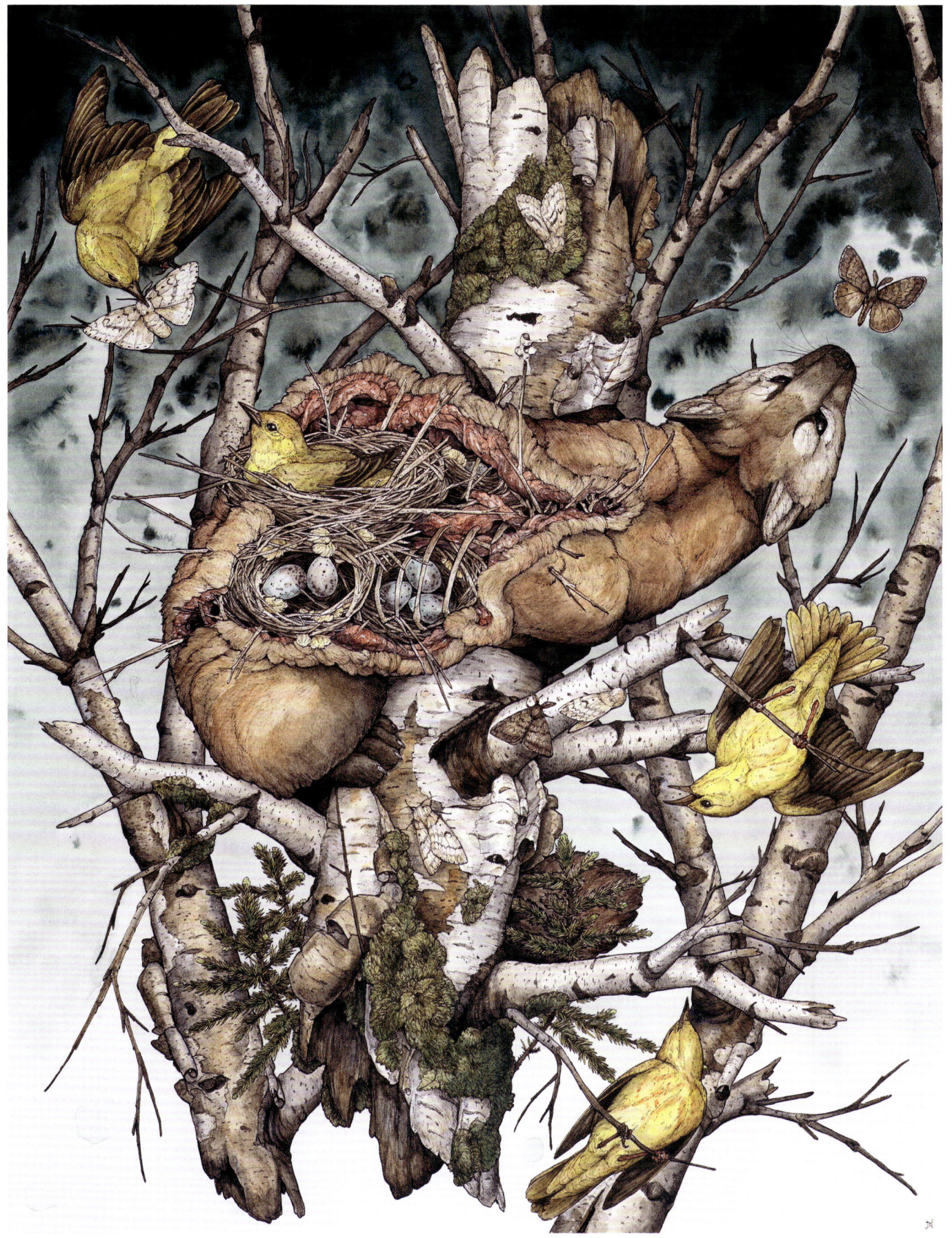

MARTES AMERICANA

18.25" x 24"

Pen, ink, colored pencil, graphite, and gel pen on paper

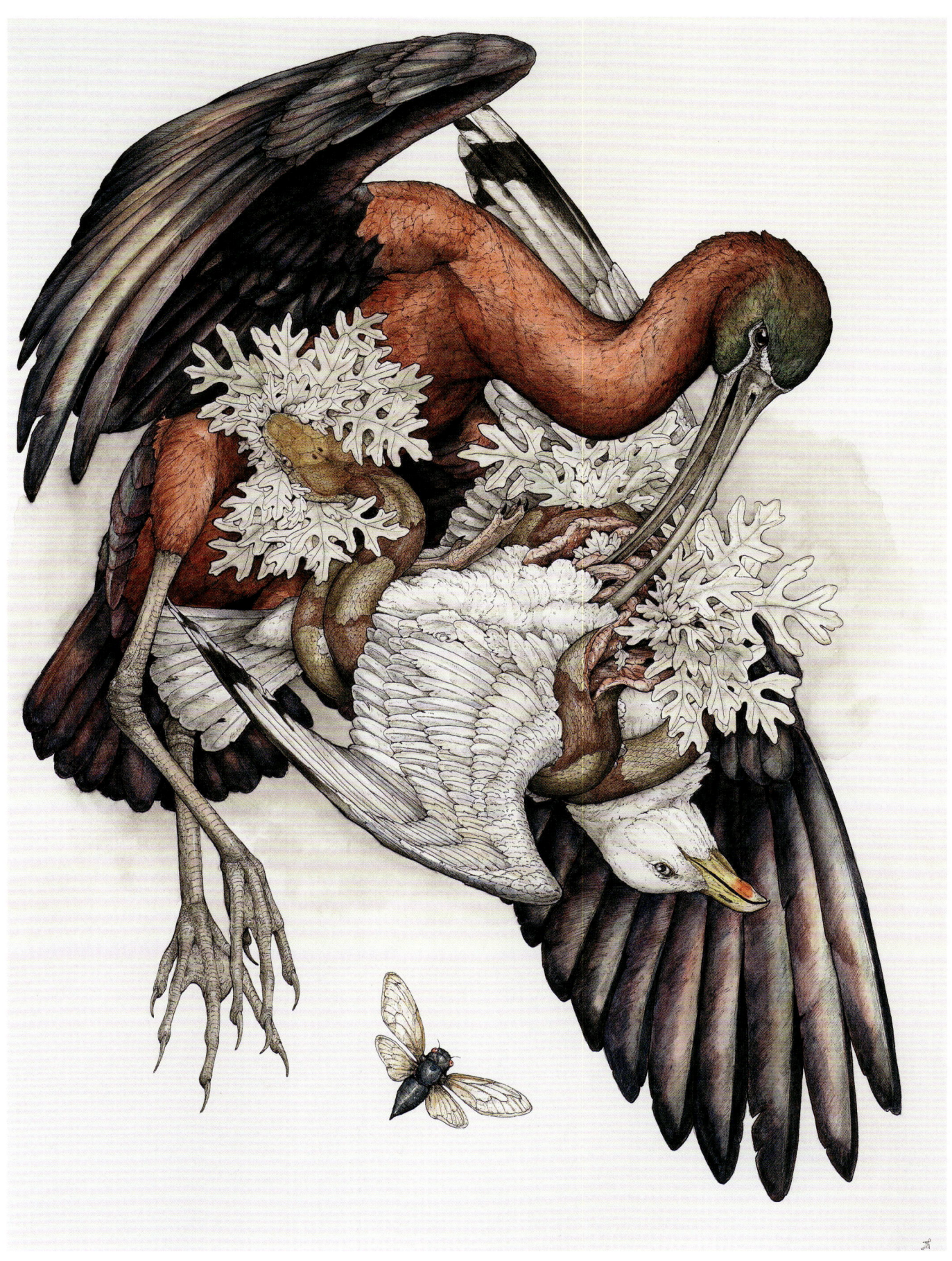

PLEGADIS FALCINELLUS

18.25″ x 24″

Pen, ink, colored pencil, graphite, and gel pen on paper

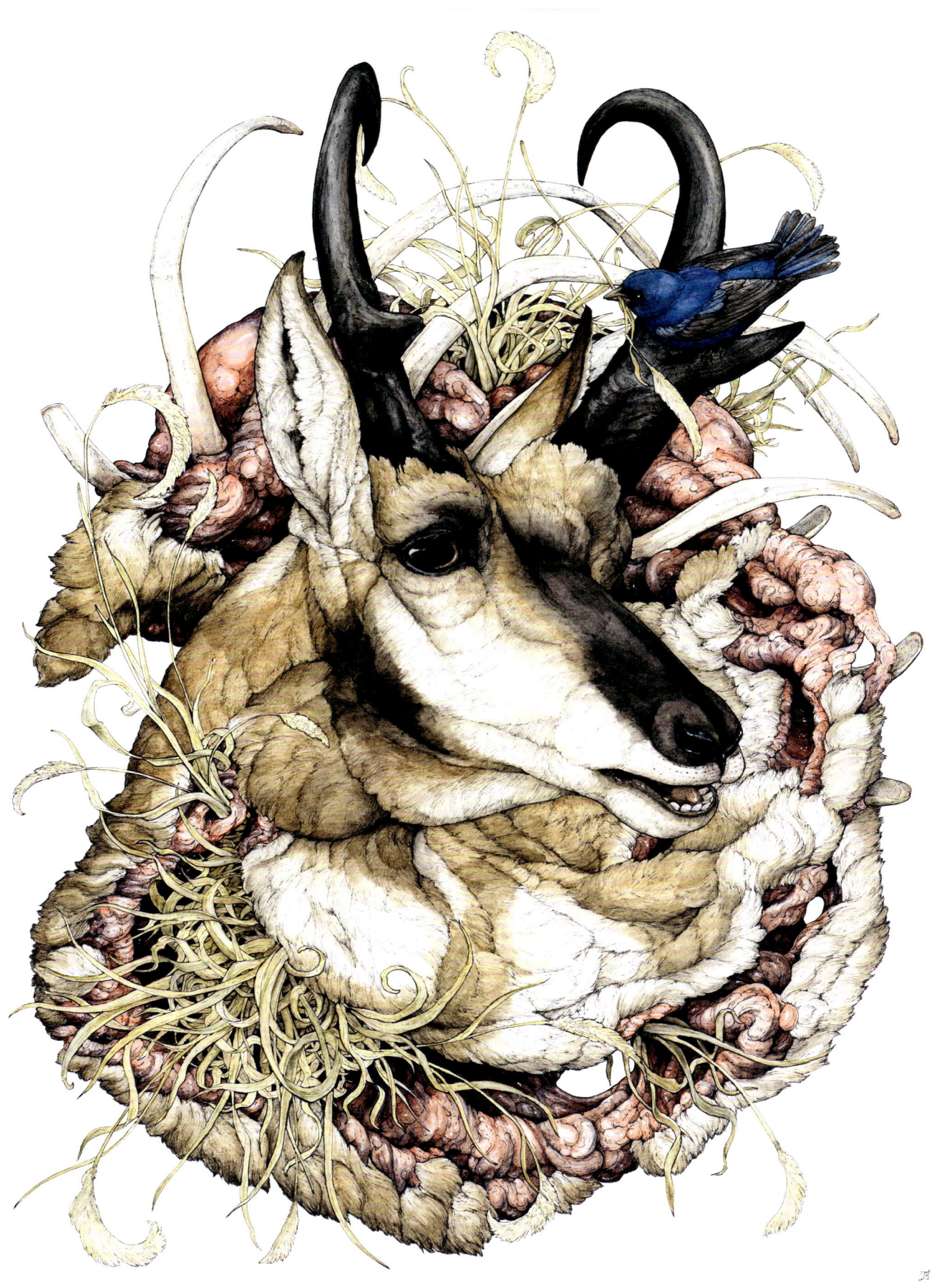

ANTILOCAPRA AMERICANA

18.25″ x 24″

Pen, ink, colored pencil, graphite, and gel pen on paper

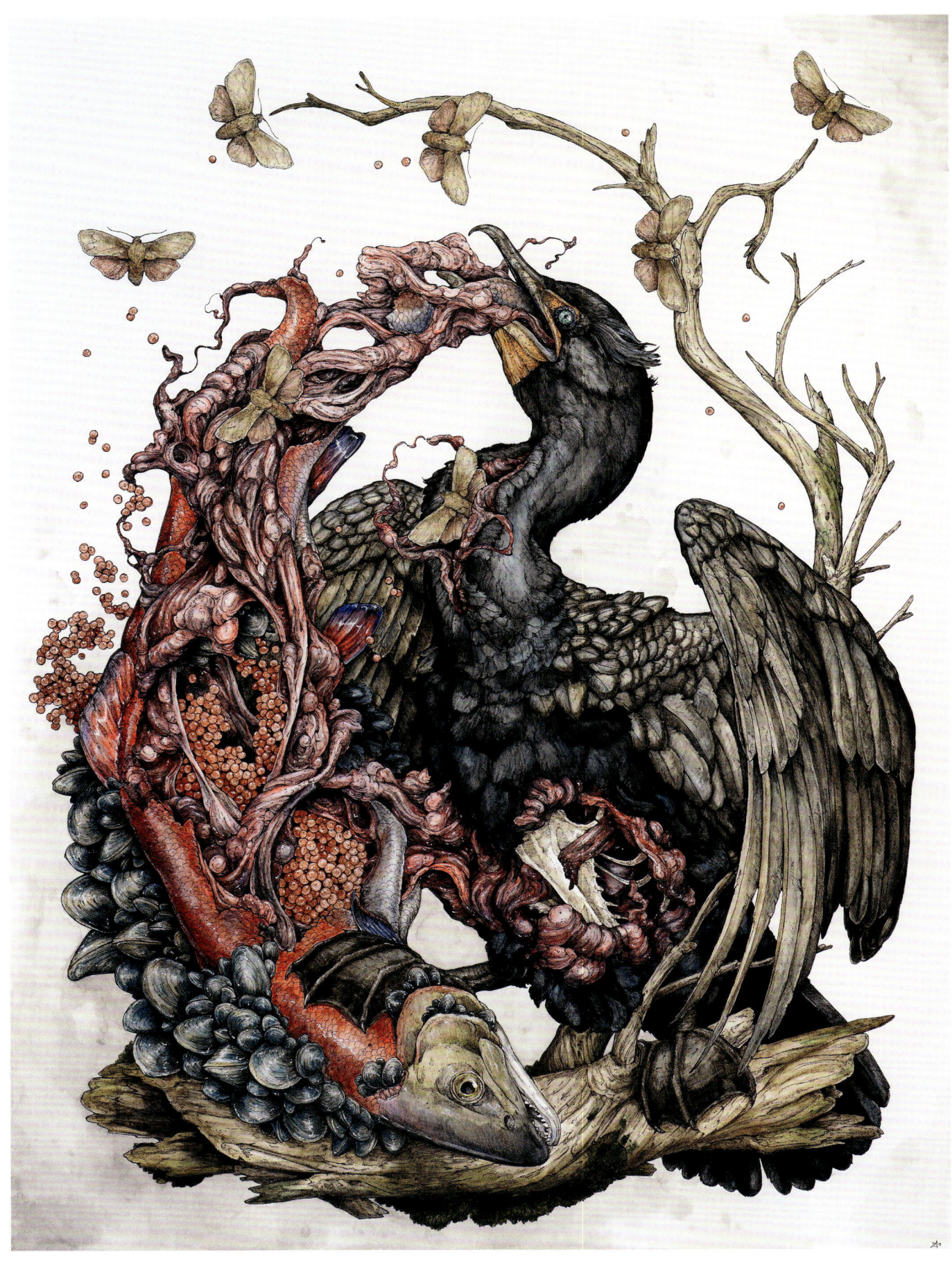

PHALACROCORAX AURITUS

18.25″ x 24″

Pen, ink, colored pencil, graphite, and gel pen on paper

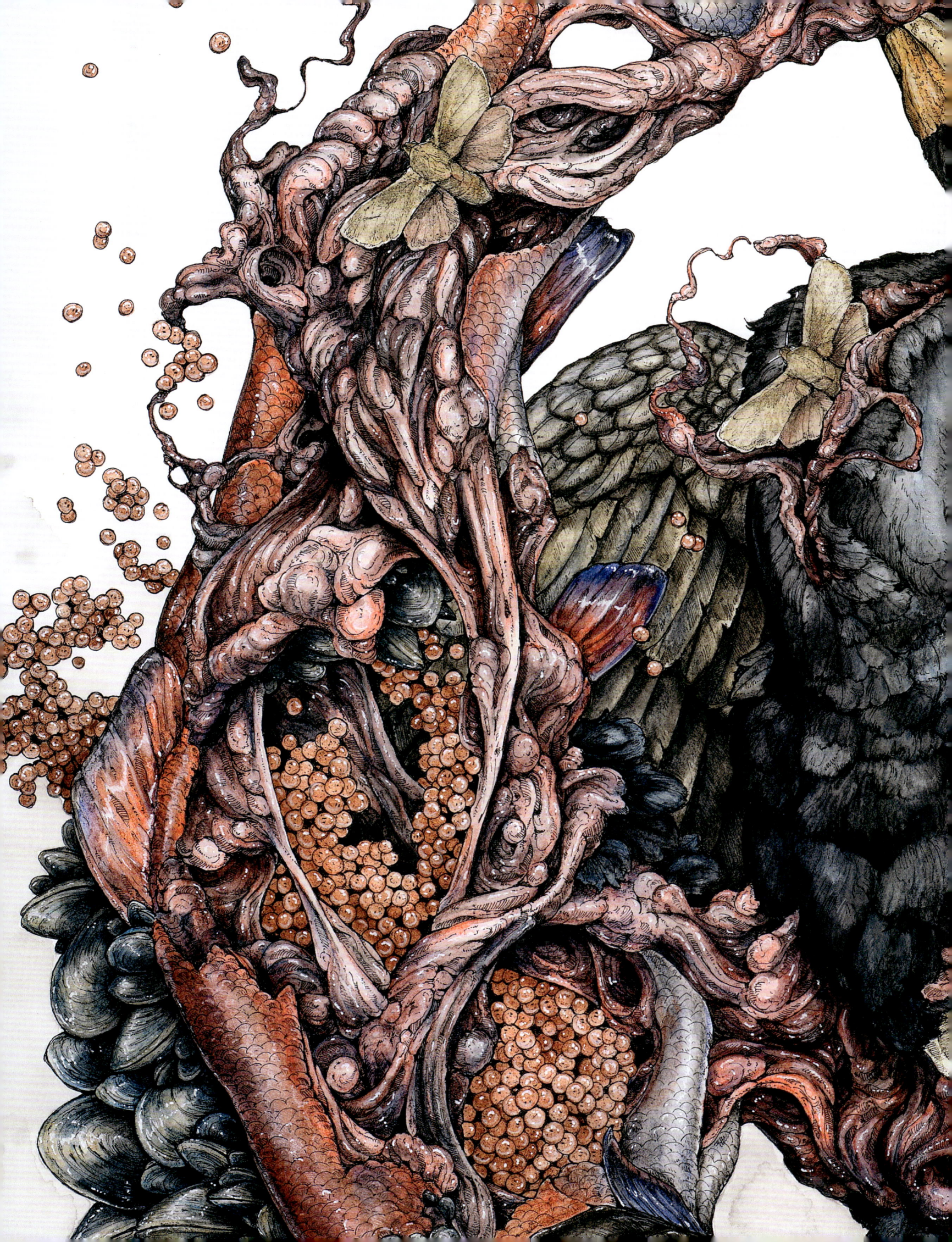

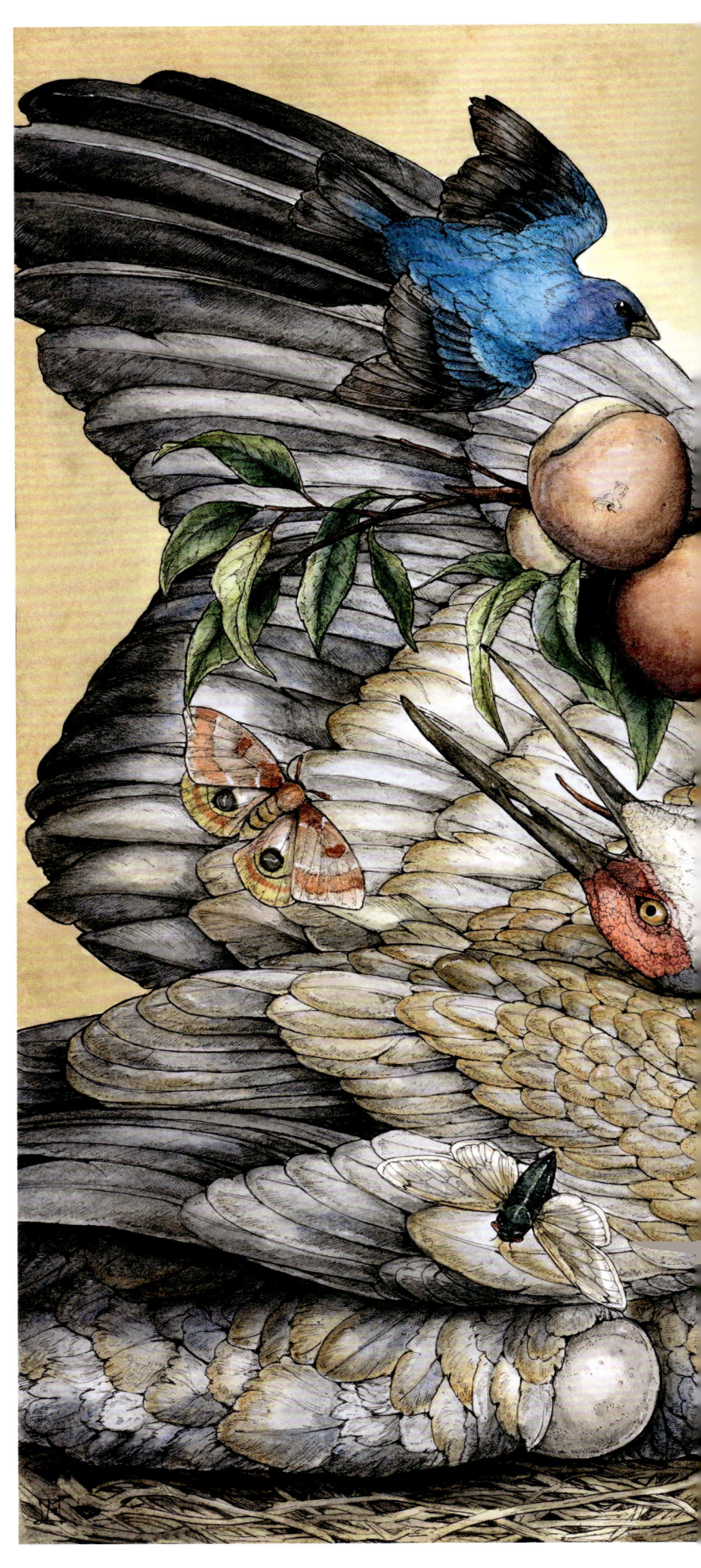

**THE SWEET SONG
OF SUMMER**

24" x 18.25"

Pen, ink, colored pencil, graphite, and
gel pen on paper

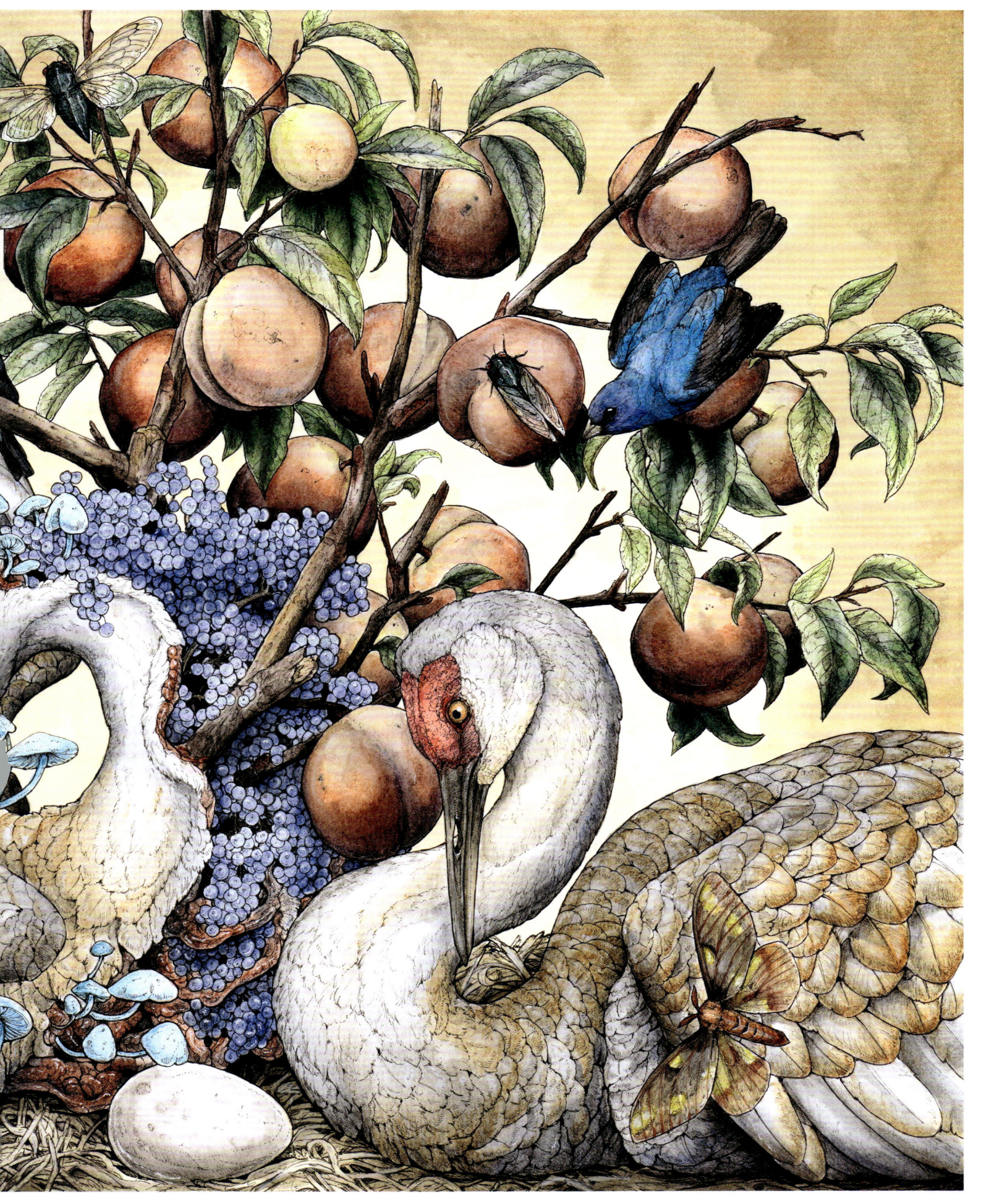

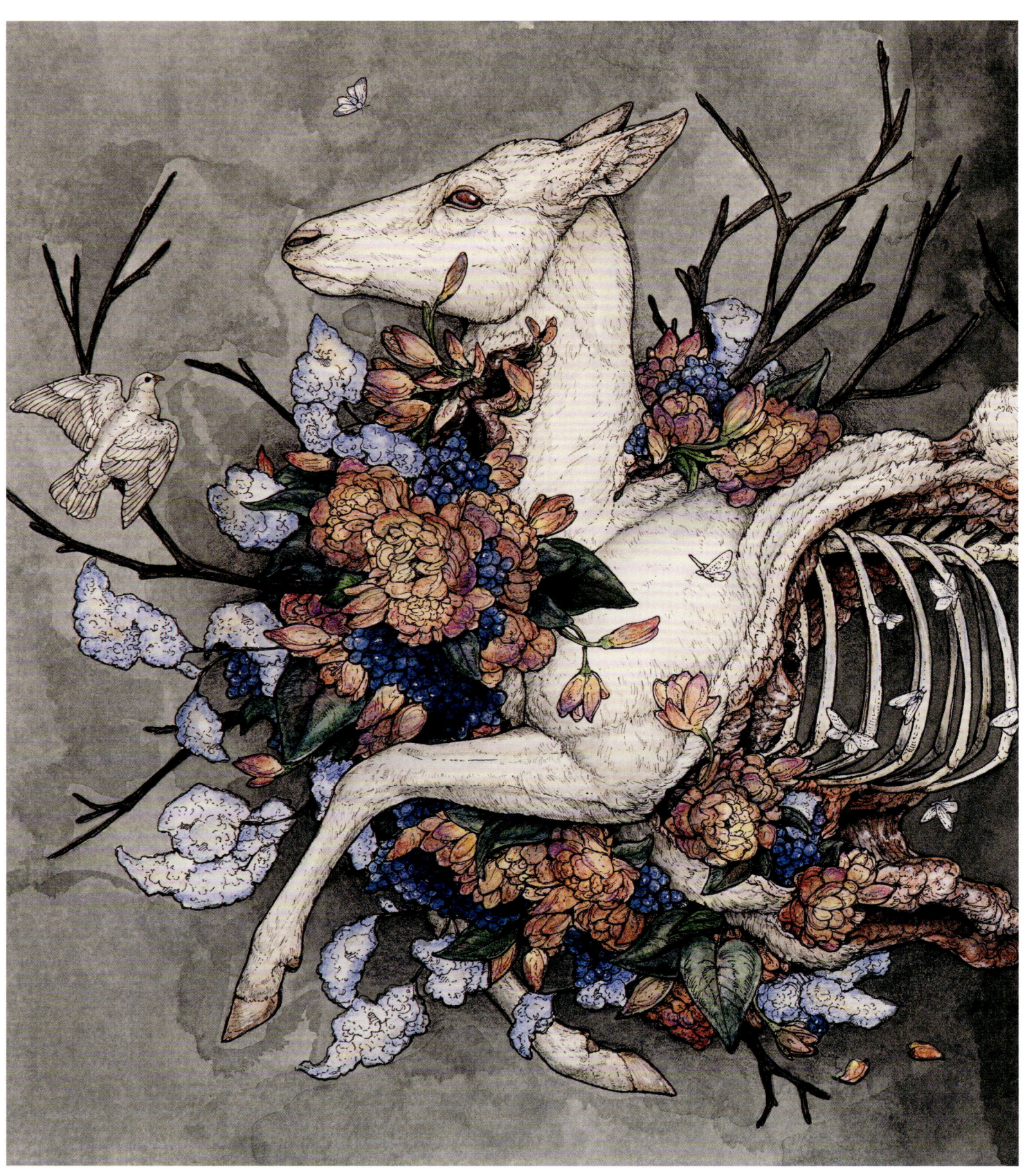

FROM OUR FLESH – DOE

10" x 17.75"

Pen, ink, colored pencil, graphite, and gel pen on paper

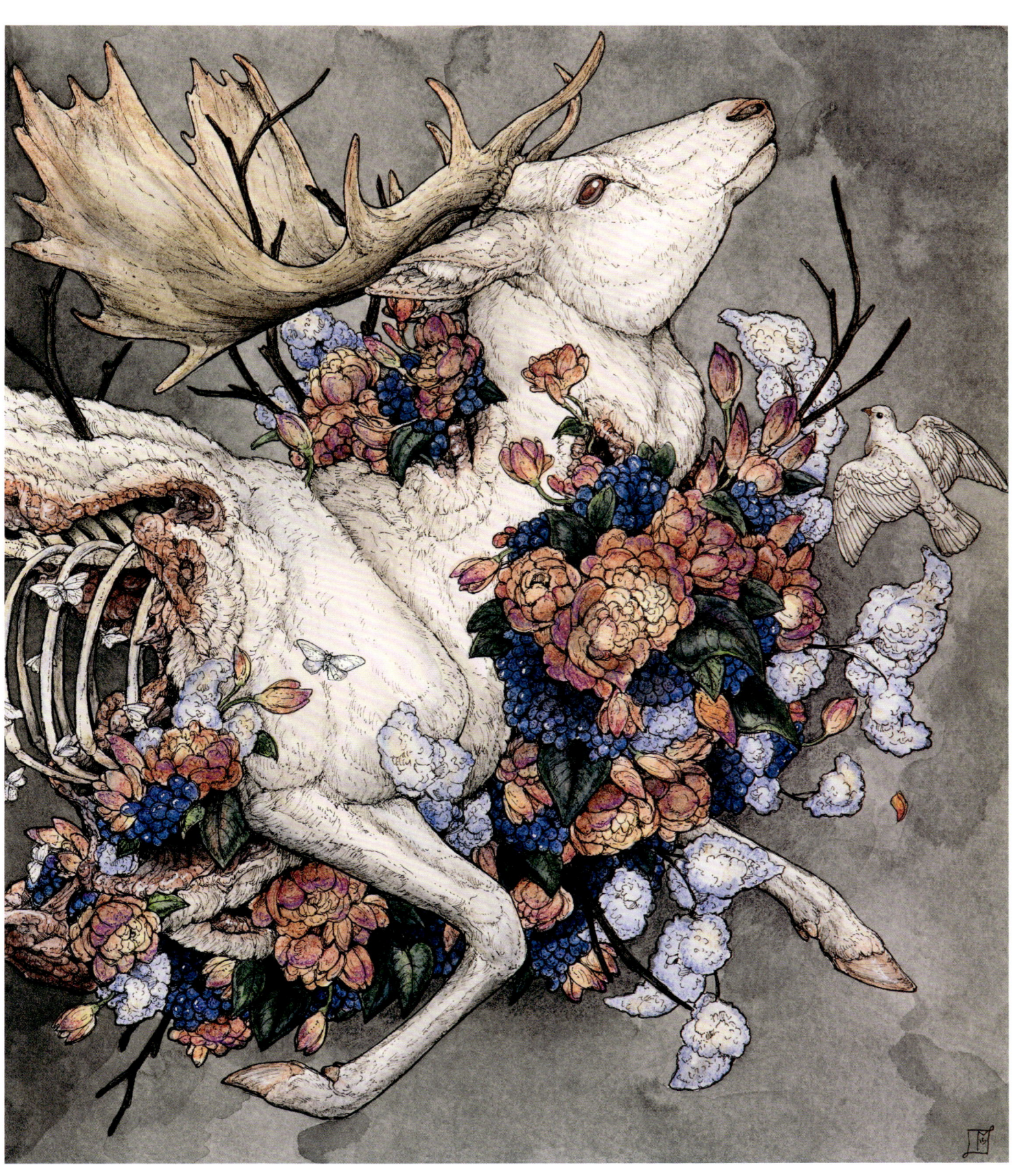

FROM OUR FLESH – BUCK

10" x 17.75"

Pen, ink, colored pencil, graphite, and gel pen on paper

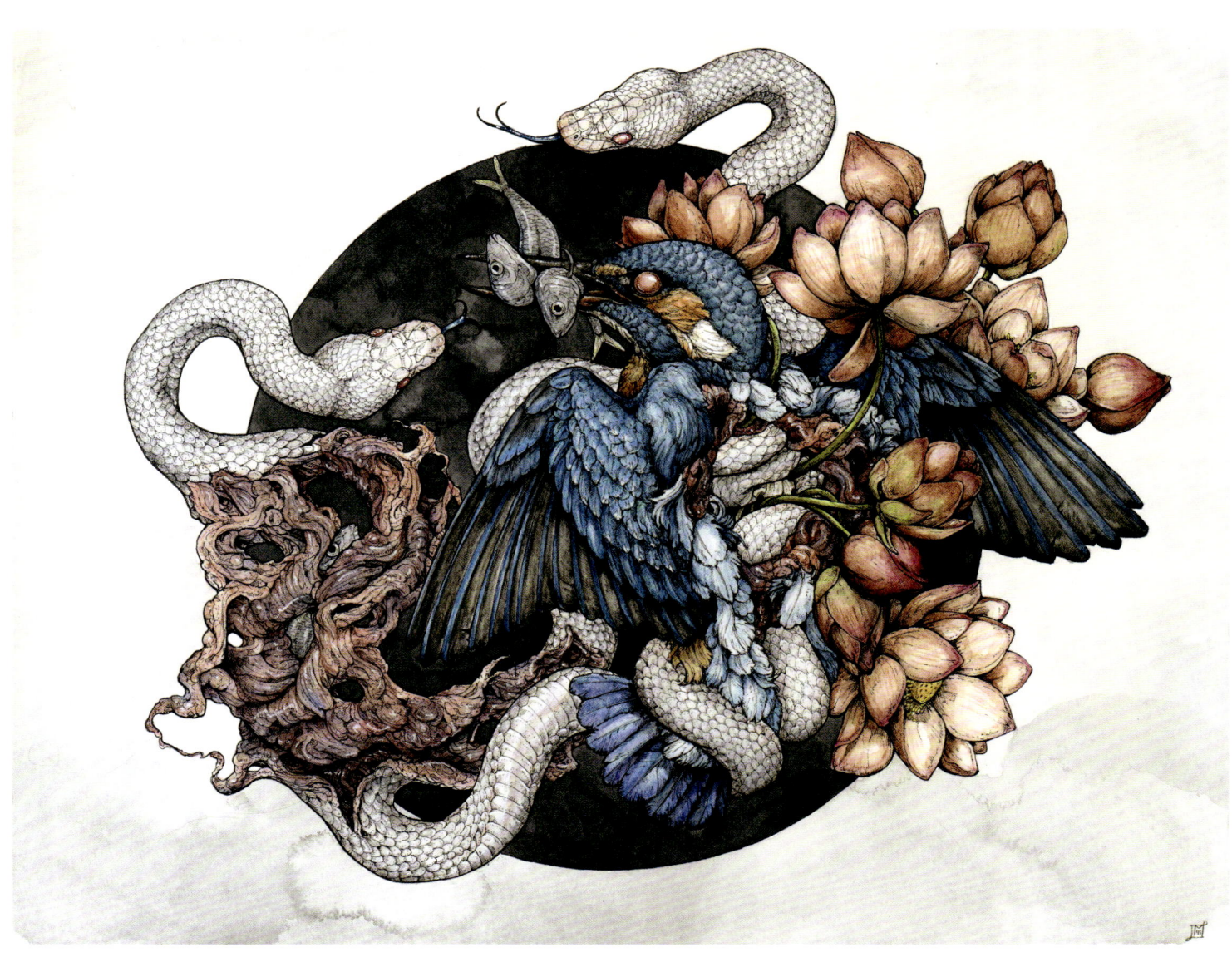

KINGFISHER

24" x 18"

Pen, ink, colored pencil, graphite, and gel pen on paper

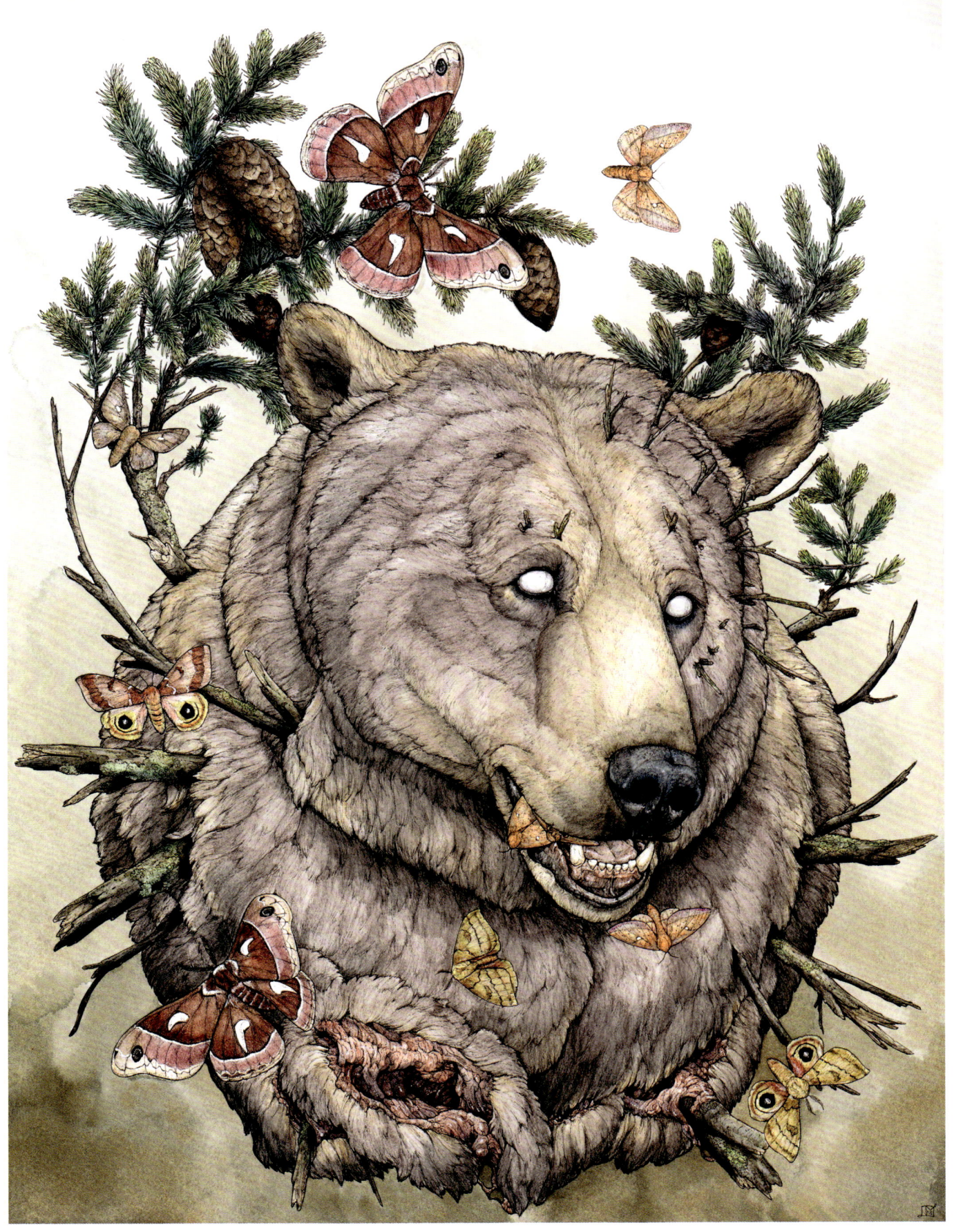

MOTH MOTHER

18″ x 24″

Pen, ink, colored pencil, graphite, and gel pen on paper

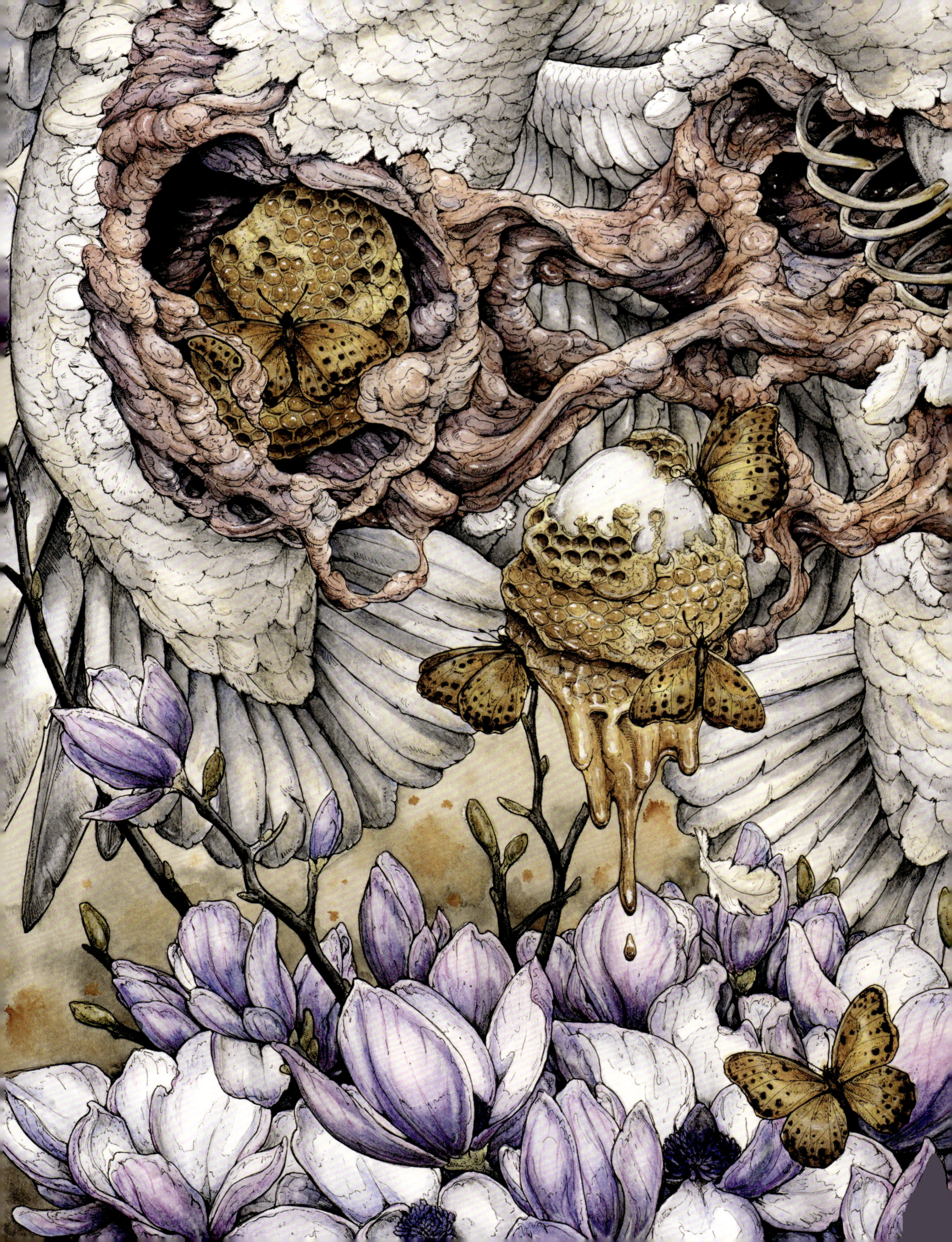

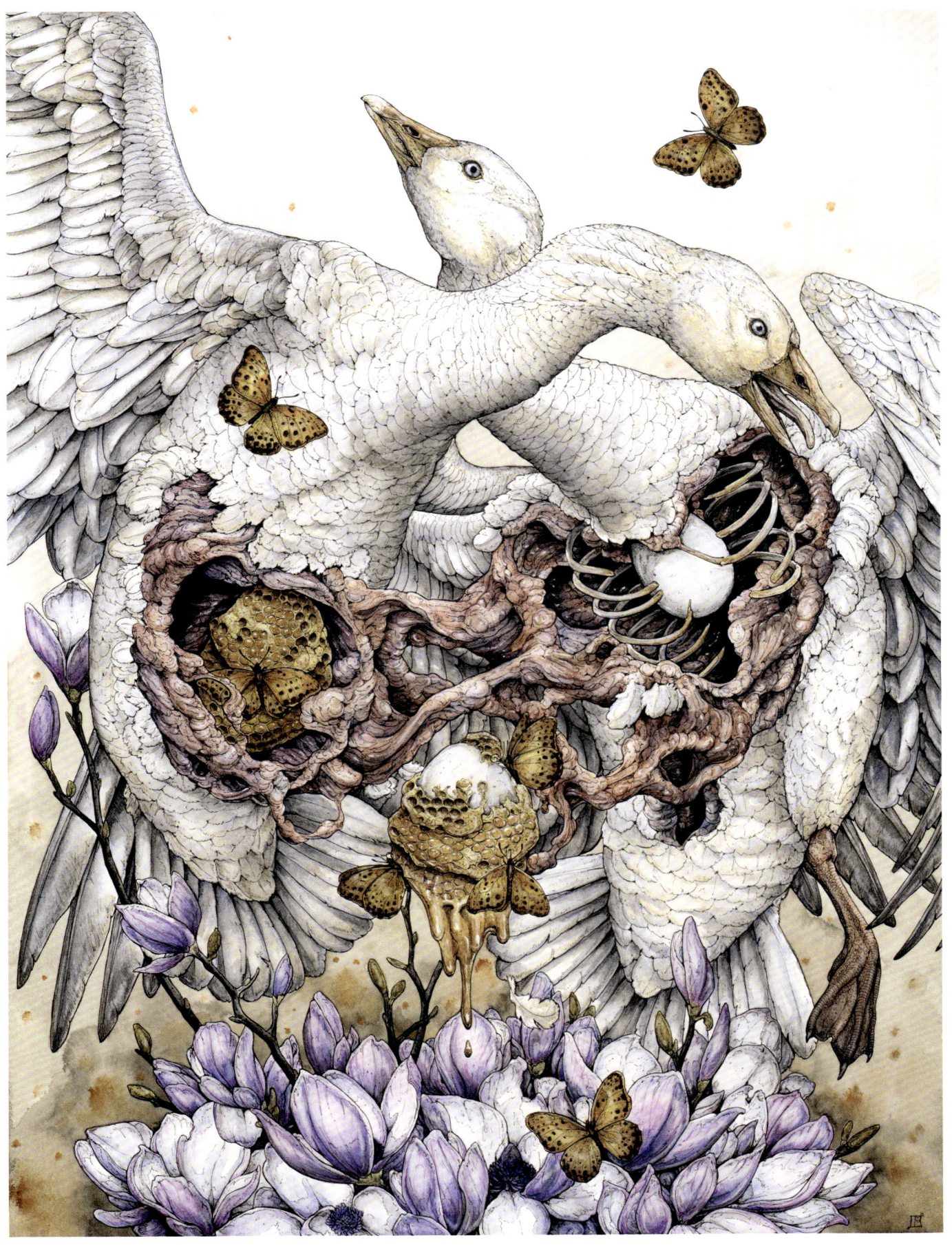

TO KILL THE GOOSE THAT LAID THE GOLDEN EGG

18.25" x 24"

Pen, ink, colored pencil, graphite, and gel pen on paper

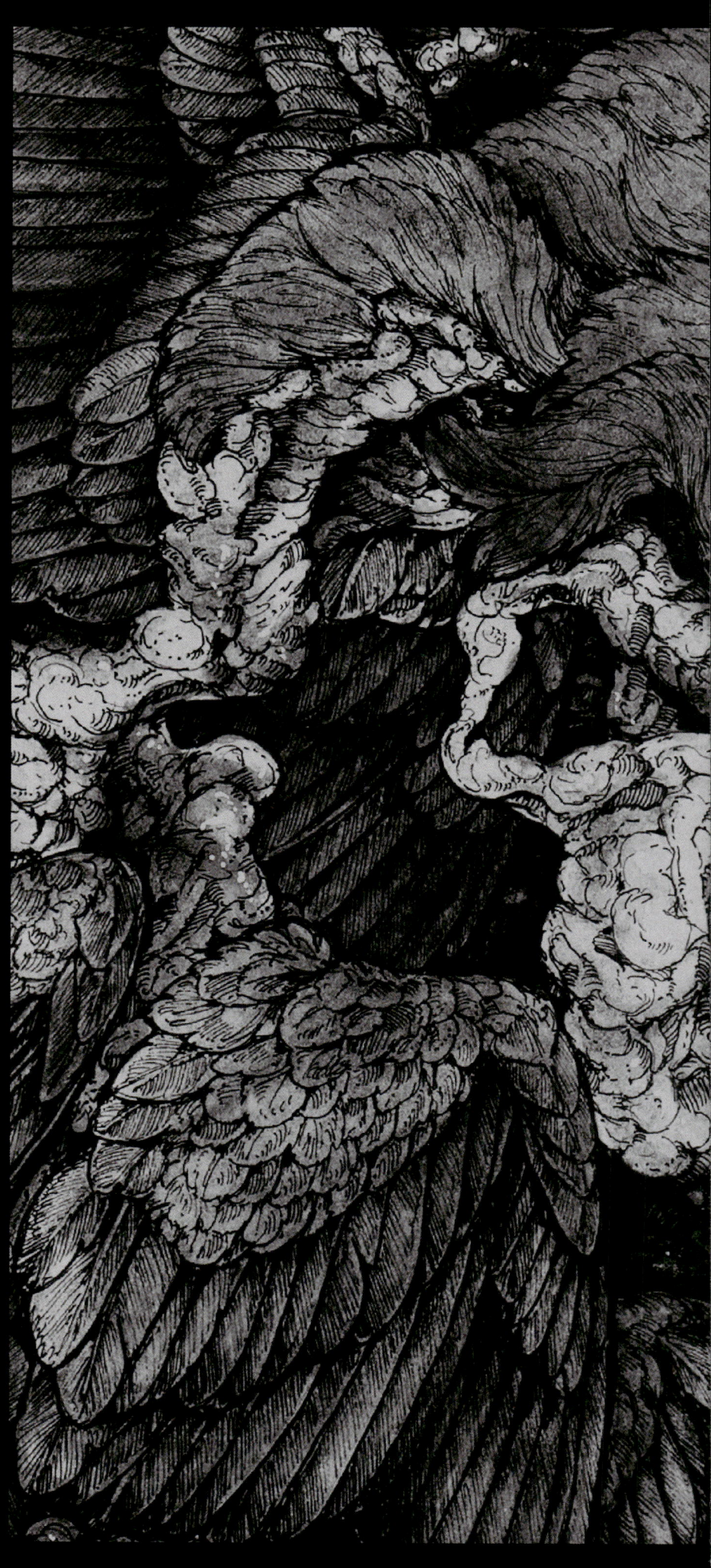

SACRED DECAY
2016

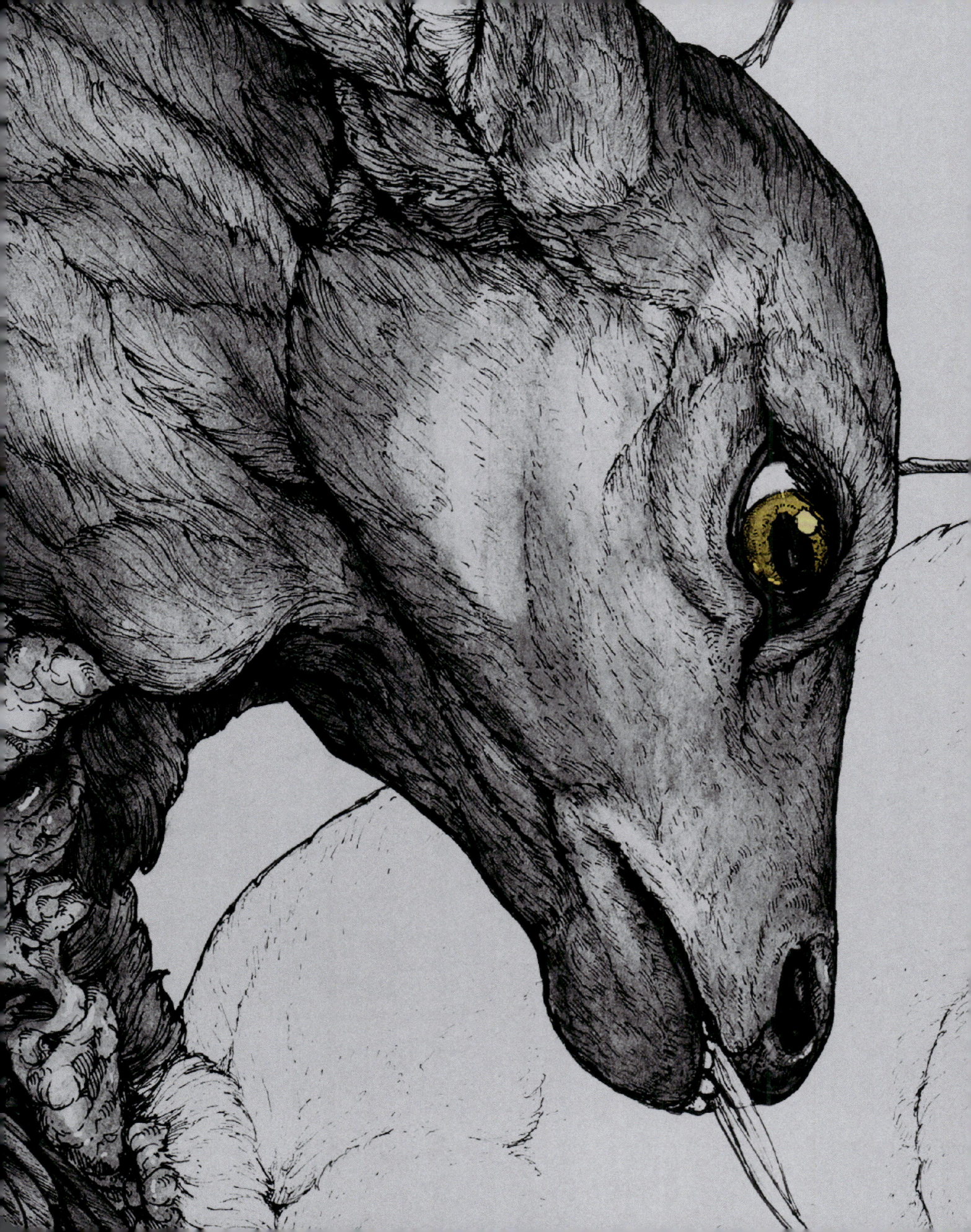

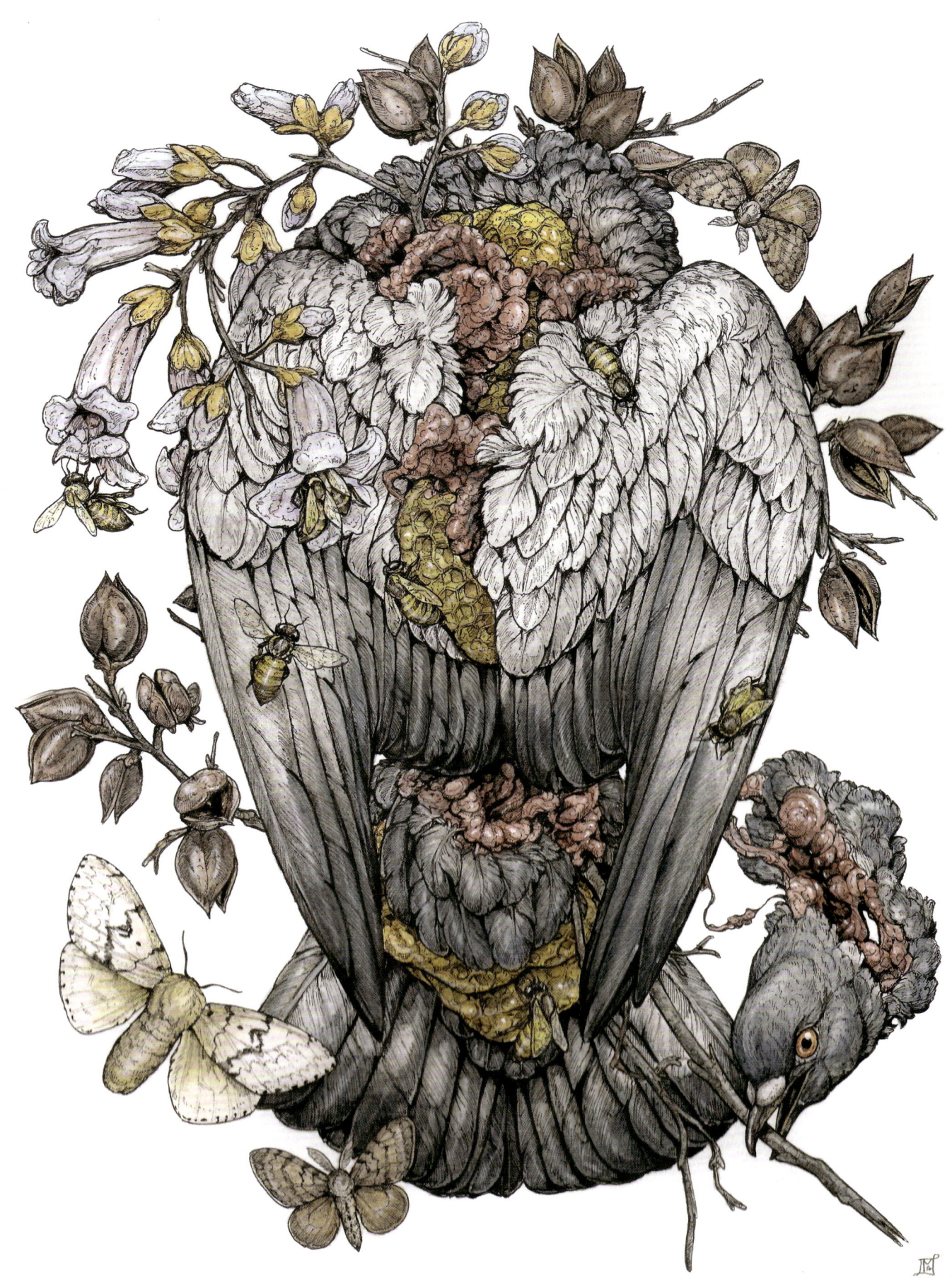

NEW HOME

9" x 12"

Pen, watercolor, ink, graphite, colored pencil, and gel pen on paper

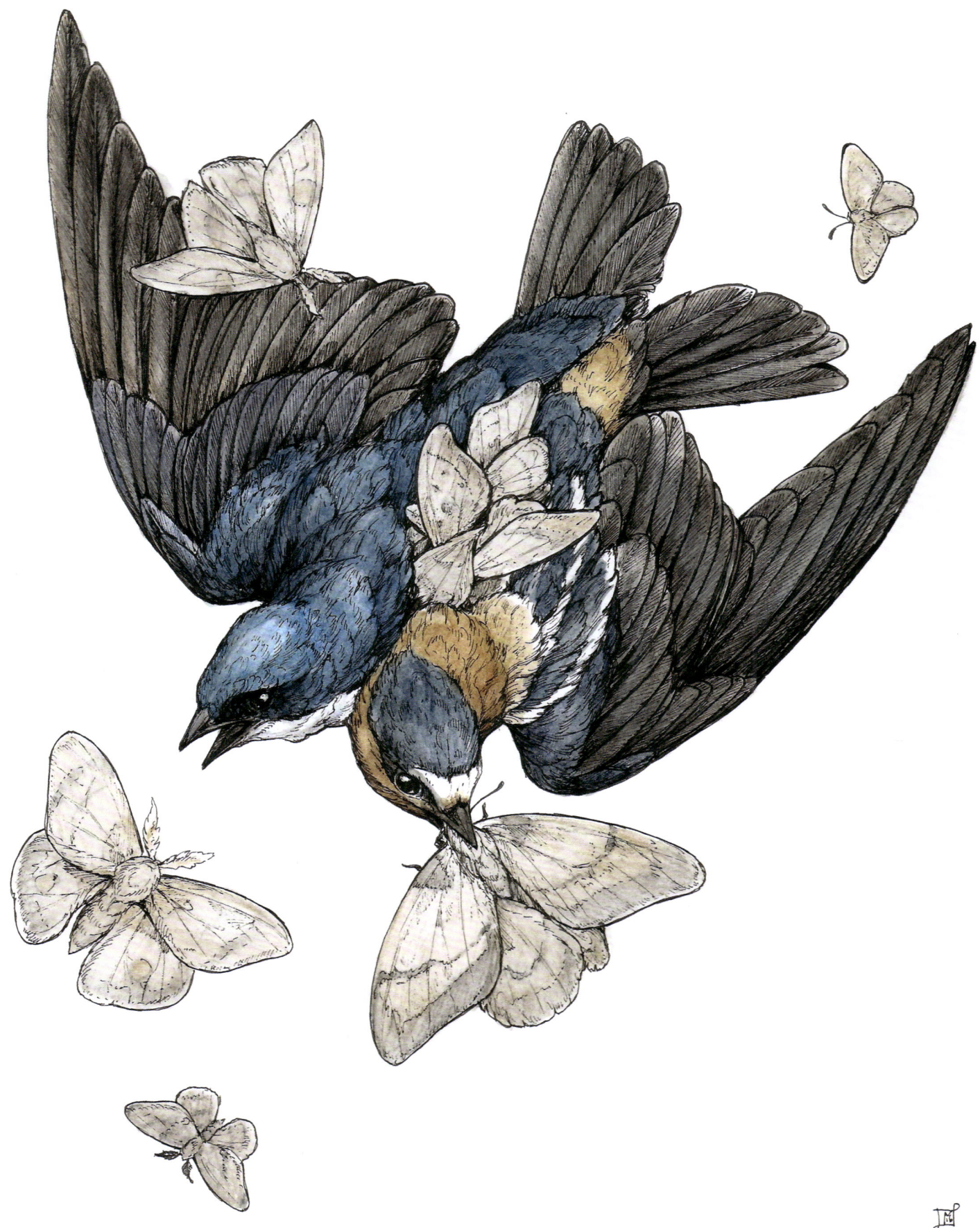

SWALLOWS

8″ x 10″

Pen, ink, colored pencil, graphite, and gel pen on paper

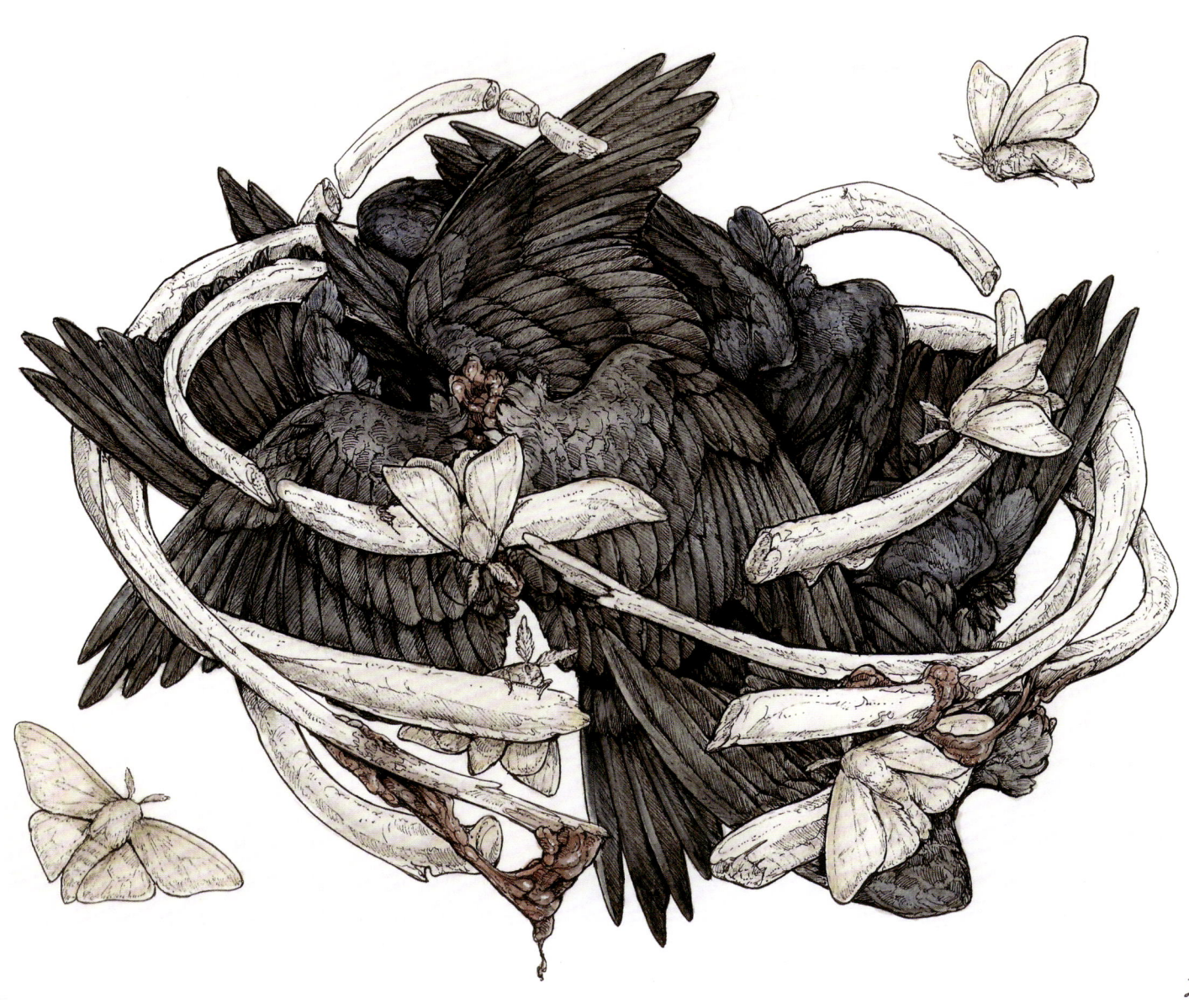

MY ANXIOUS LUNGS I

10″ x 8″

Pen, ink, colored pencil, graphite, and gel pen on paper

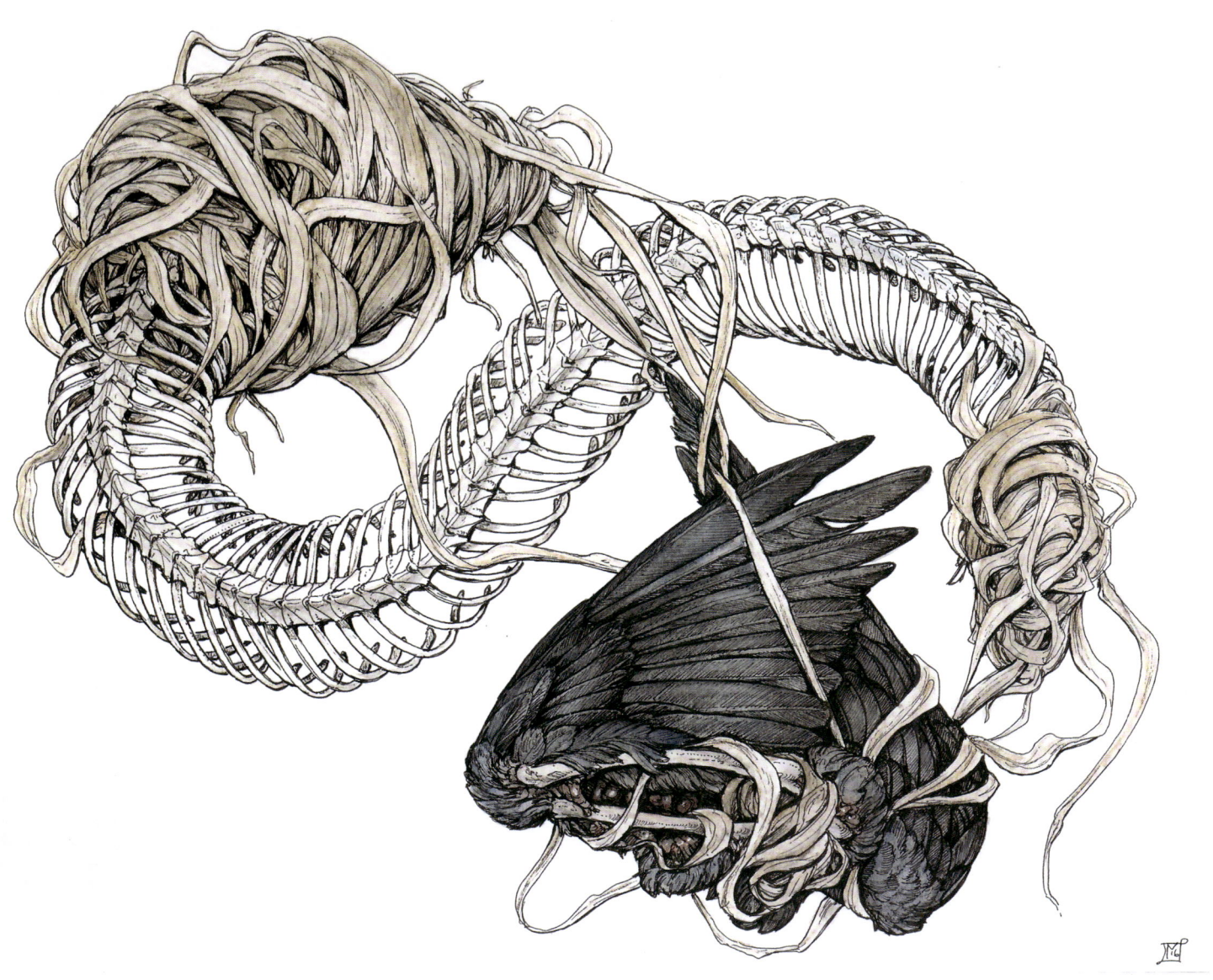

MY ANXIOUS LUNGS II

10″ x 8″

Pen, ink, colored pencil, graphite, and gel pen on paper

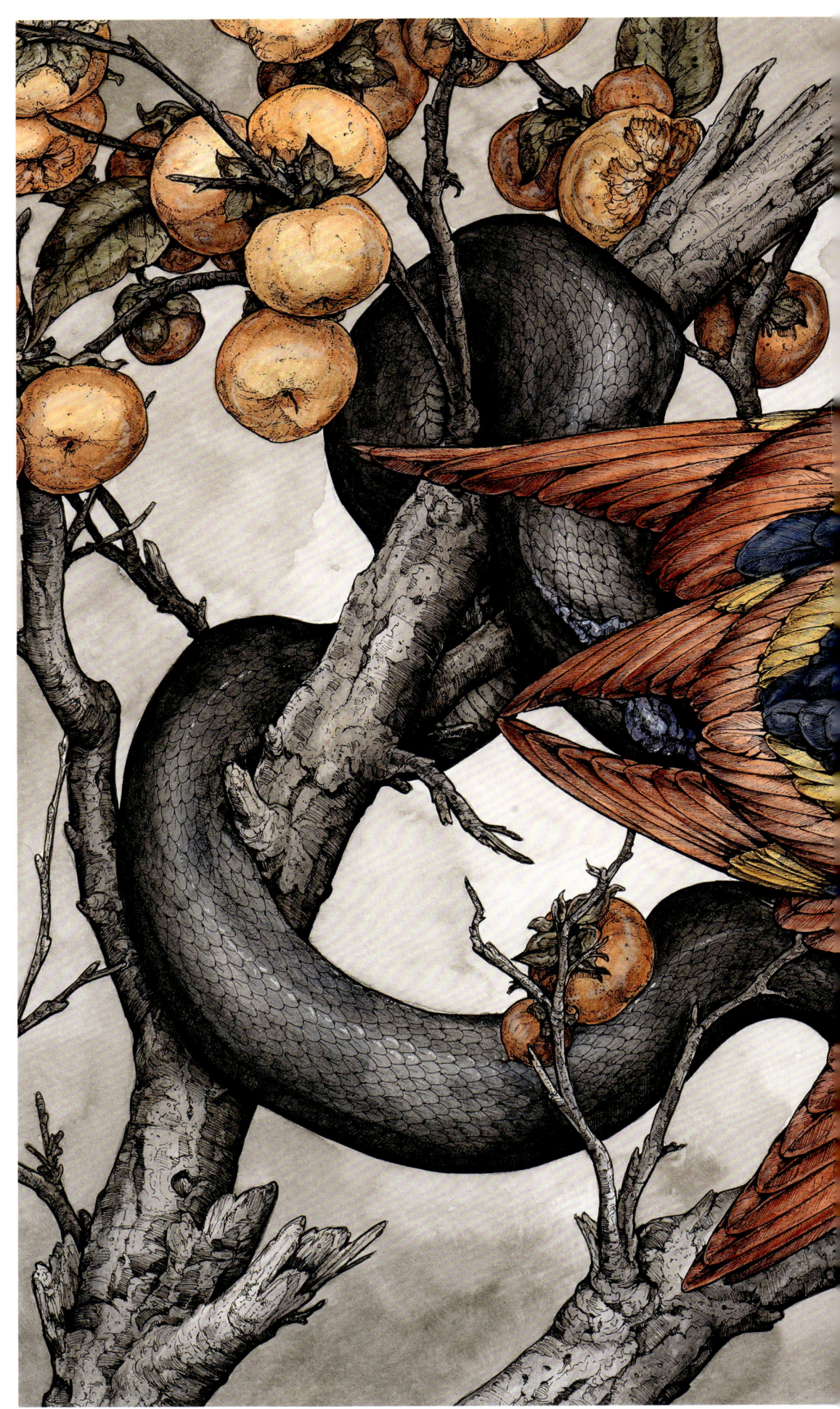

SWEET DAMNATION

24" x 16"

Pen, ink, graphite, colored pencil, and
gel pen on paper

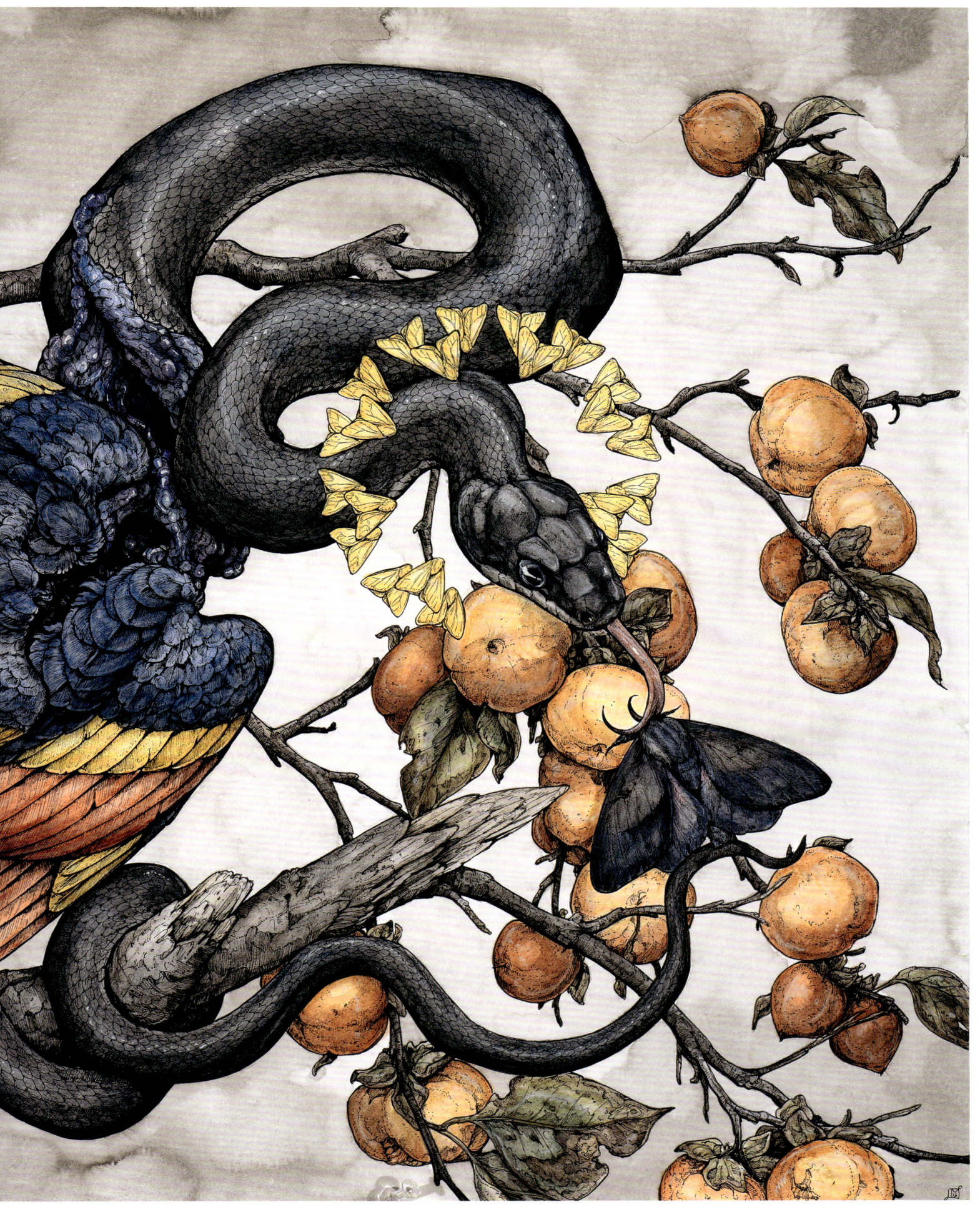

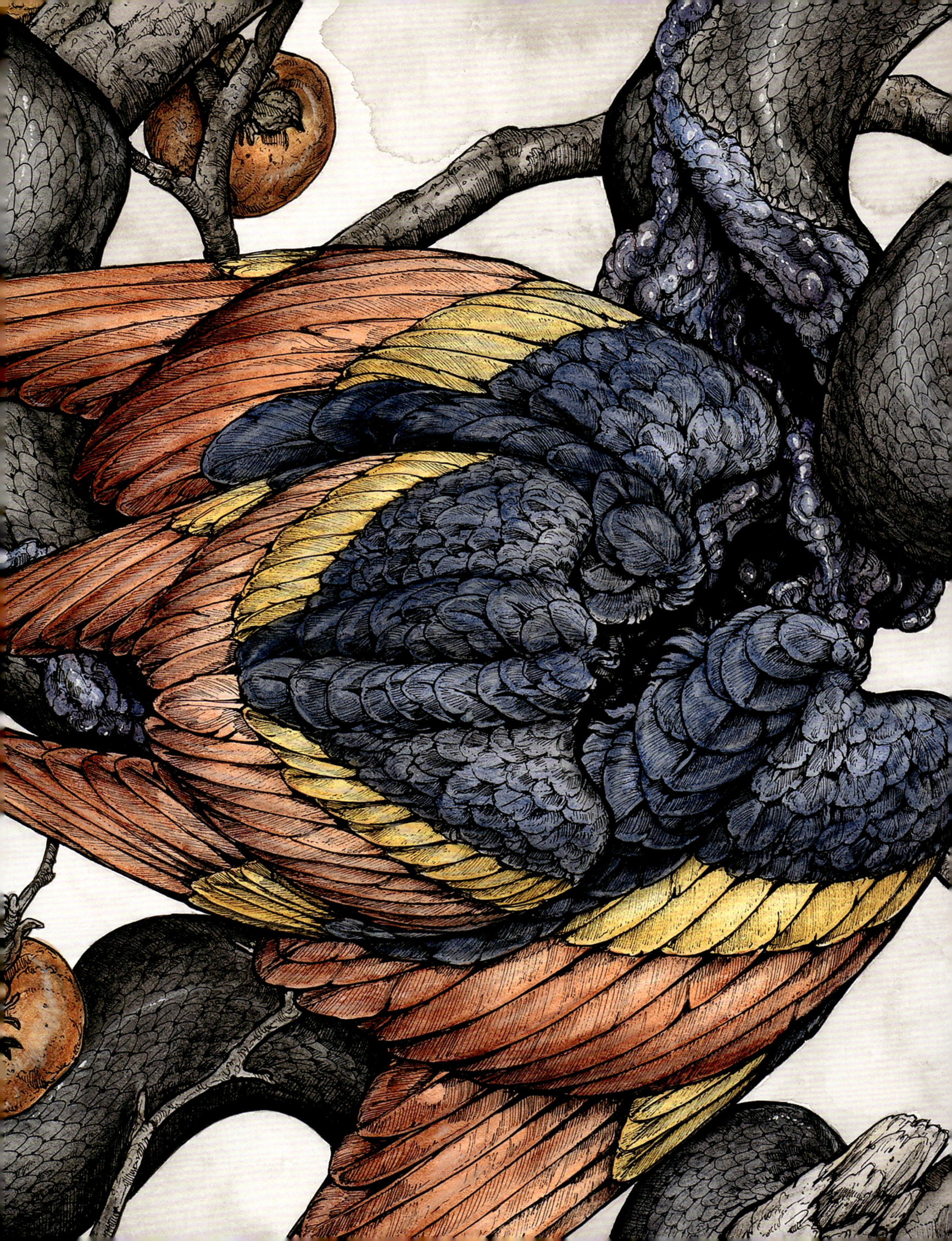

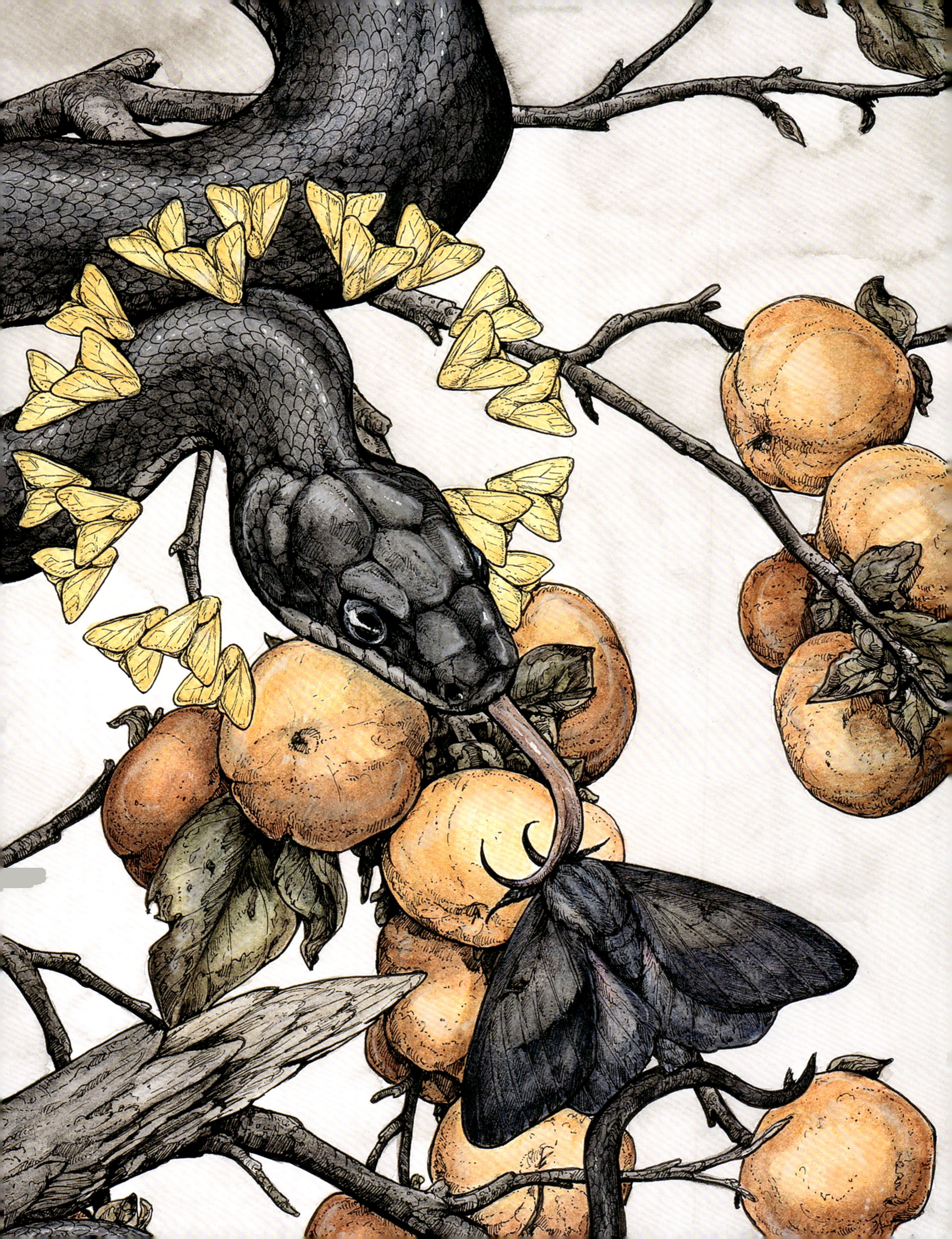

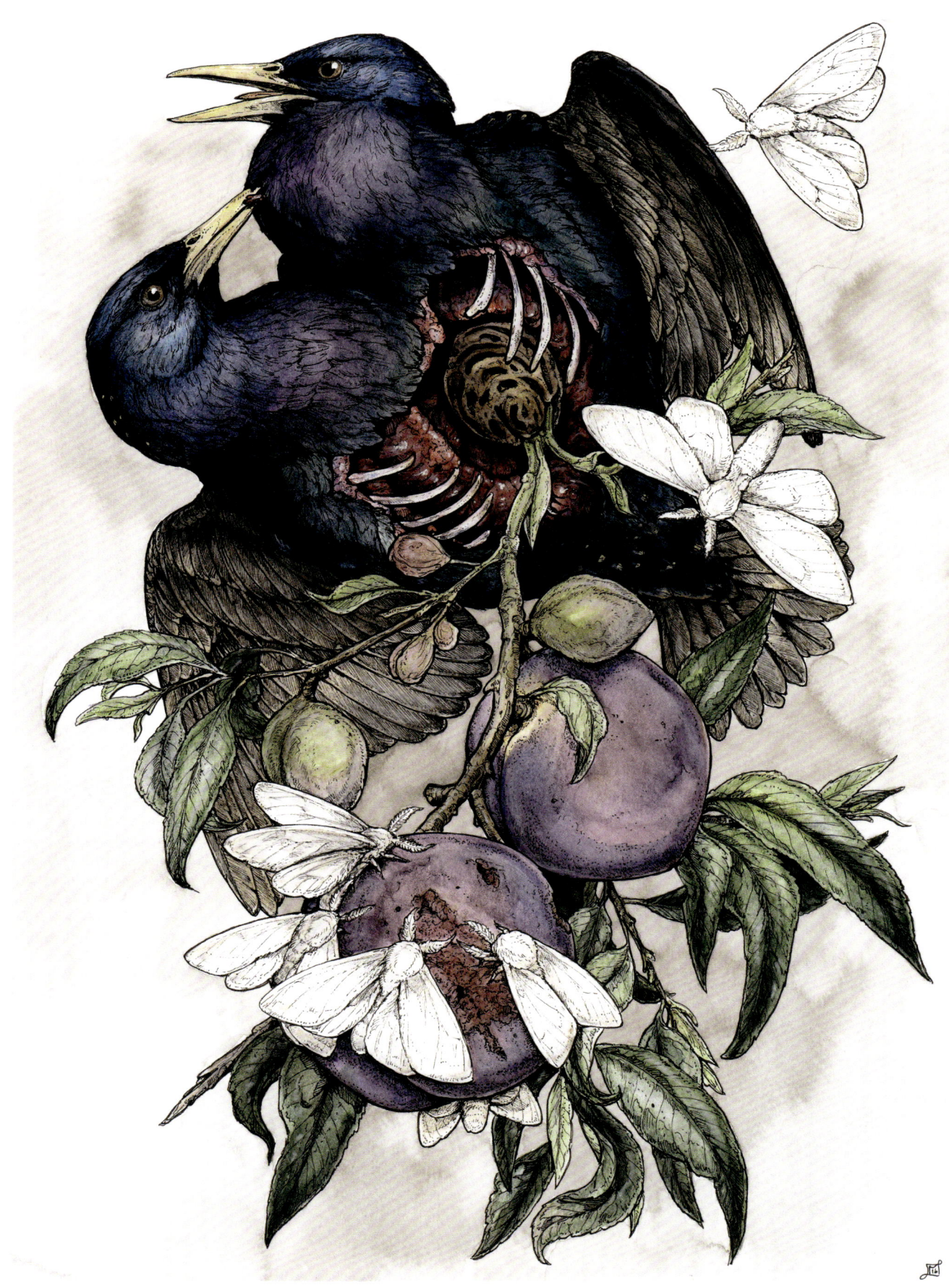

ATTACHED

8.5" x 11.75"

Pen, ink, graphite, colored pencil, gel pen, and acrylic on paper
From the exhibition "Flesh Blood Bone"

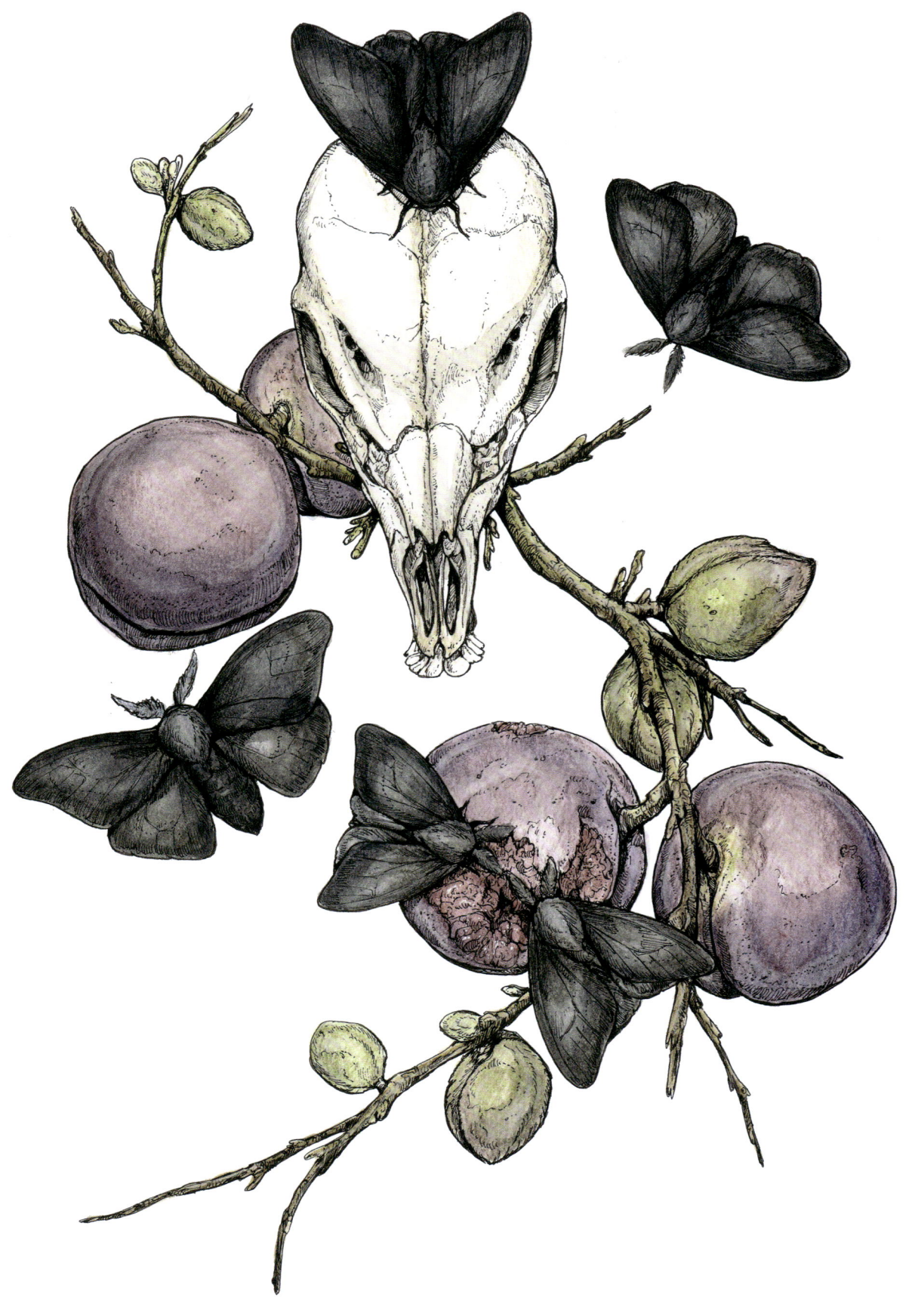

ONE CAN ONLY HOPE

9" x 12"

Pen, ink, graphite, colored pencil, and gel pen on paper
From the exhibition "Flesh Blood Bone"

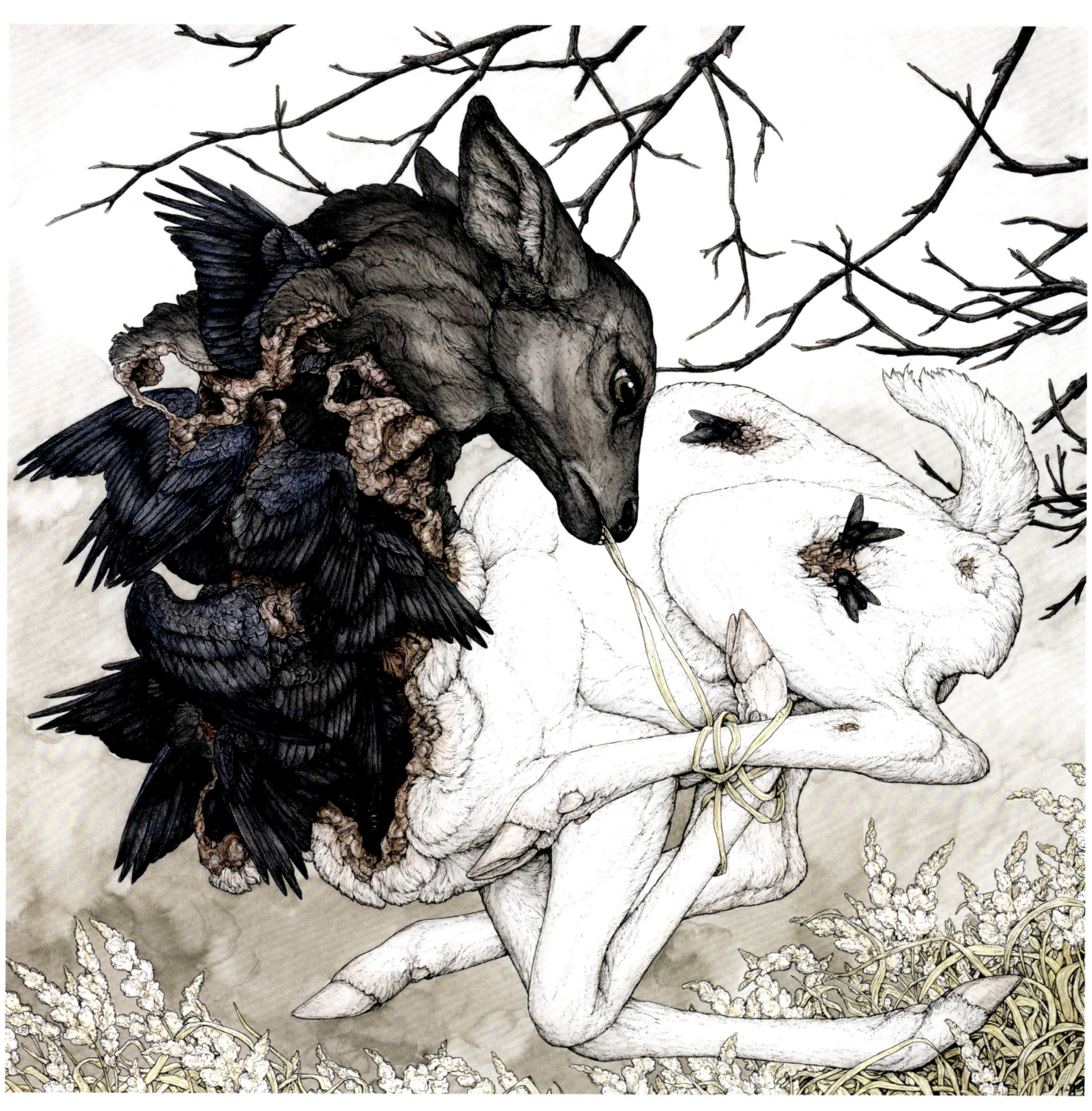

SELF-INFLICTED

20″ x 20″

Pen, ink, graphite, colored pencil, and gel pen on paper
From the exhibition "Flesh Blood Bone"

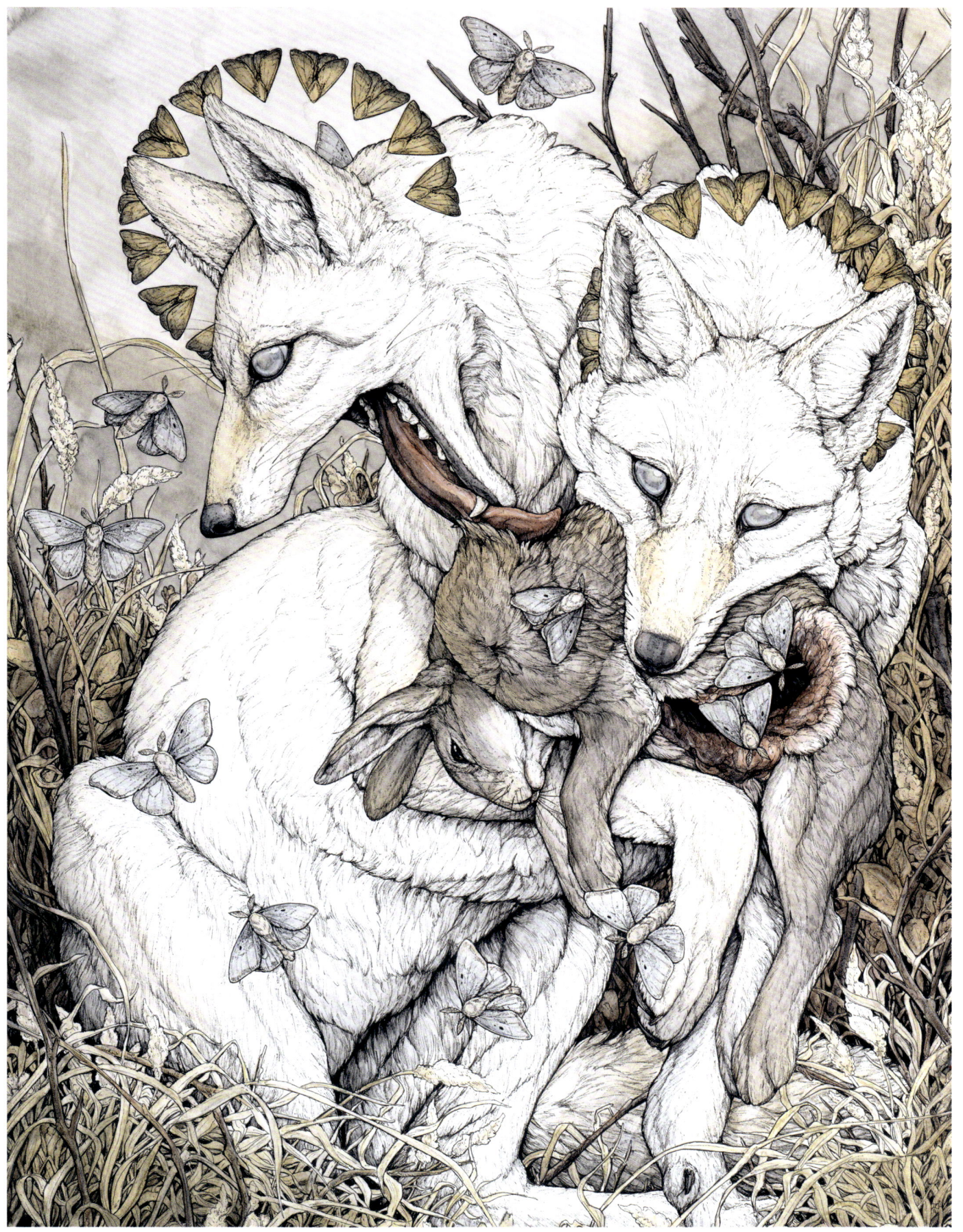

FORTUNA

15" x 19"

Pen, ink, colored pencil, graphite, and gel pen on paper

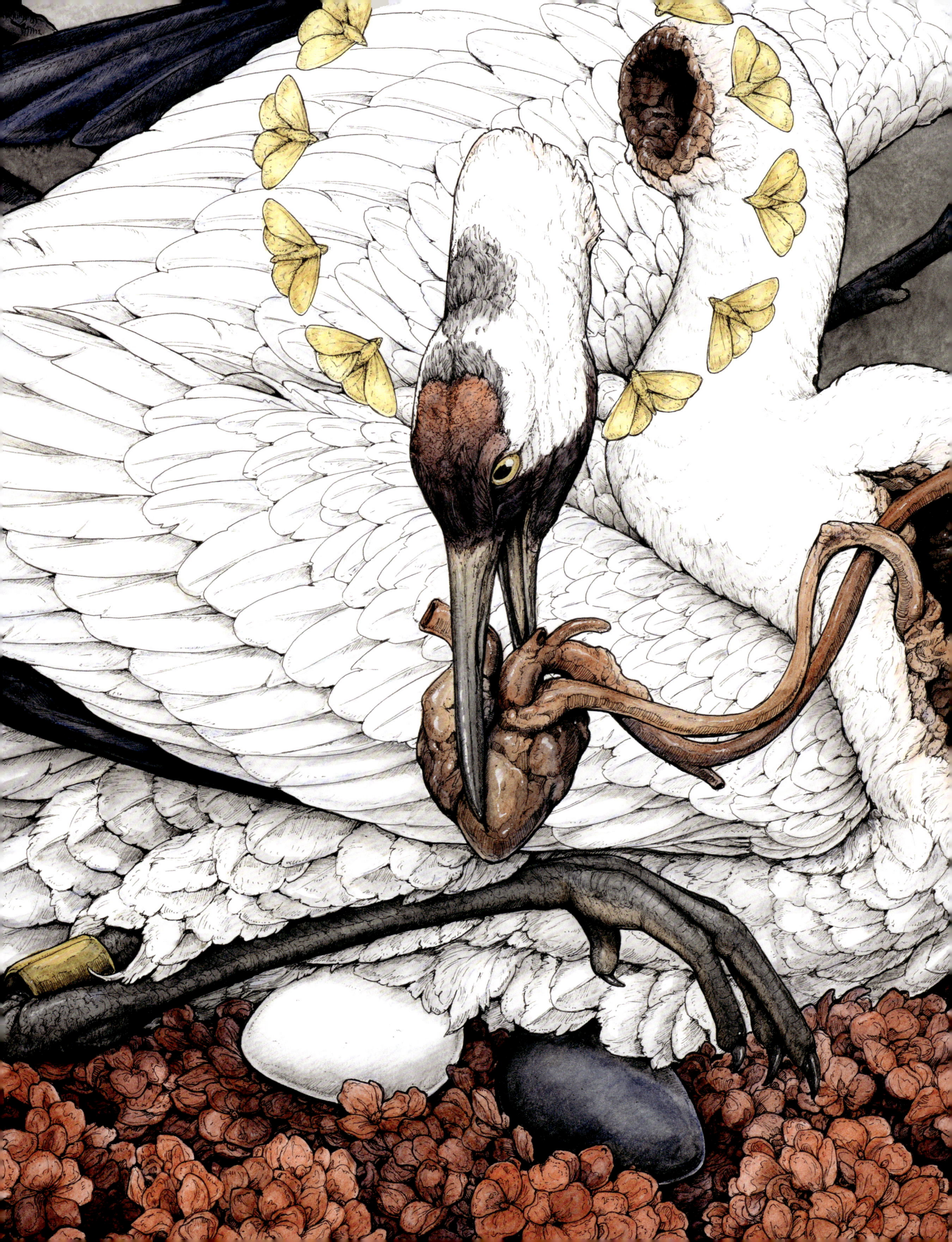

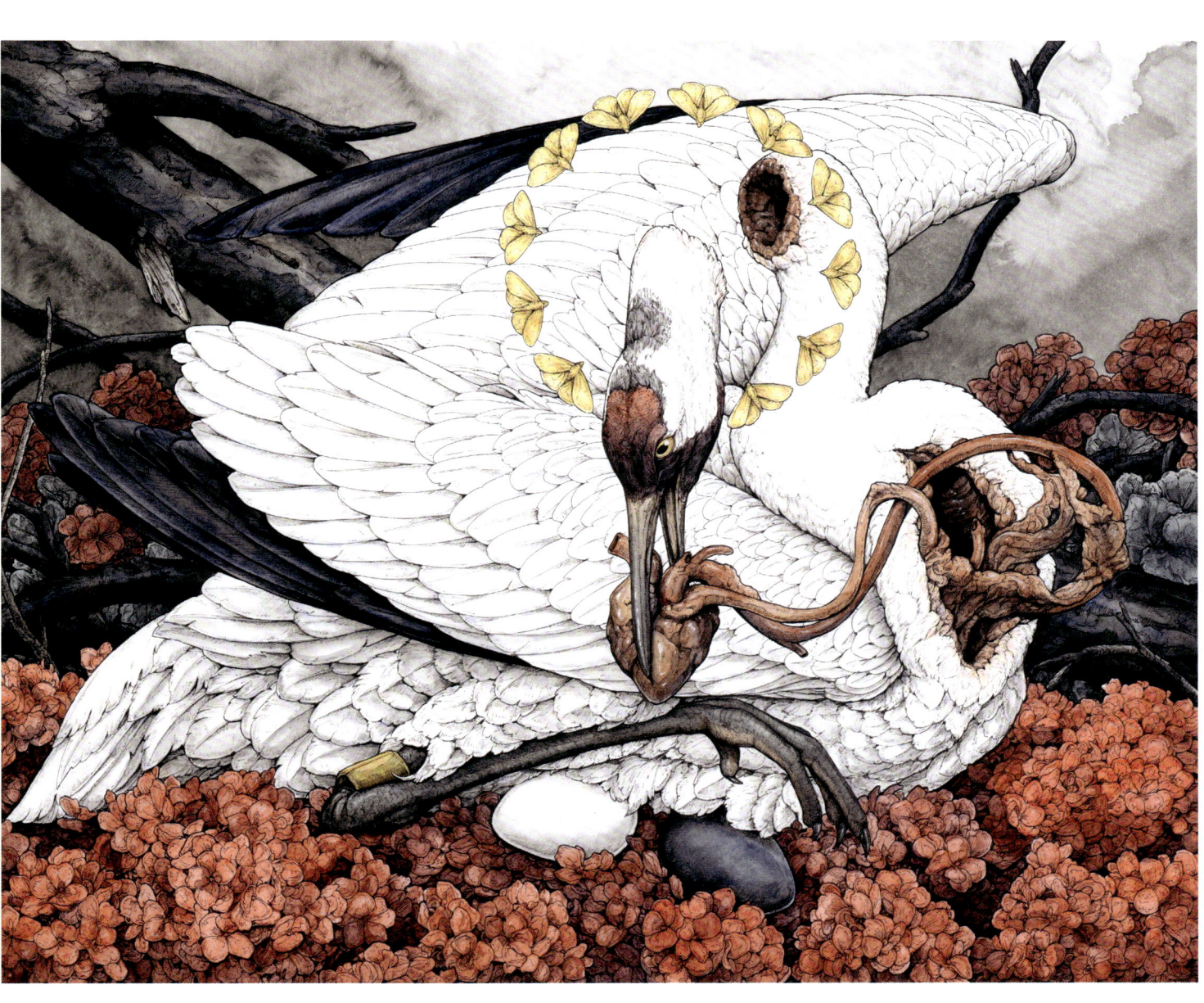

THE SACRIFICE OF THE BLOOD-RED SAINT

20" x 16"

Pen, ink, graphite, colored pencil, and gel pen on paper
From the exhibition "Flesh Blood Bone"

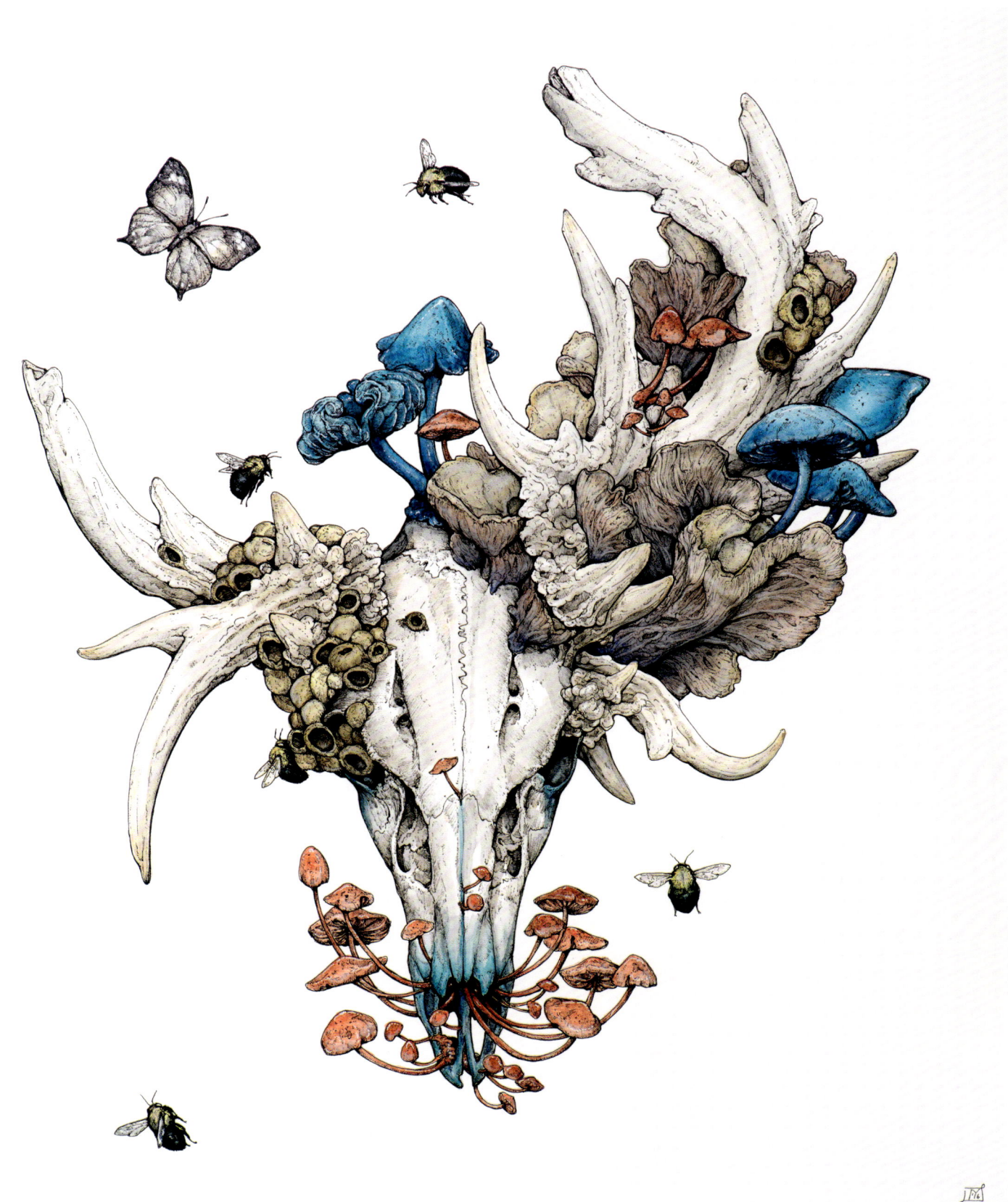

PERUKE

15" x 17.25"

Pen, ink, colored pencil, graphite, and gel pen on paper

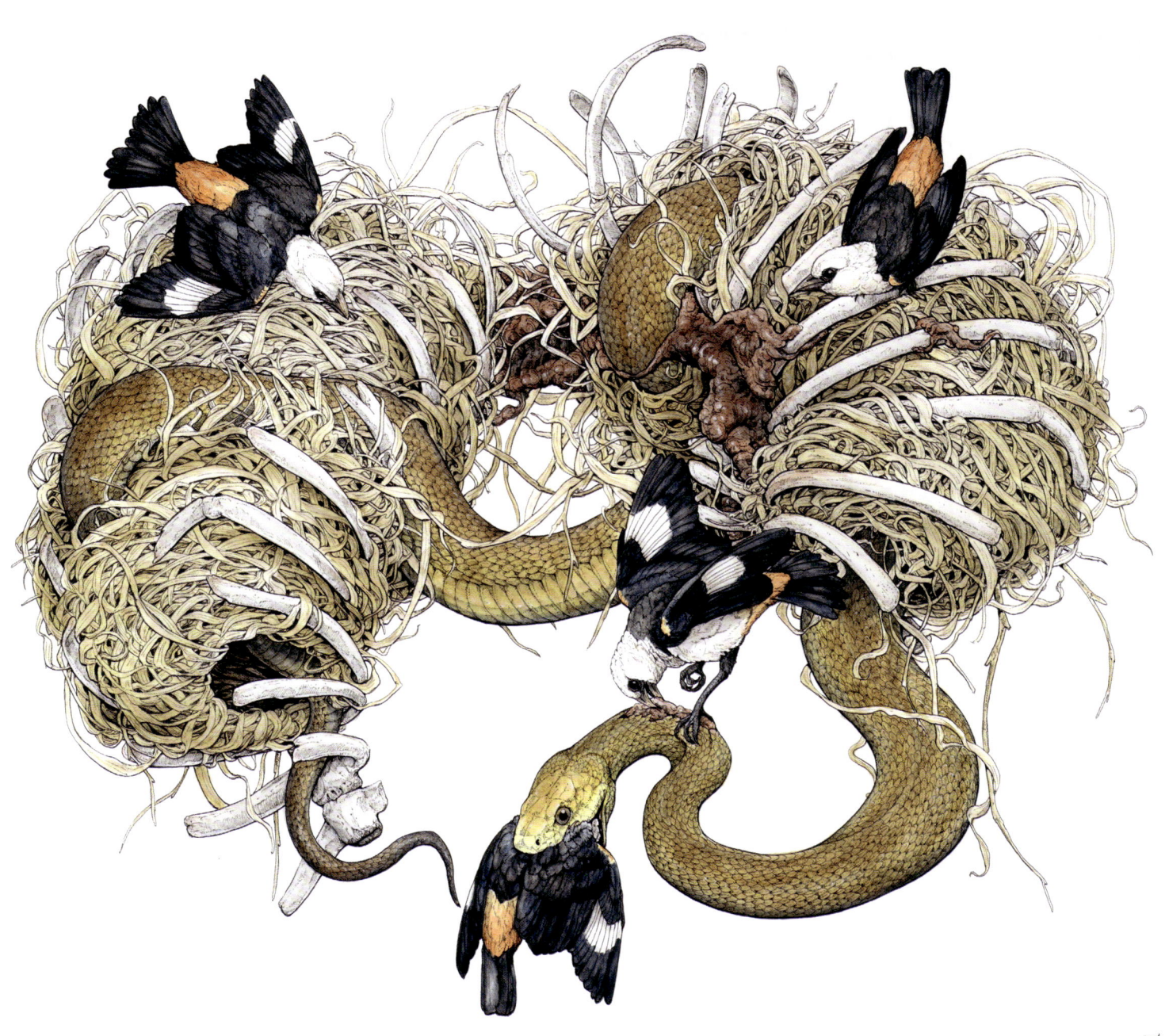

INHALE EXHALE CHOKE

20" x 17.75"

Pen, ink, graphite, colored pencil, and gel pen on paper
From the exhibition "Flesh Blood Bone"

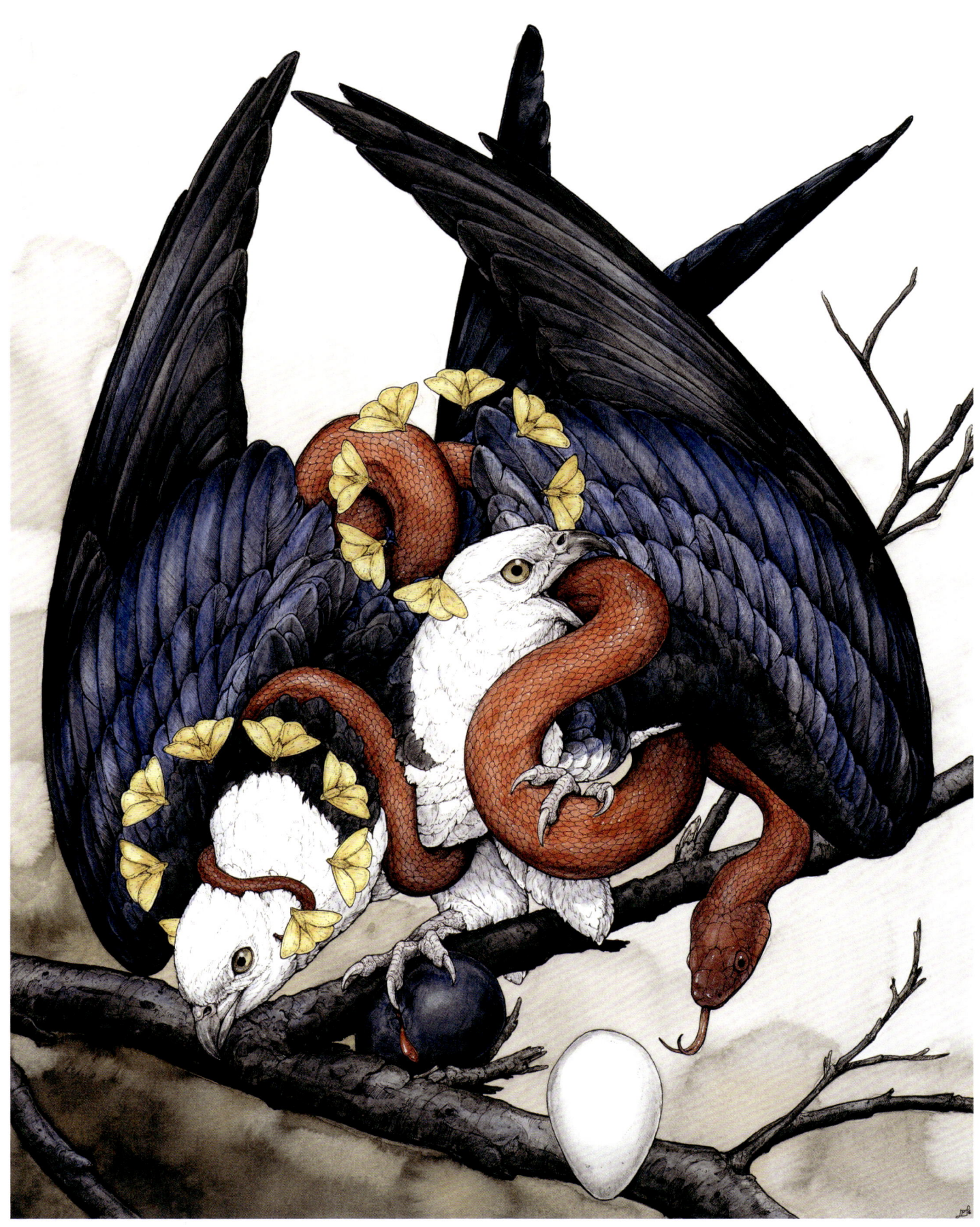

THE STRUGGLE OF THE APATHETIC SAINT

15.75" x 20"

Pen, ink, graphite, colored pencil, and gel pen on paper
From the exhibition "Flesh Blood Bone"

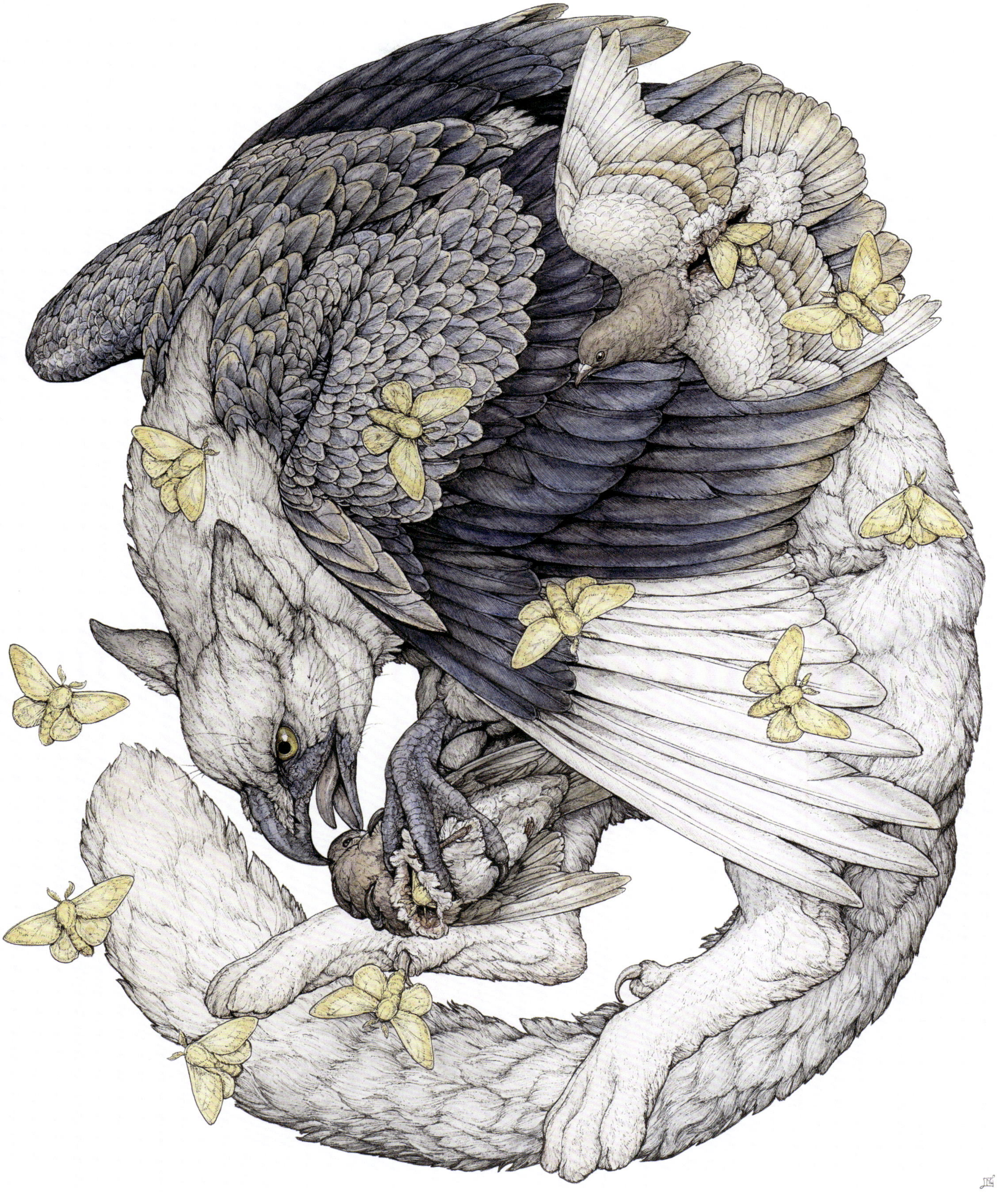

PIGEON GRYPHON

15.5" x 19.25"

Pen, ink, colored pencil, graphite, and gel pen on paper

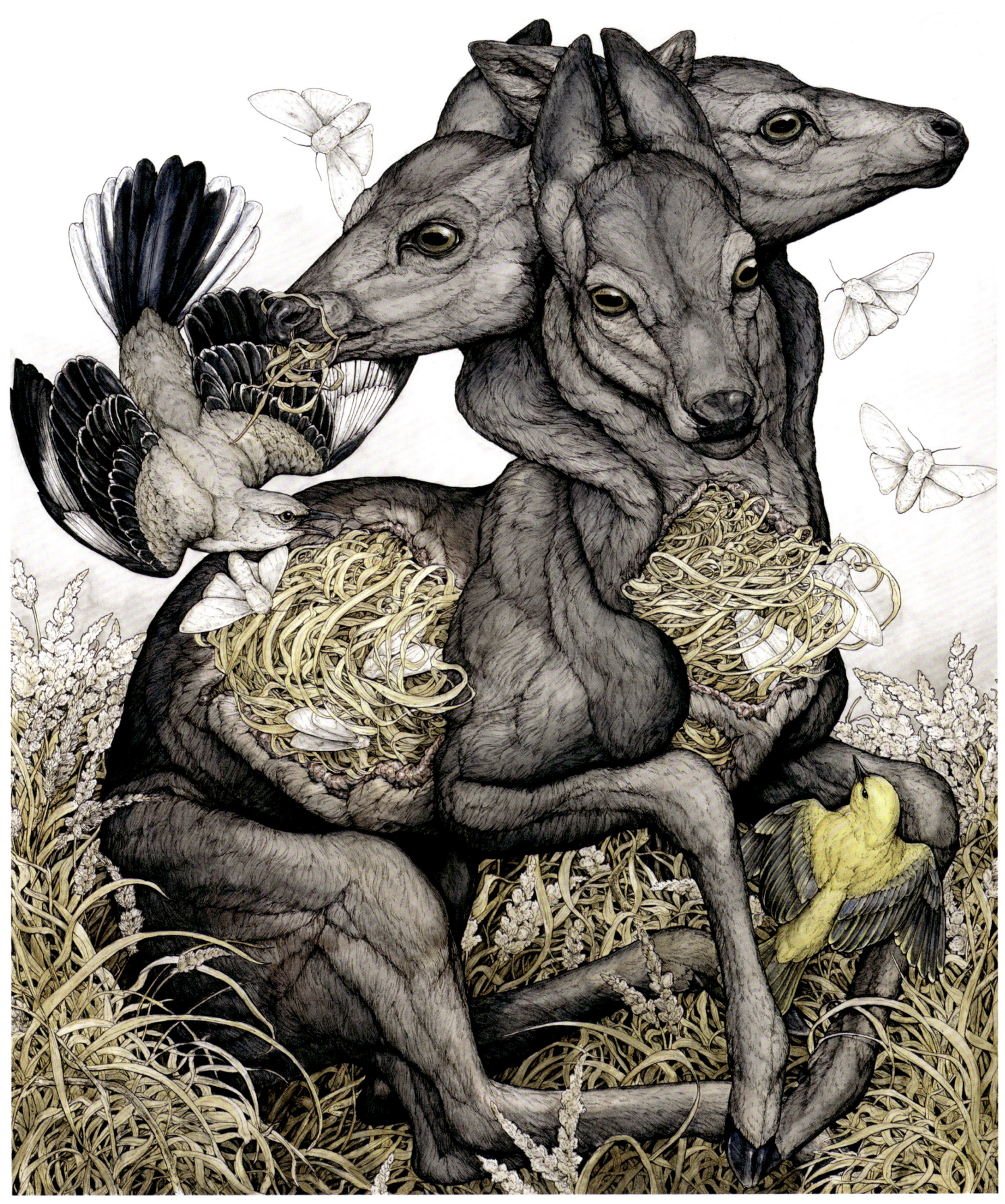

THE FIRST

20" x 24"

Pen, ink, graphite, colored pencil, and gel pen on paper
From the exhibition "Flesh Blood Bone"

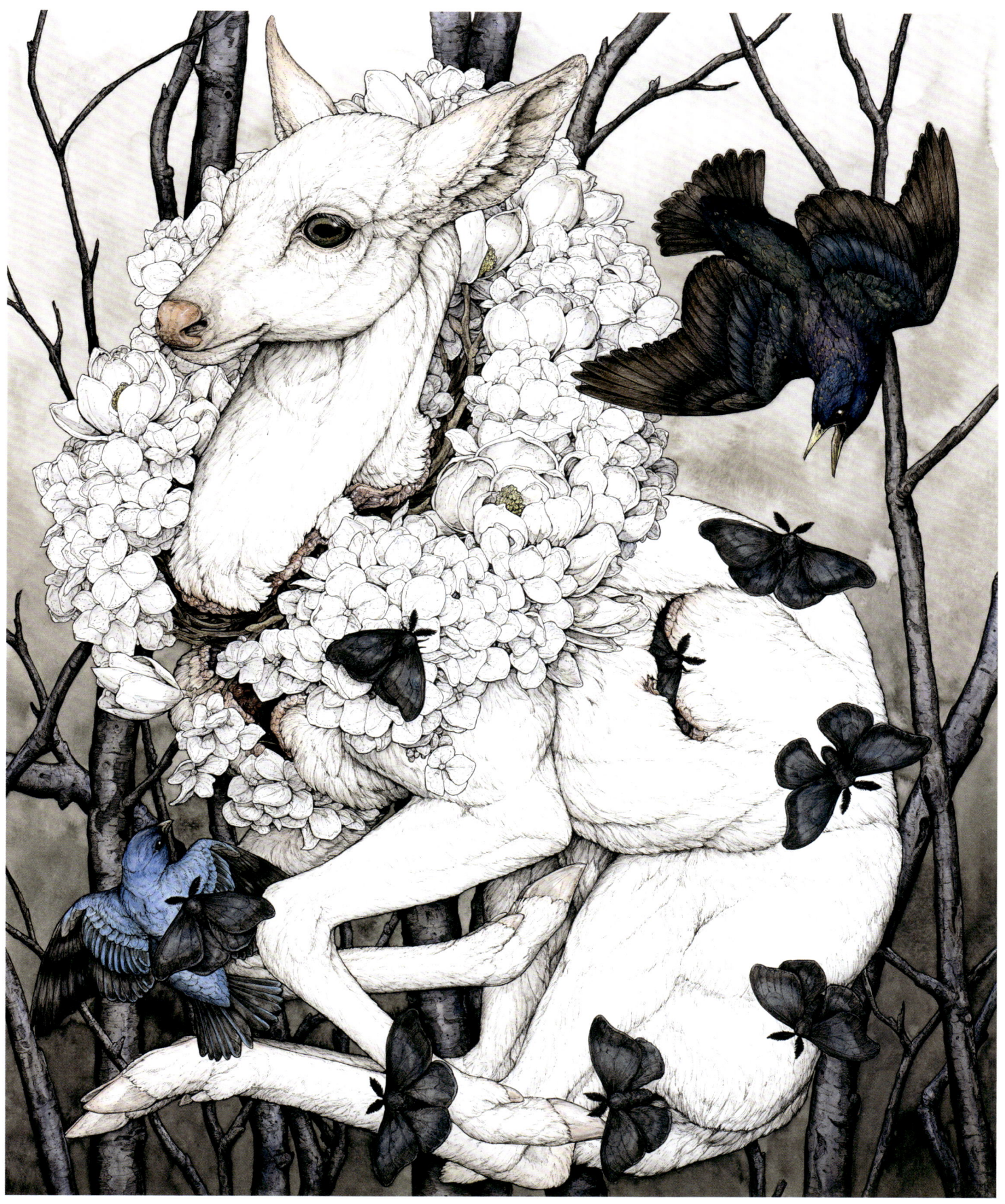

THE SECOND

20" x 24"

Pen, ink, graphite, colored pencil, gel pen, and acrylic on paper
From the exhibition "Flesh Blood Bone"

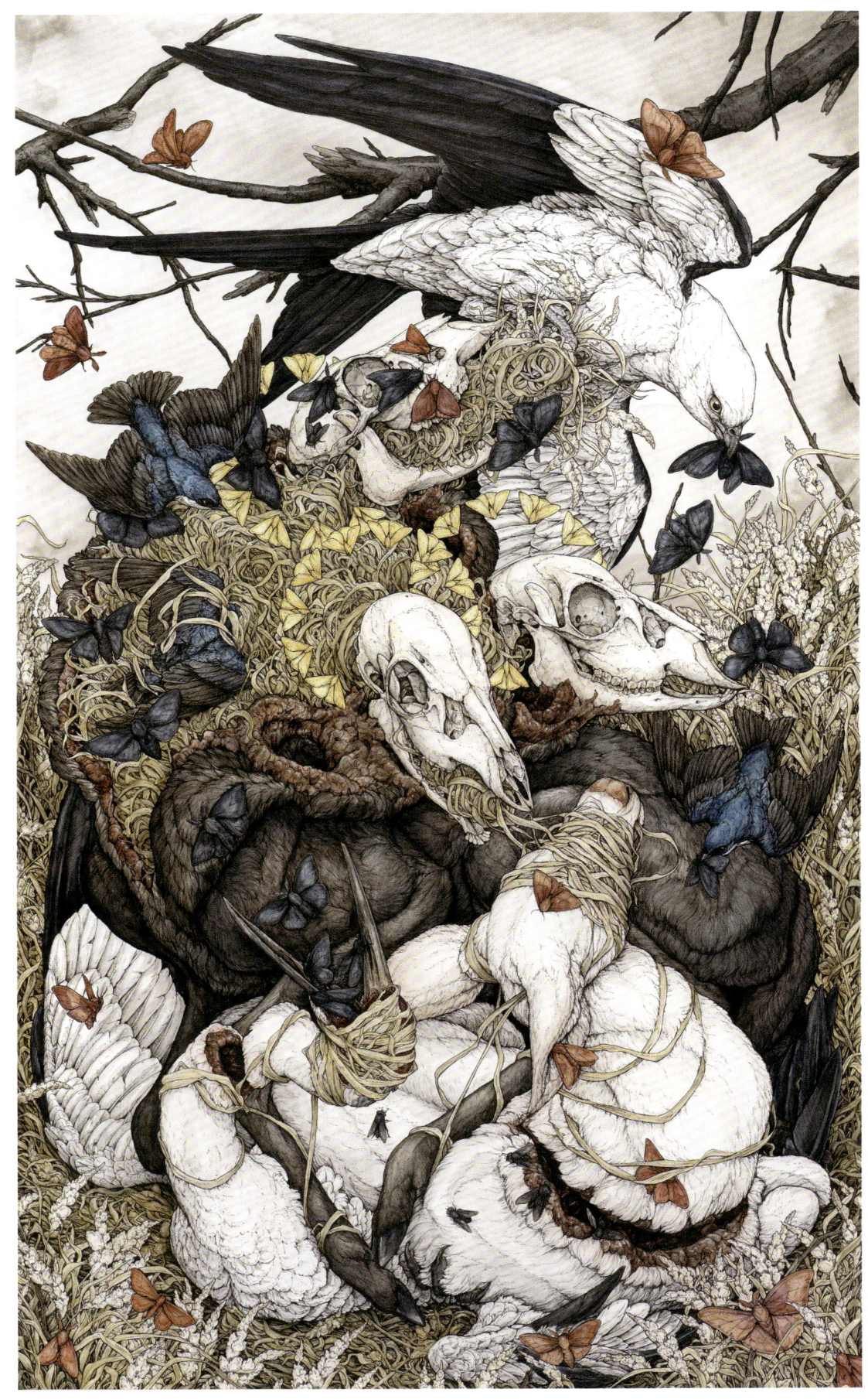

WHEN THE FIRST BECAME DIVINE

24" x 40"

Pen, ink, graphite, colored pencil, and gel pen on paper
From the exhibition "Flesh Blood Bone"

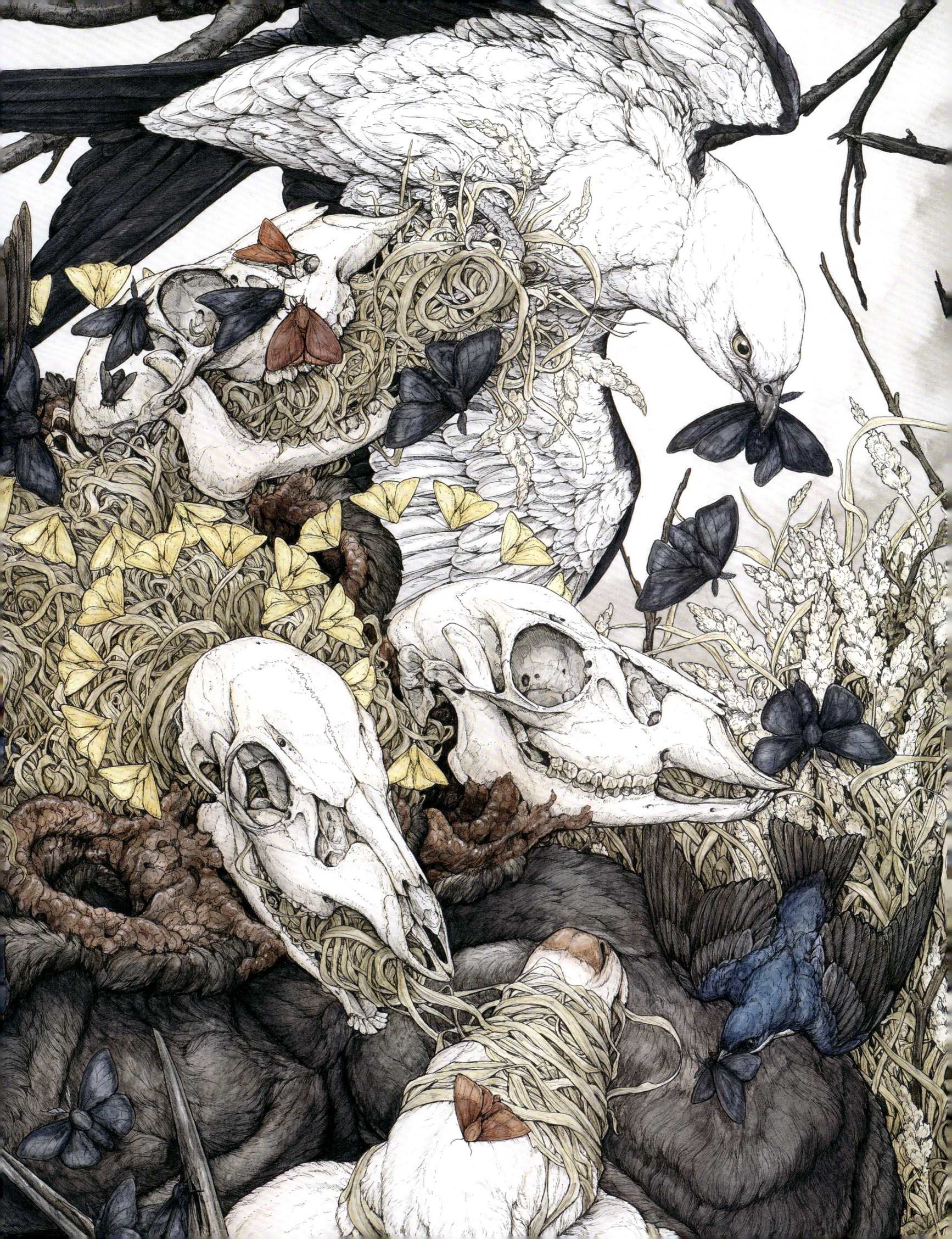

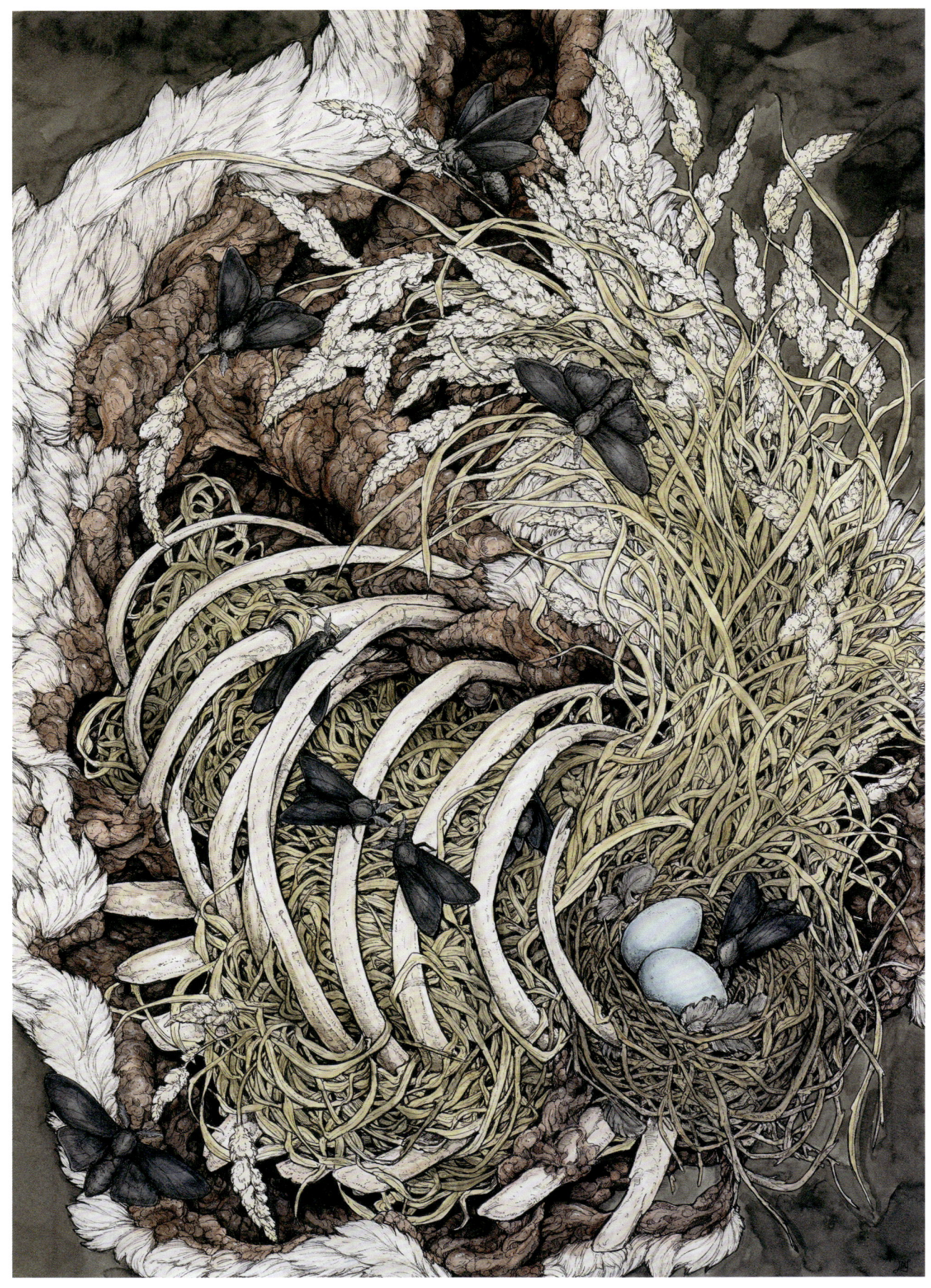

IN MY BONES

13.75" x 19.25"

Pen, ink, graphite, colored pencil, and gel pen on paper
From the exhibition "Flesh Blood Bone"

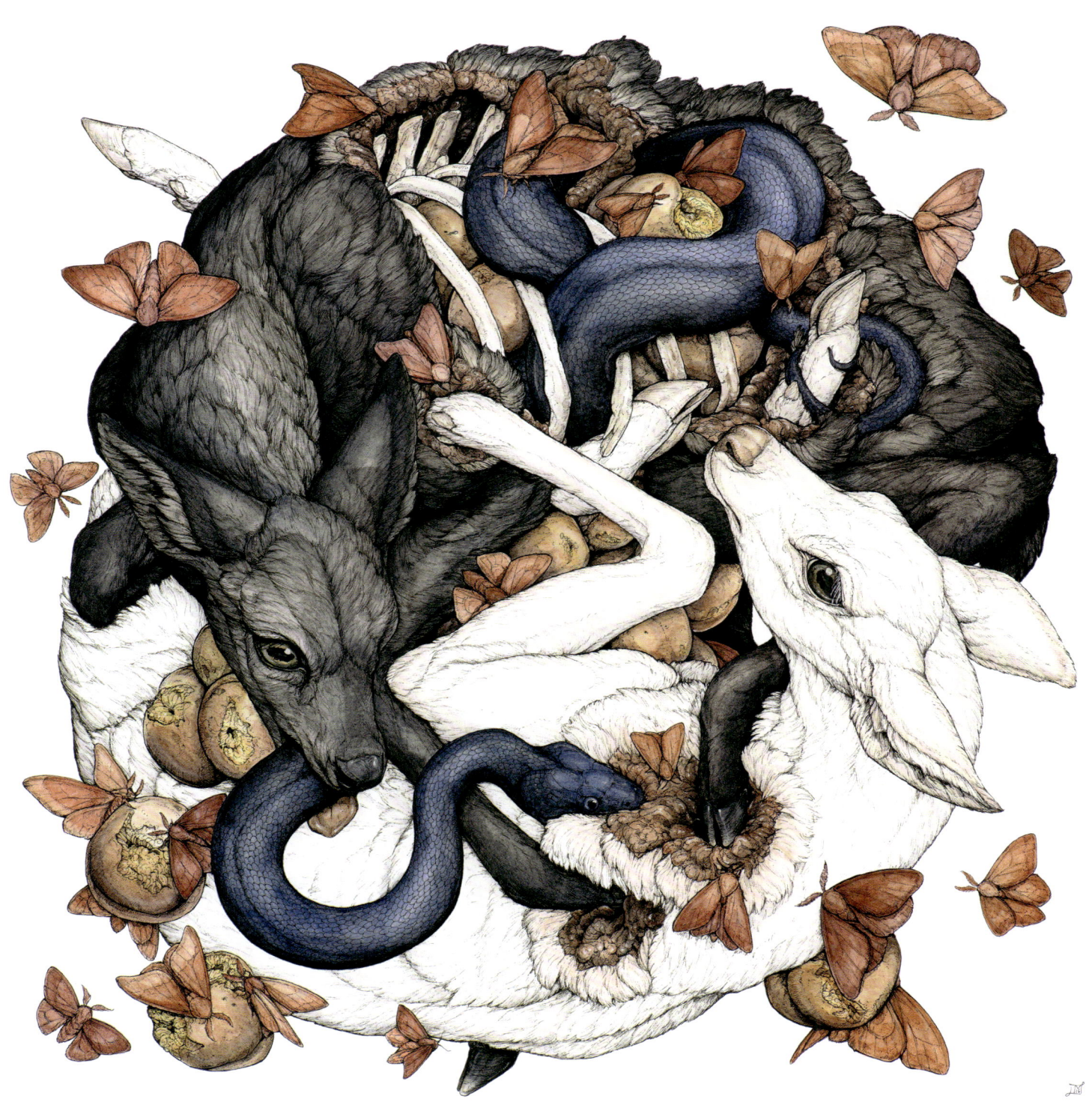

FALL APART LIKE ME

20" x 20"

Pen, ink, graphite, colored pencil, and gel pen on paper
From the exhibition "Flesh Blood Bone"

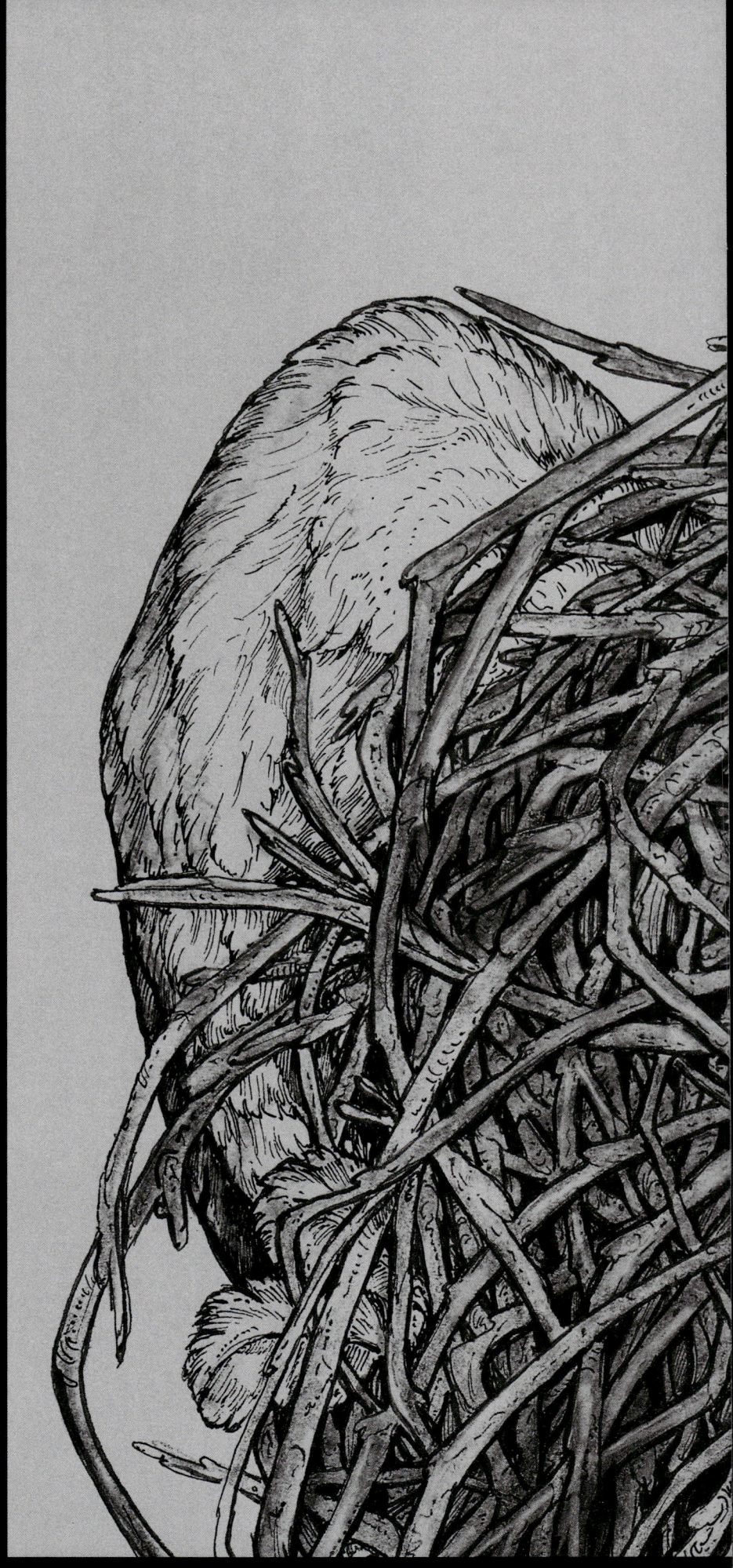

SACRED DECAY

2017

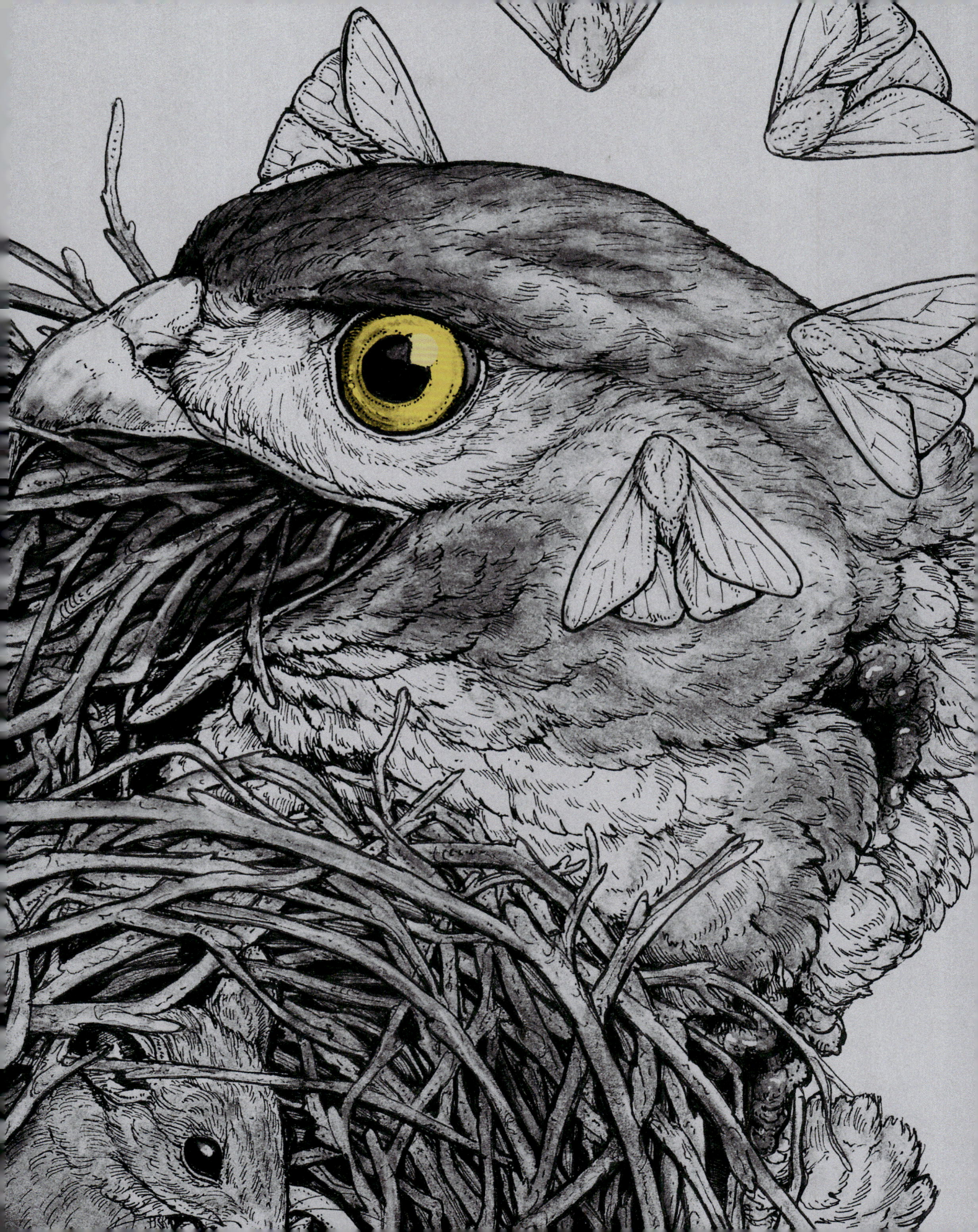

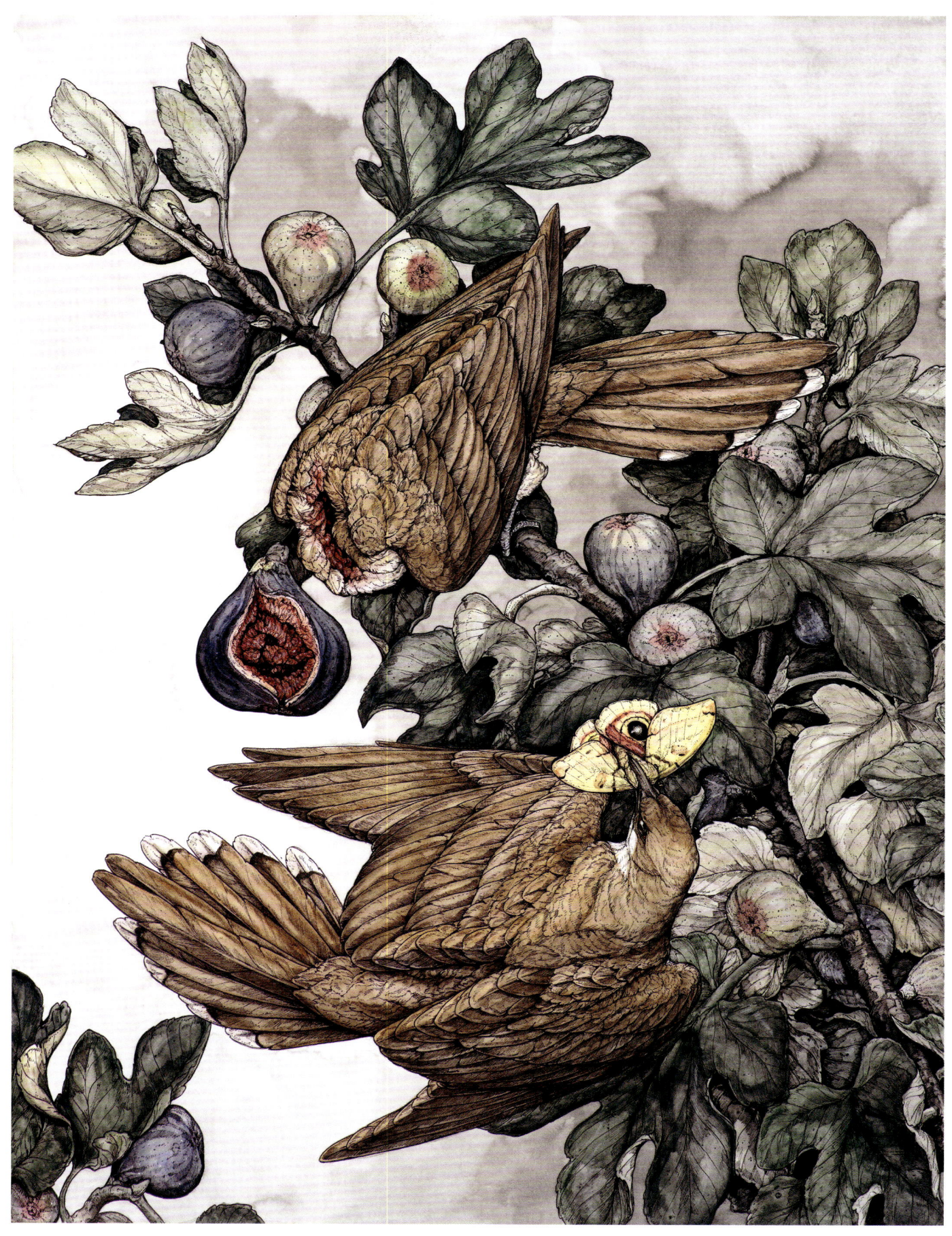

FIG

18" x 23.5"

Pen, watercolor, ink, colored pencil, graphite, and gel pen on paper

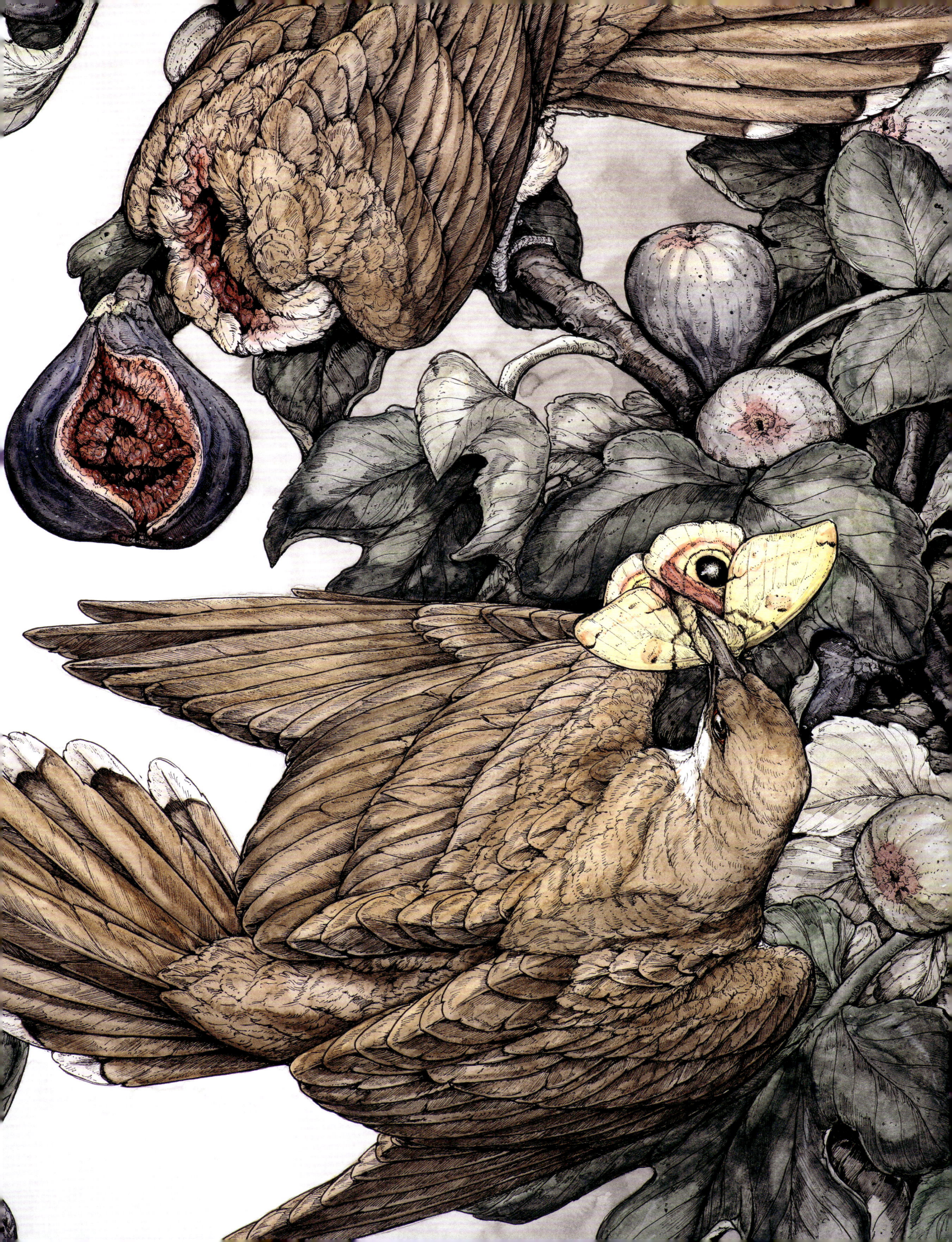

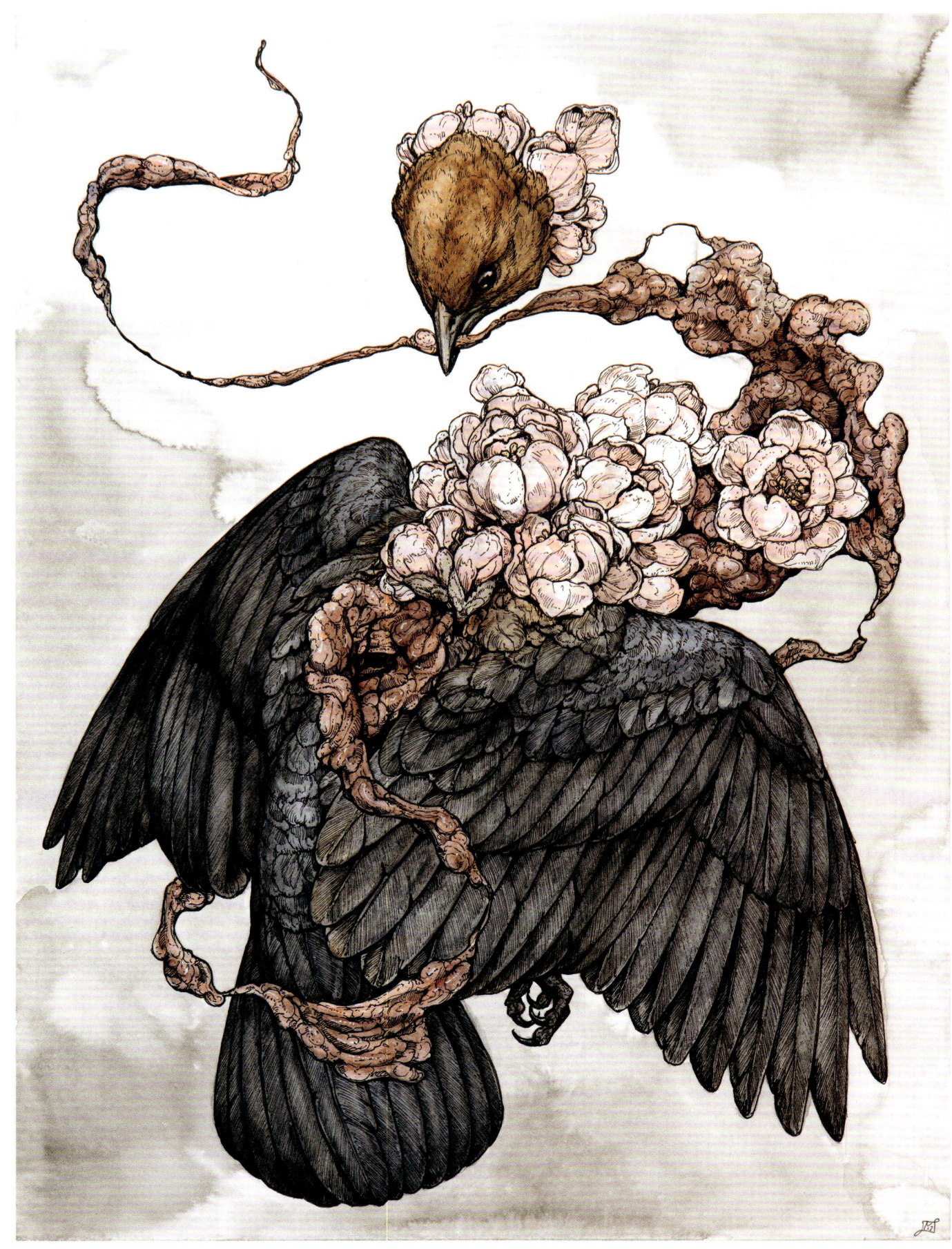

PEACH BLOSSOM

9" x 12"

Pen, watercolor, ink, colored pencil, graphite, and gel pen on paper

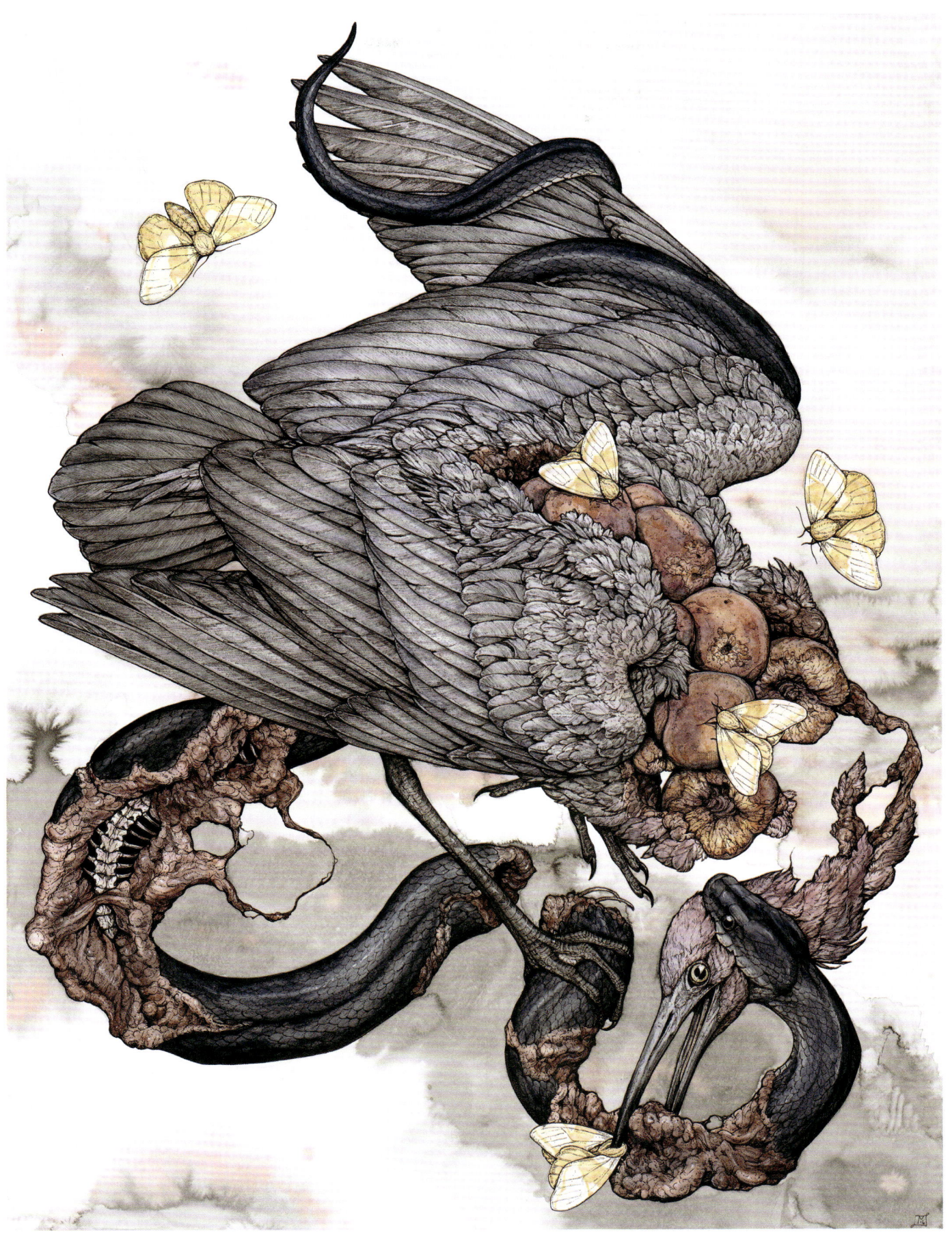

PEACH

18" x 23.75"

Pen, watercolor, ink, colored pencil, graphite, and gel pen on paper

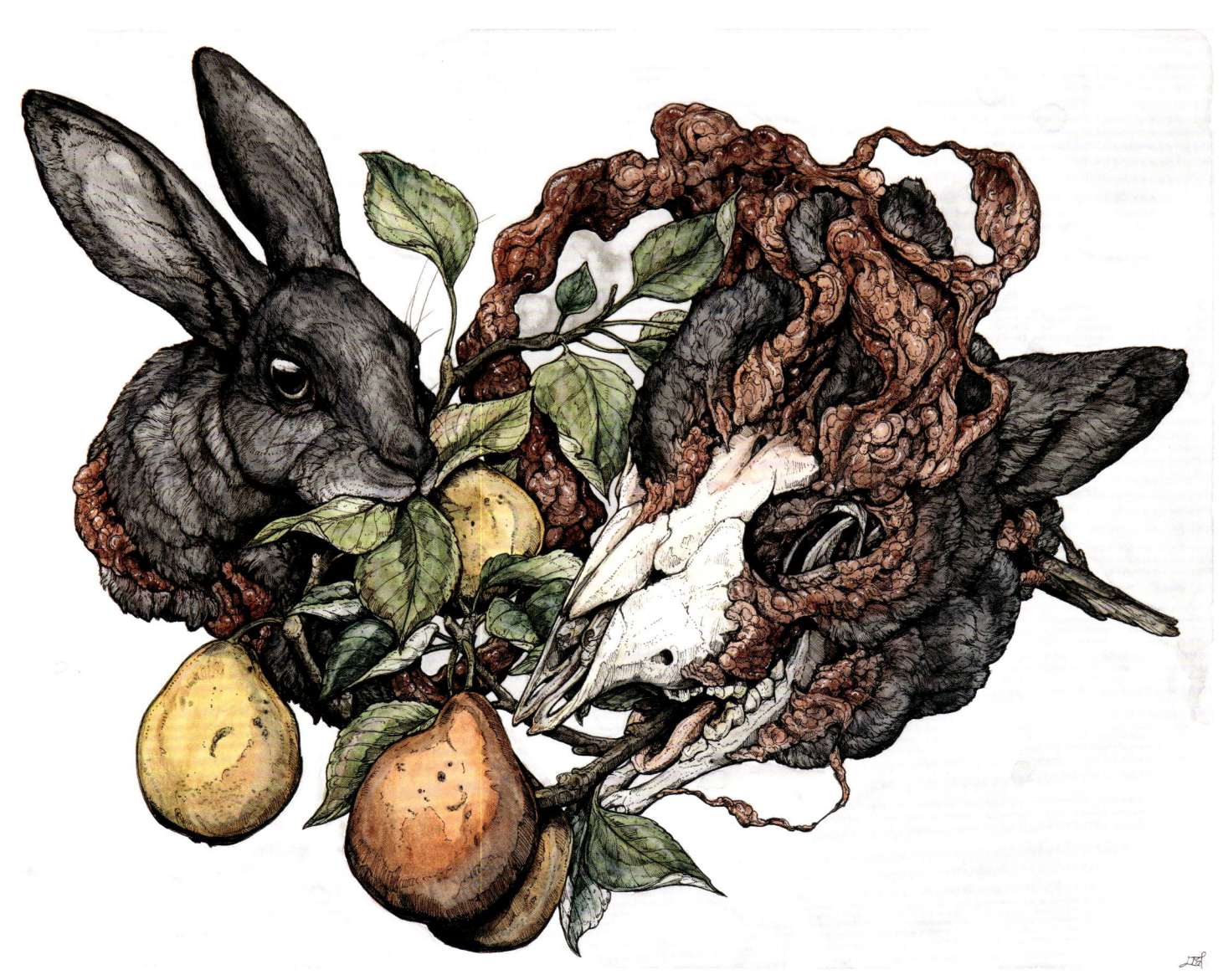

PEAR

14" x 11"

Pen, watercolor, ink, colored pencil, graphite, and gel pen on paper

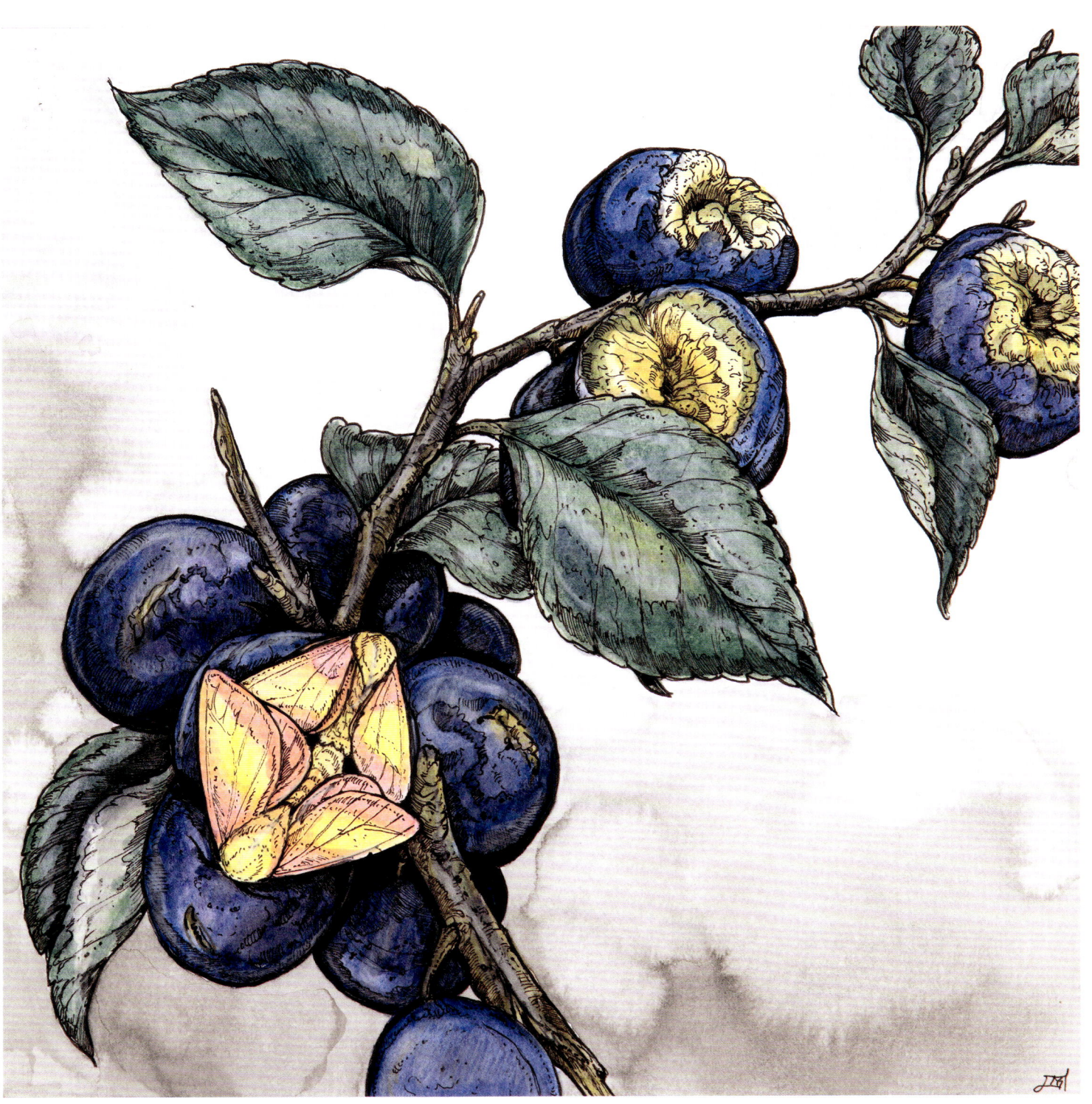

PLUM

7" x 7"

Pen, watercolor, ink, colored pencil, graphite, and gel pen on paper

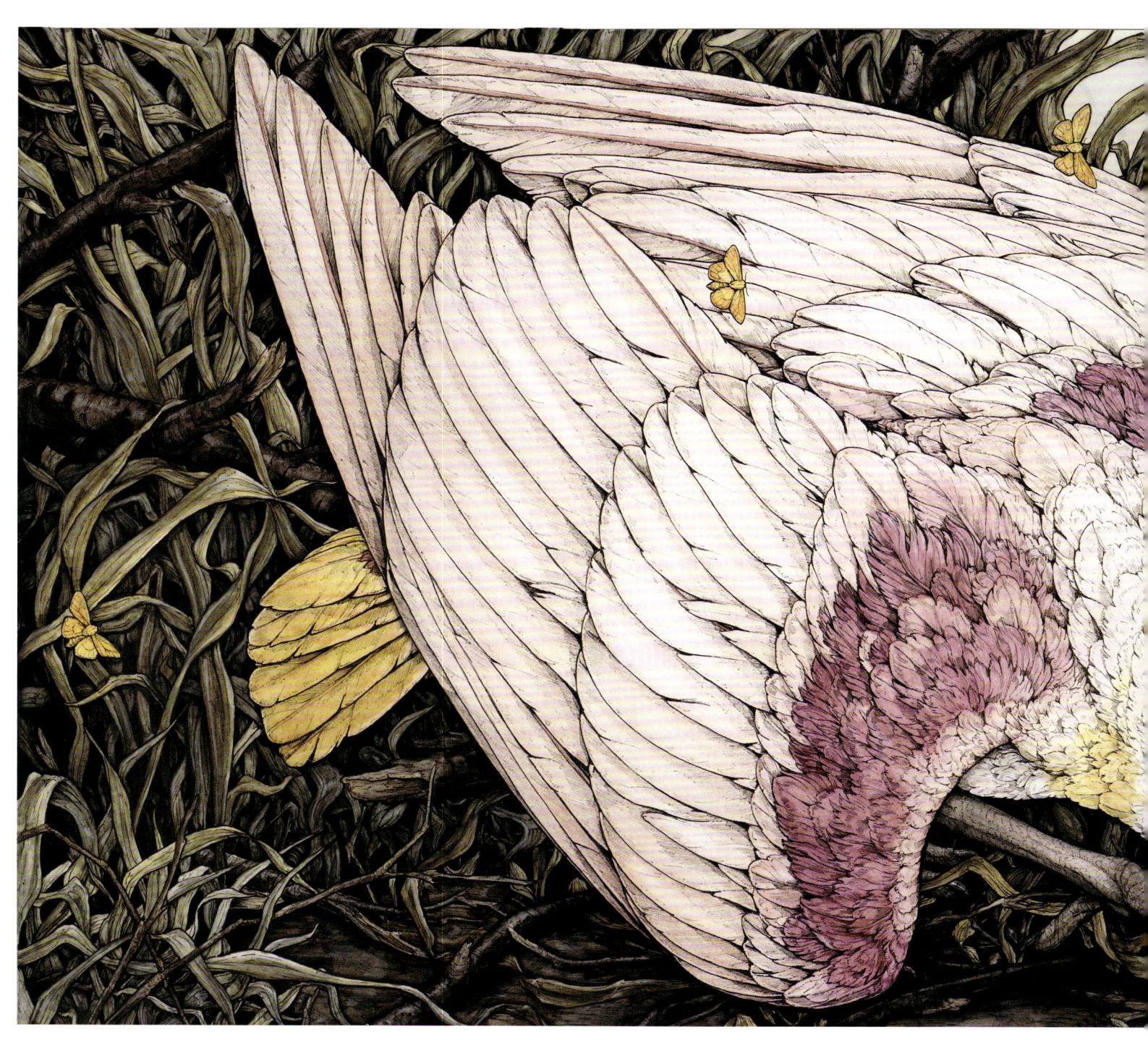

THE MARTYRDOM OF A FISH

42" x 18"

Pen, watercolor, ink, colored pencil,
gel pen, and graphite on paper

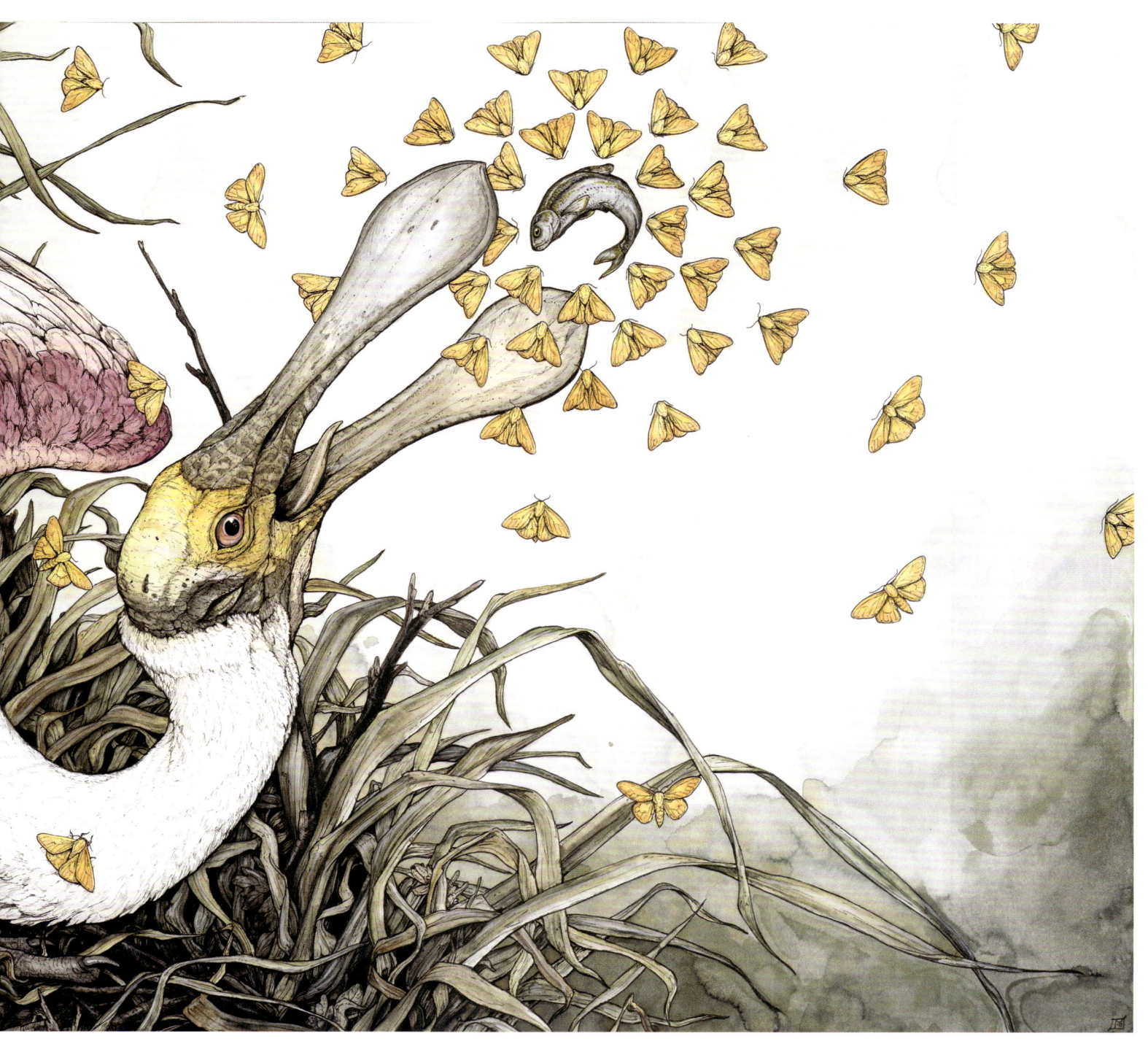

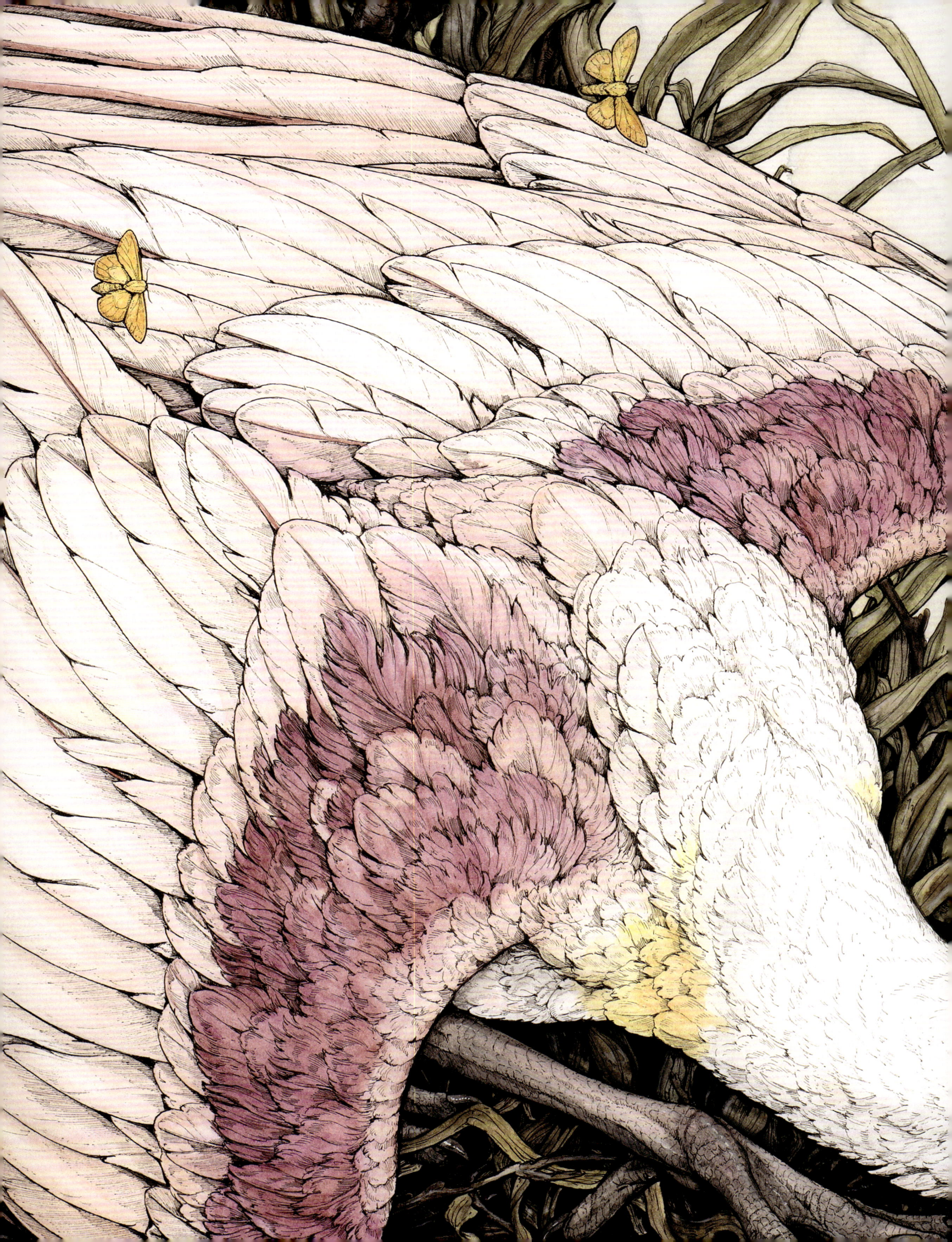

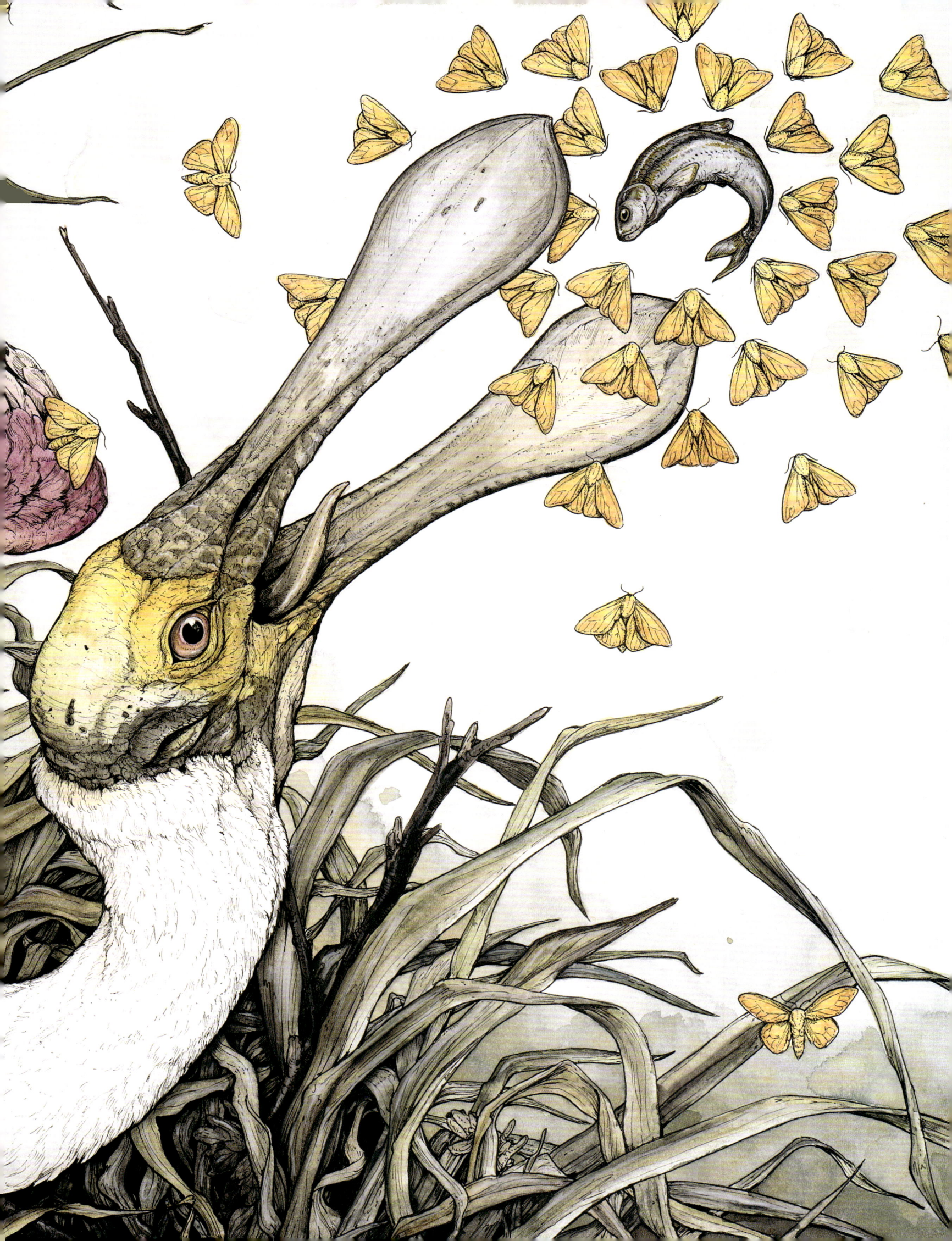

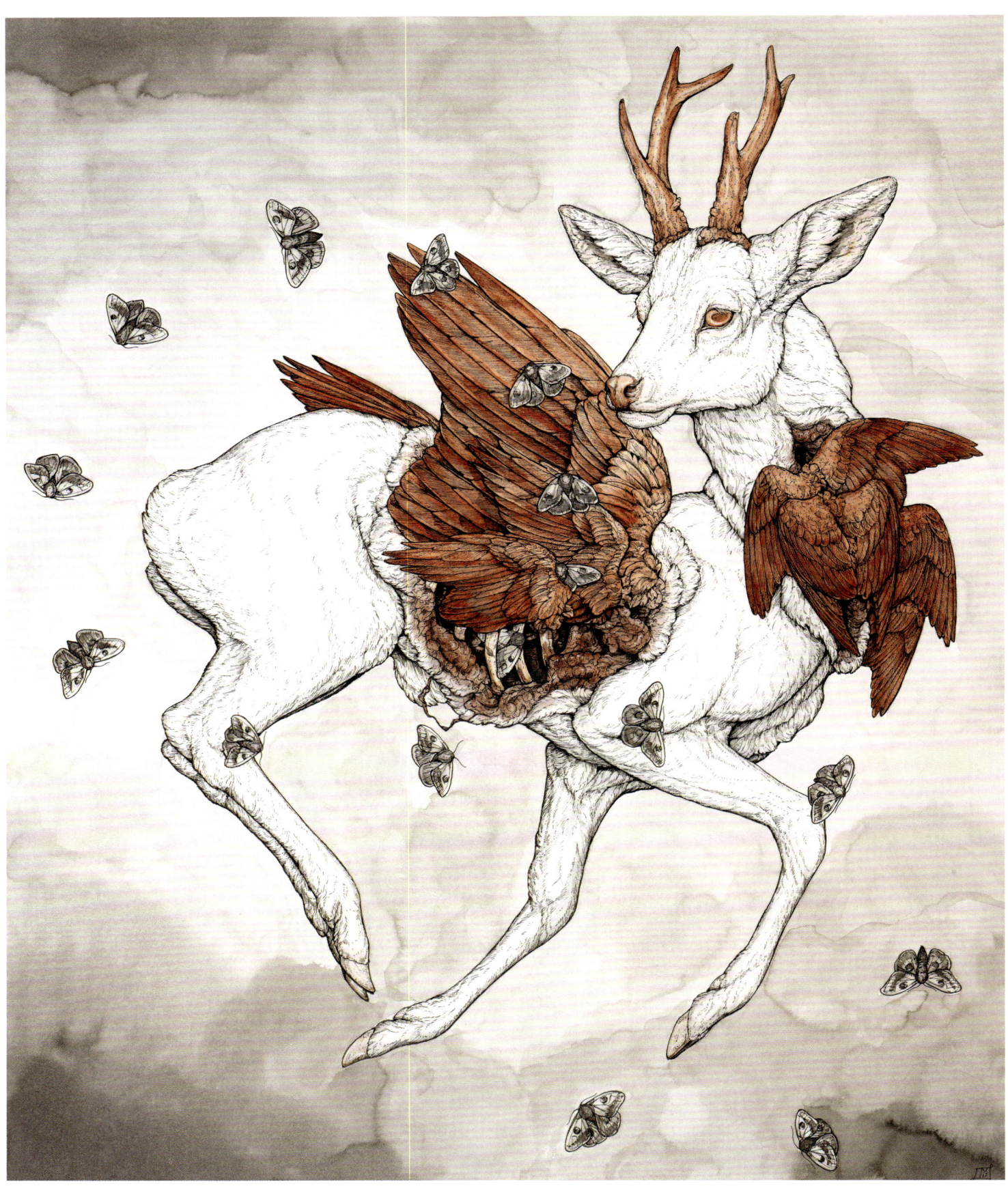

DIVINE ROE PERYTON

17.5" x 20.75"

Pen, watercolor, ink, colored pencil, graphite, and gel pen on paper

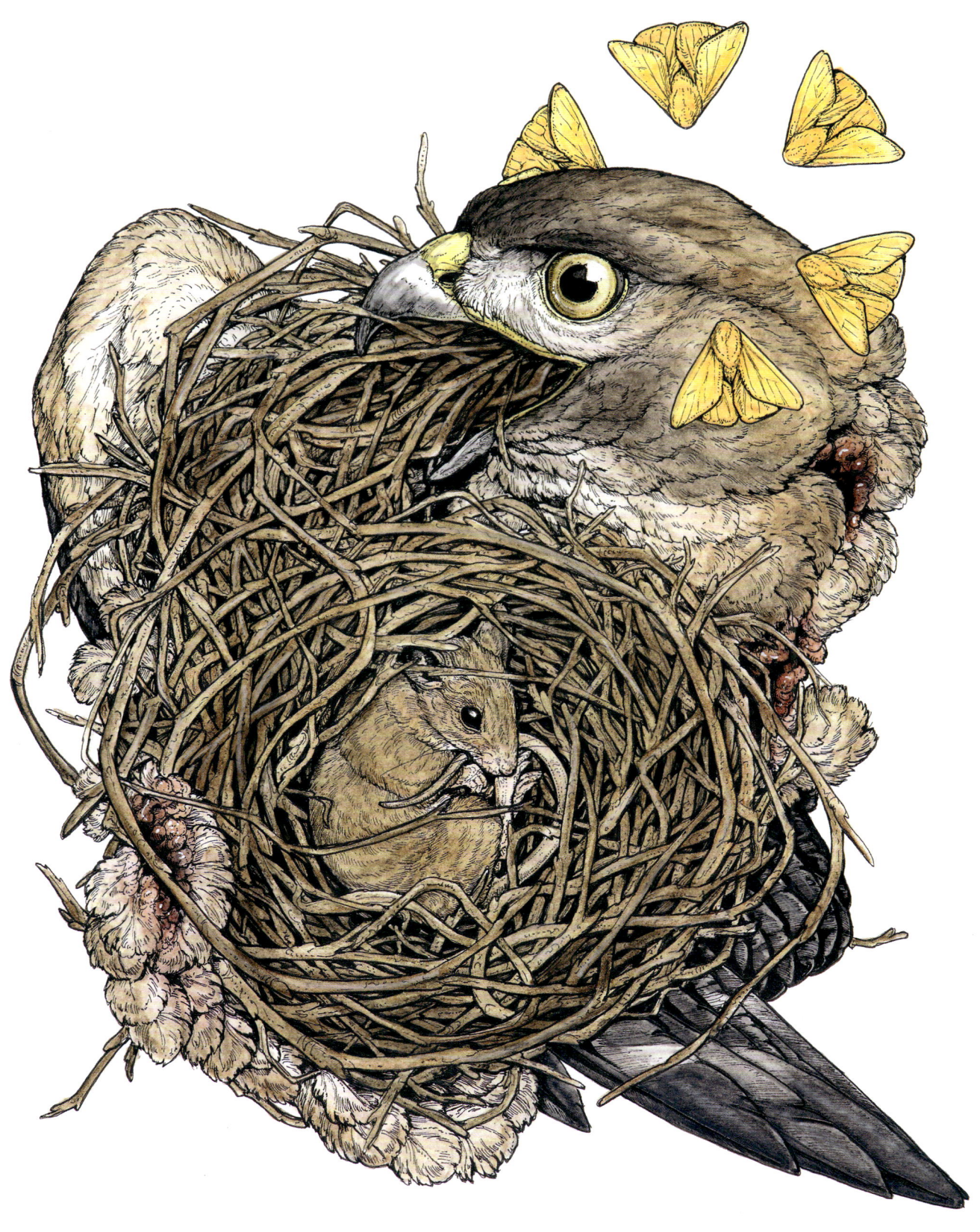

MOUSE SAINT

9.25" x 11.25"

Pen, watercolor, ink, colored pencil, gel pen, and graphite on paper

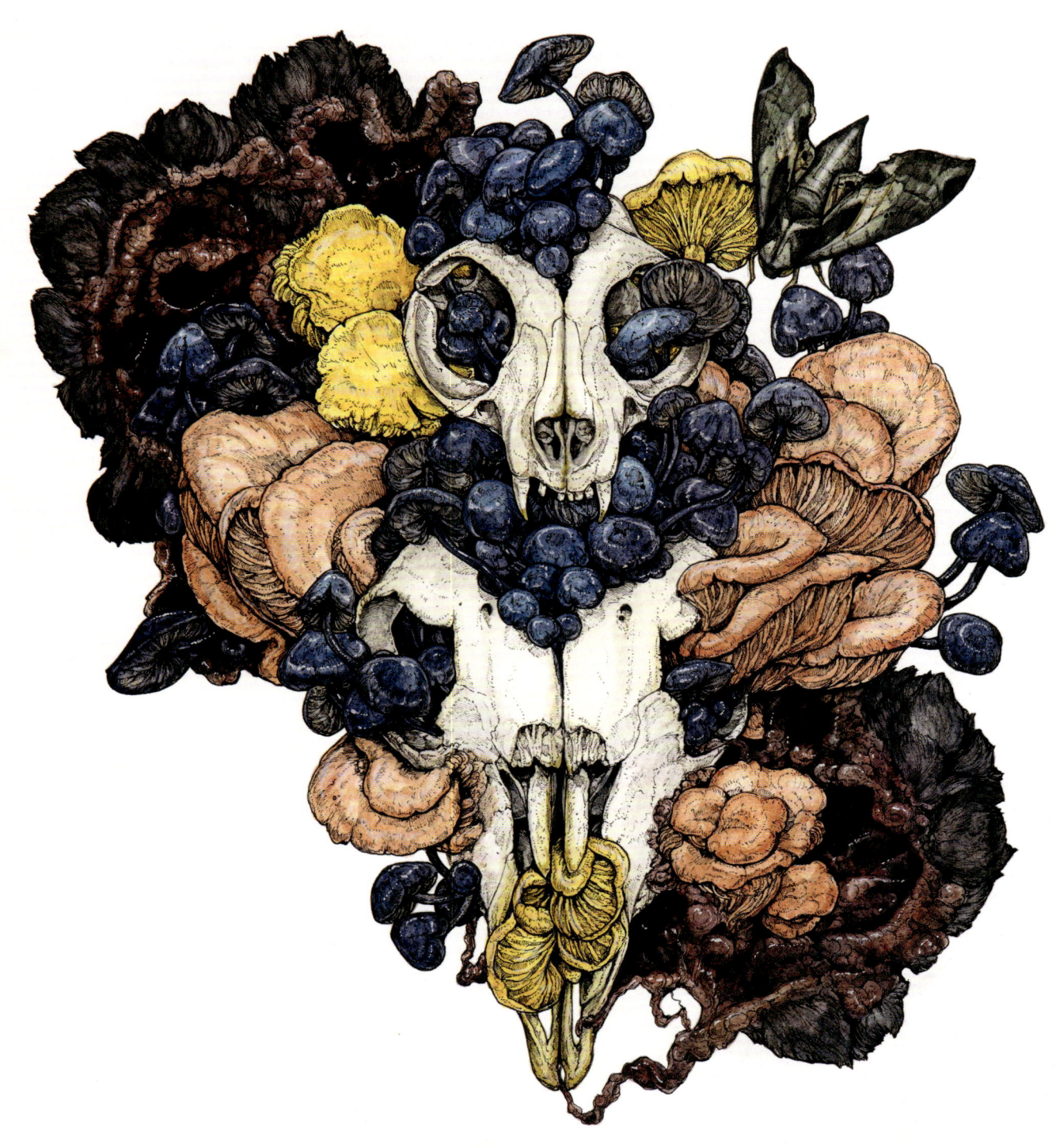

TOTEMS

12″ x 12″

Pen, ink, watercolor, colored pencil, graphite, and gel pen on paper

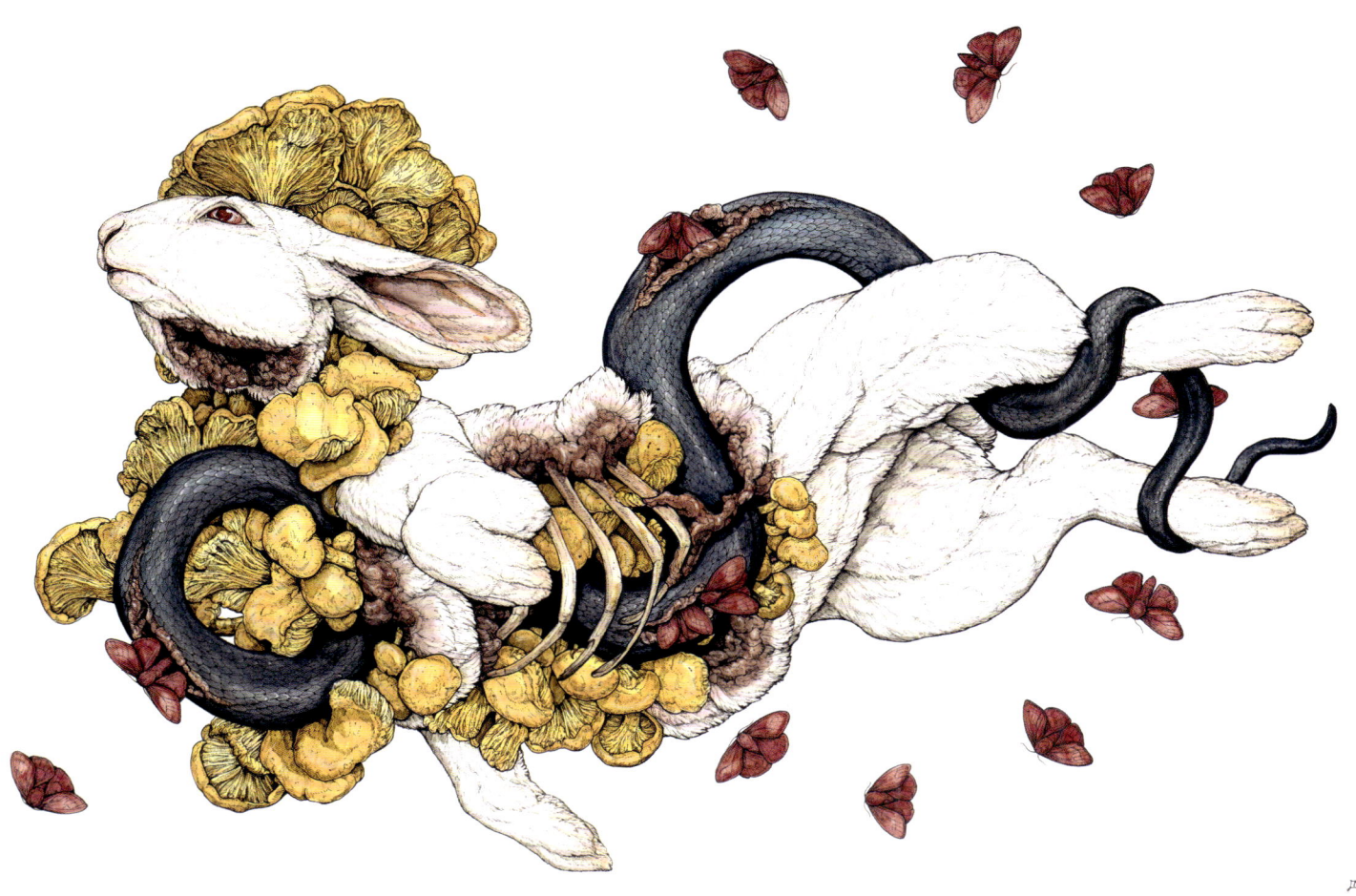

THE CONTEMPLATION OF LEPUS

23″ x 15.25″

Pen, watercolor, ink, colored pencil, gel pen, and graphite on paper

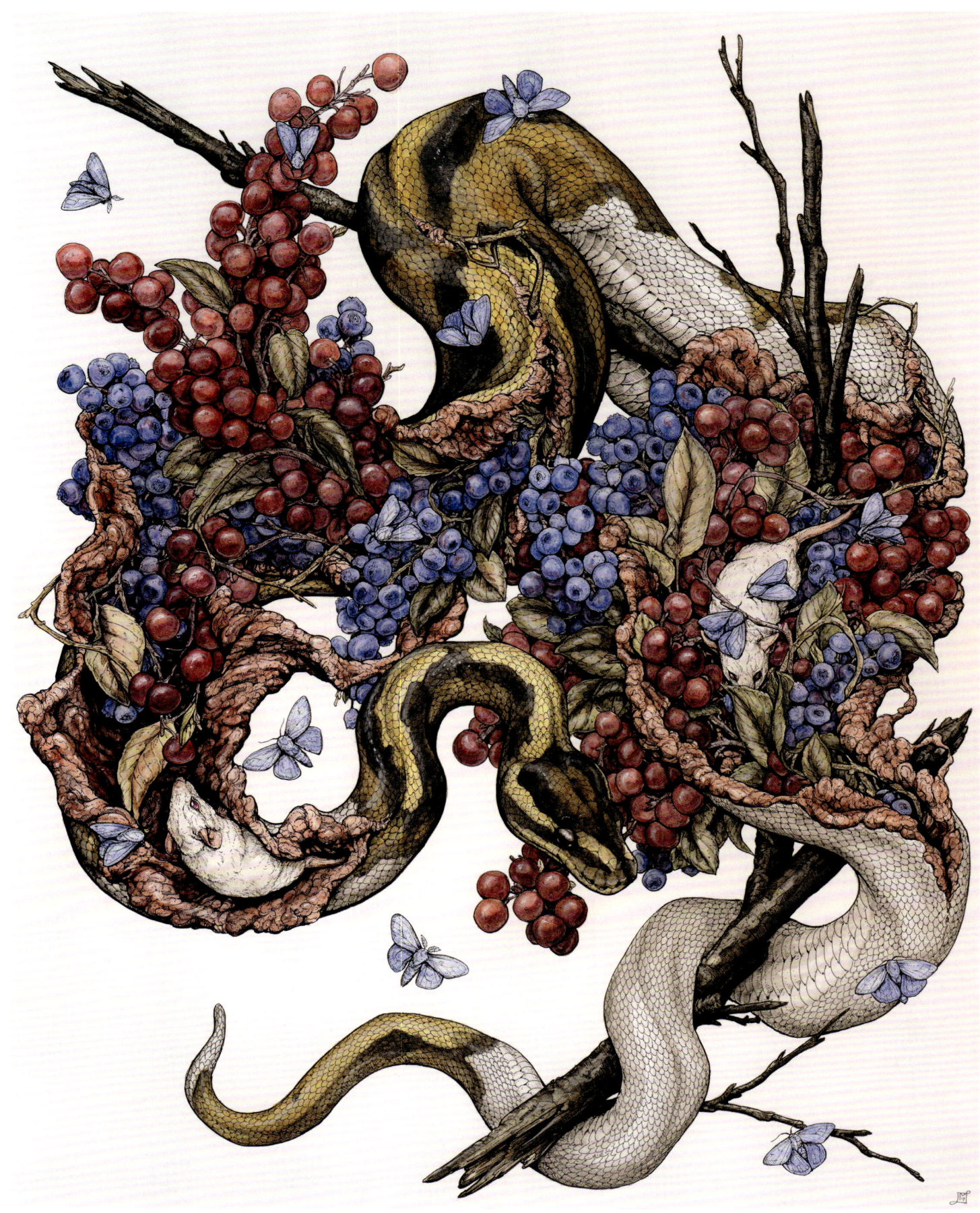

HYPOPIGMENTATION

16" x 20"

Pen, ink, watercolor, graphite, colored pencil, and gel pen on paper
Collaboration with Jason Koharik

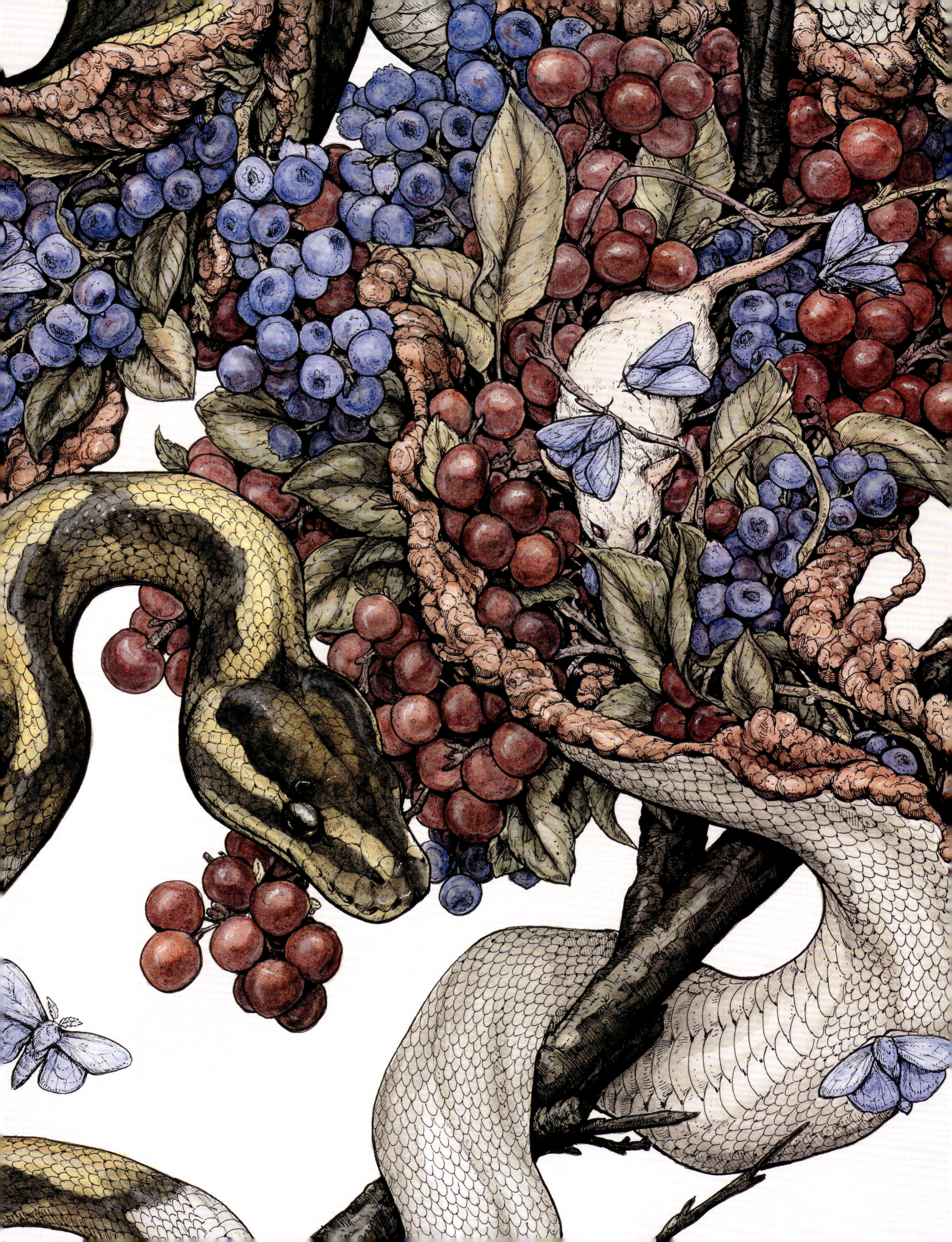

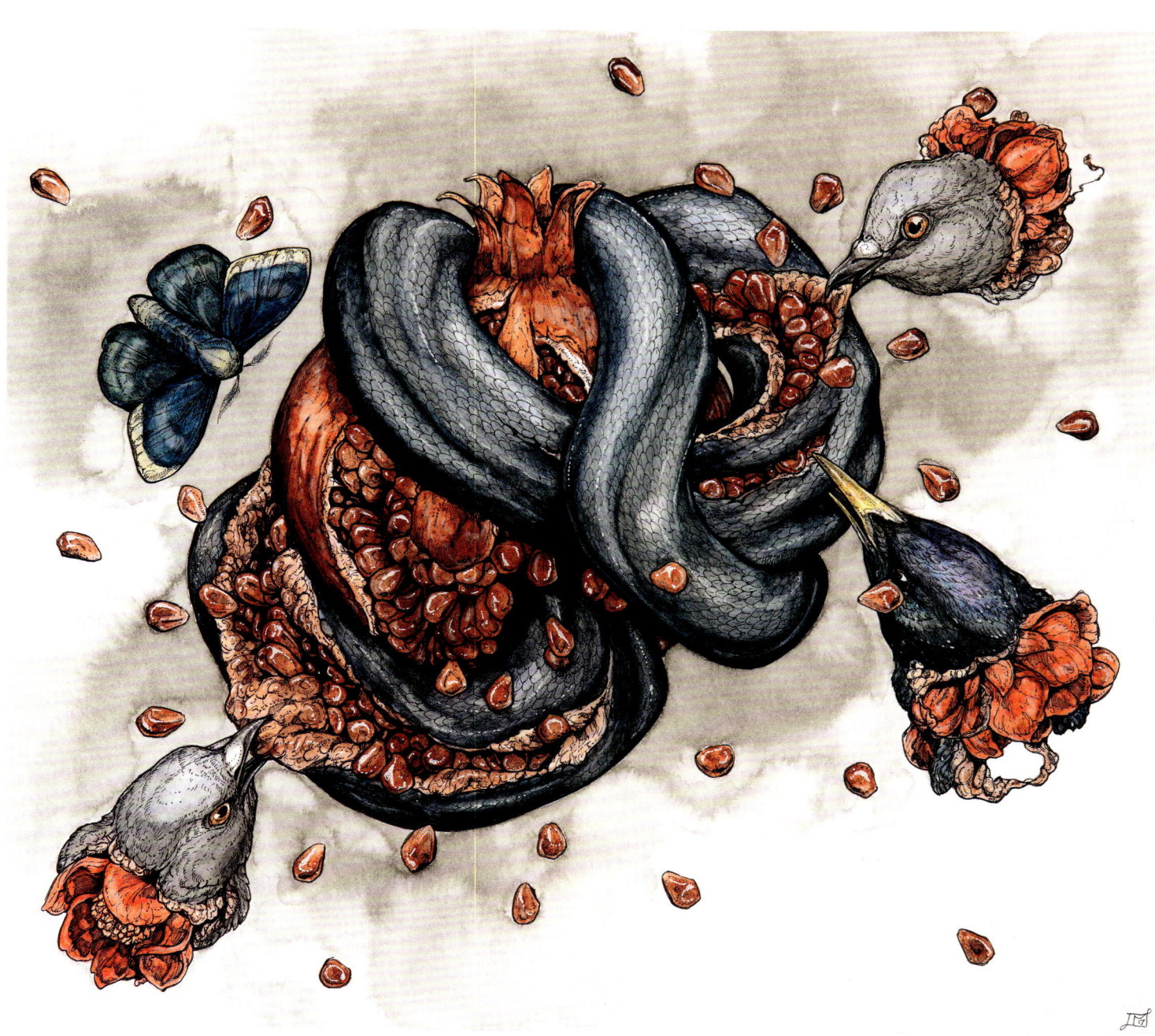

POMEGRANATE

12.5" x 11"

Pen, watercolor, ink, colored pencil, graphite, and gel pen on paper

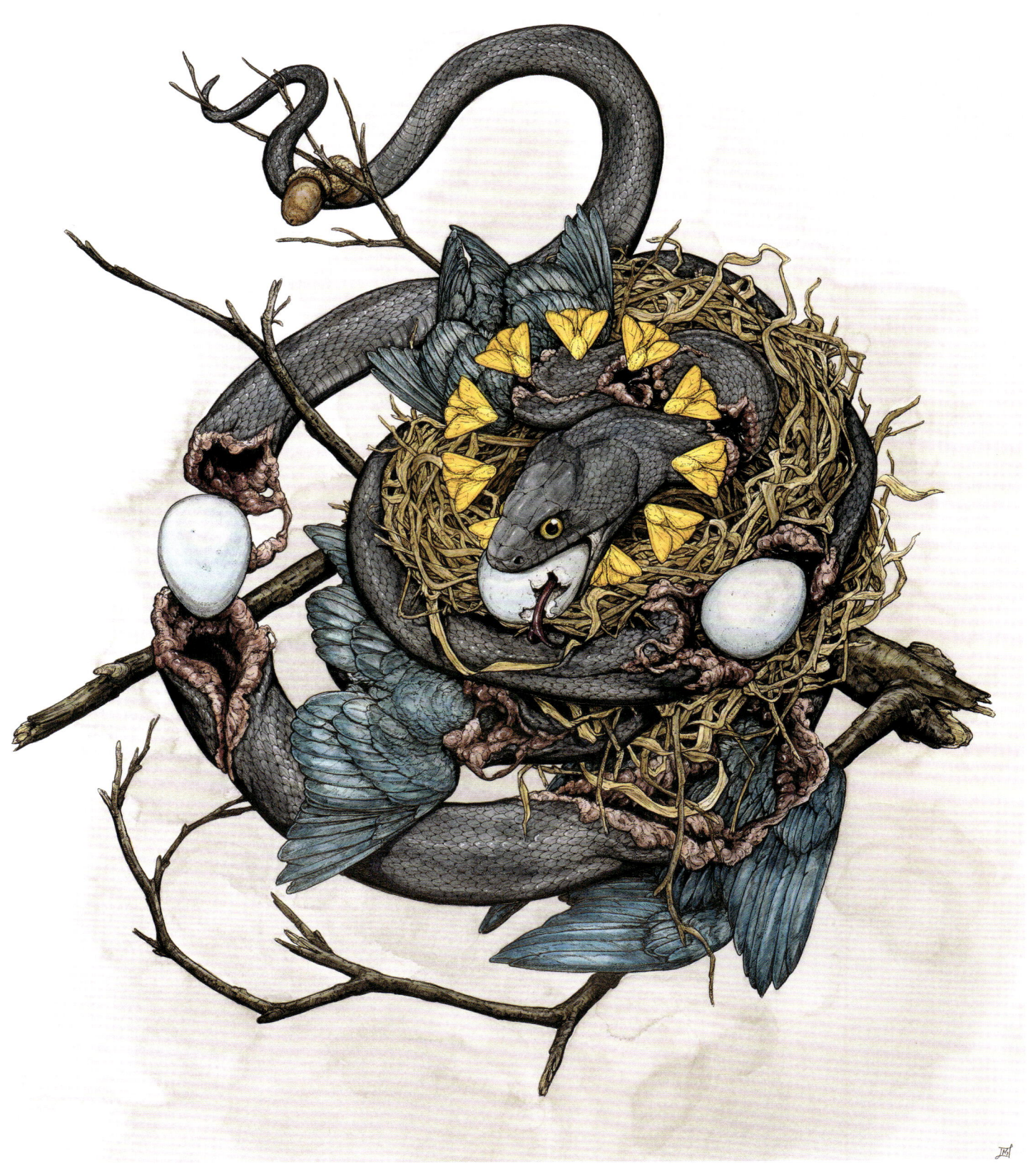

THE EGG EATER

17.25" x 20.5"

Pen, watercolor, ink, colored pencil, gel pen, and graphite on paper

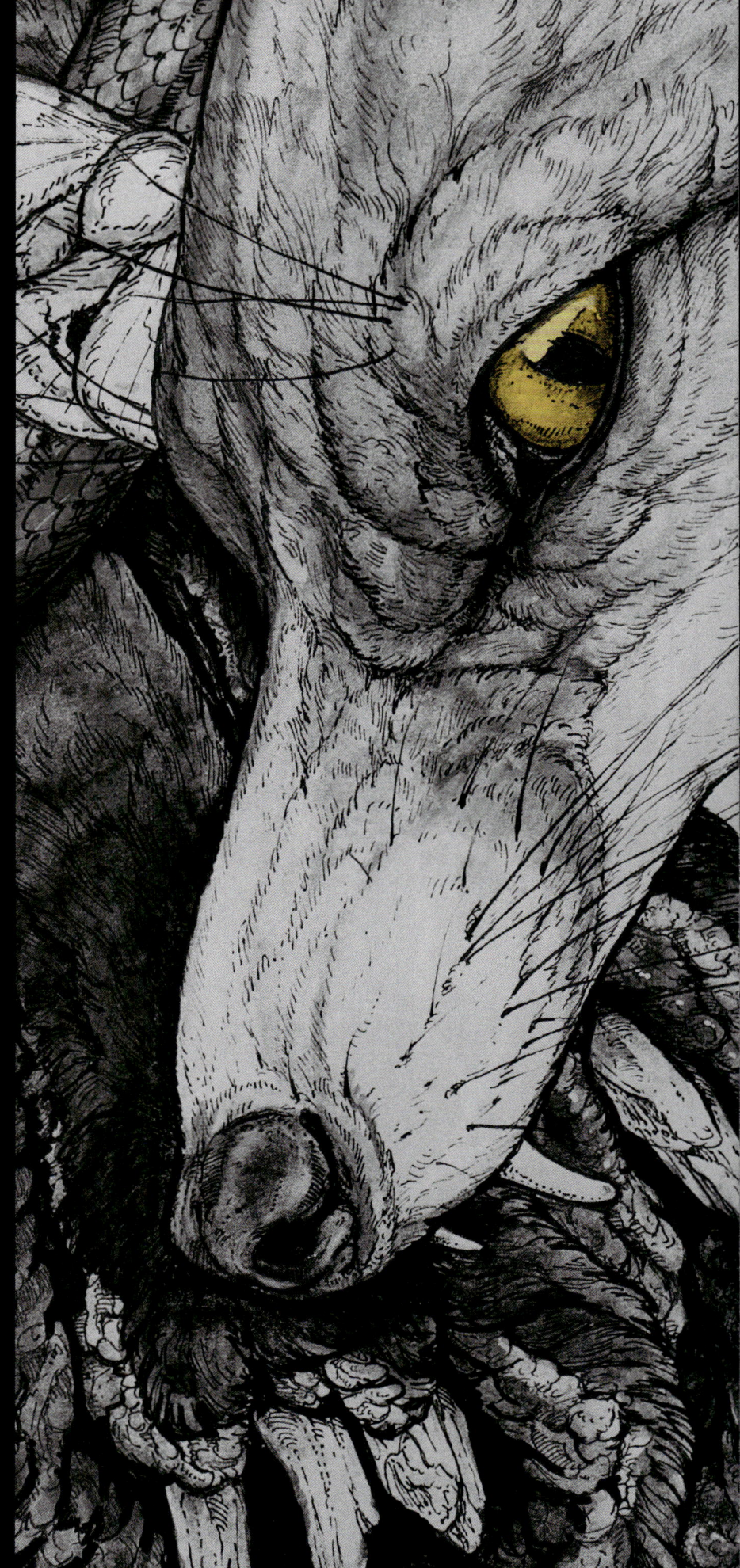

SACRED DECAY

2018

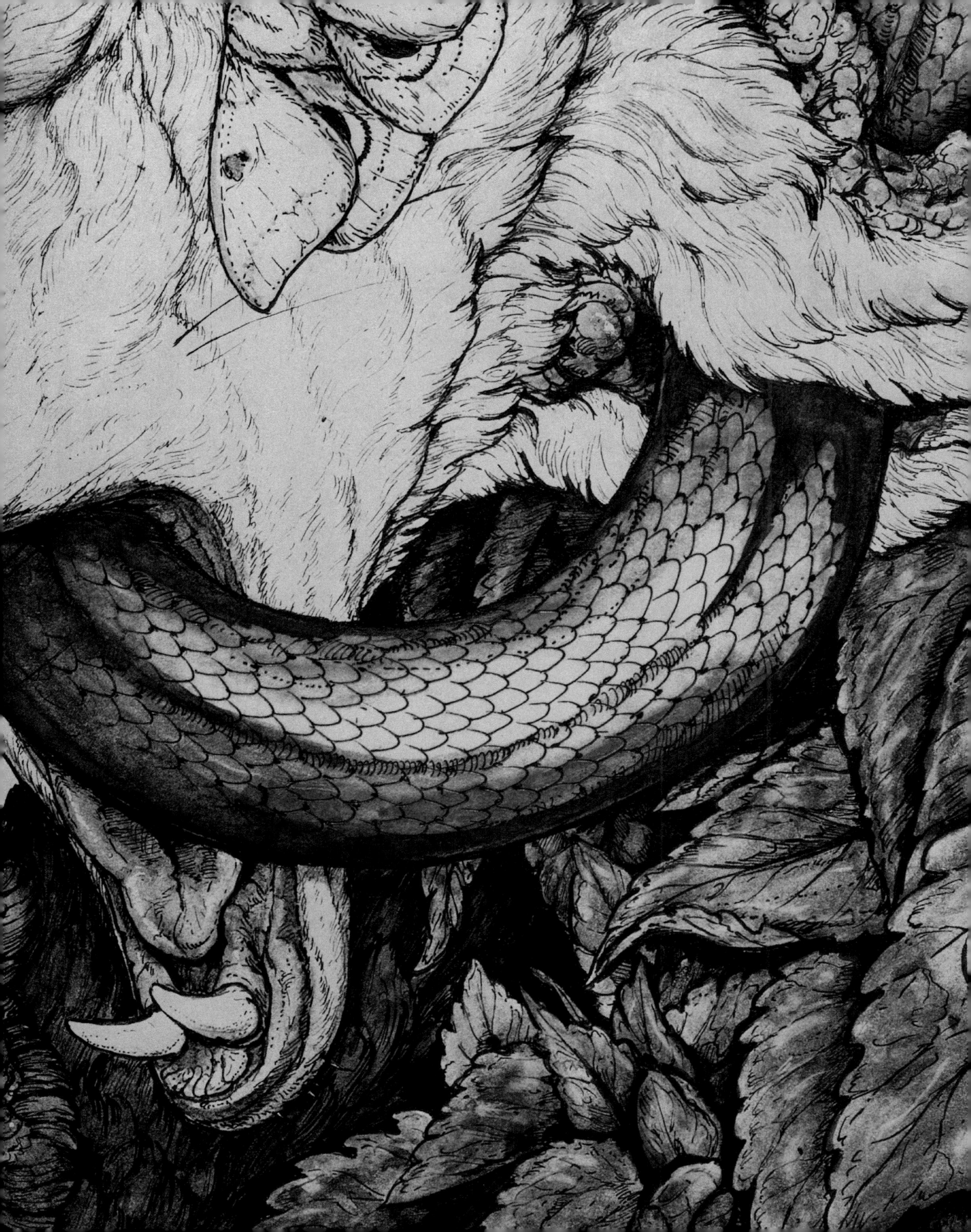

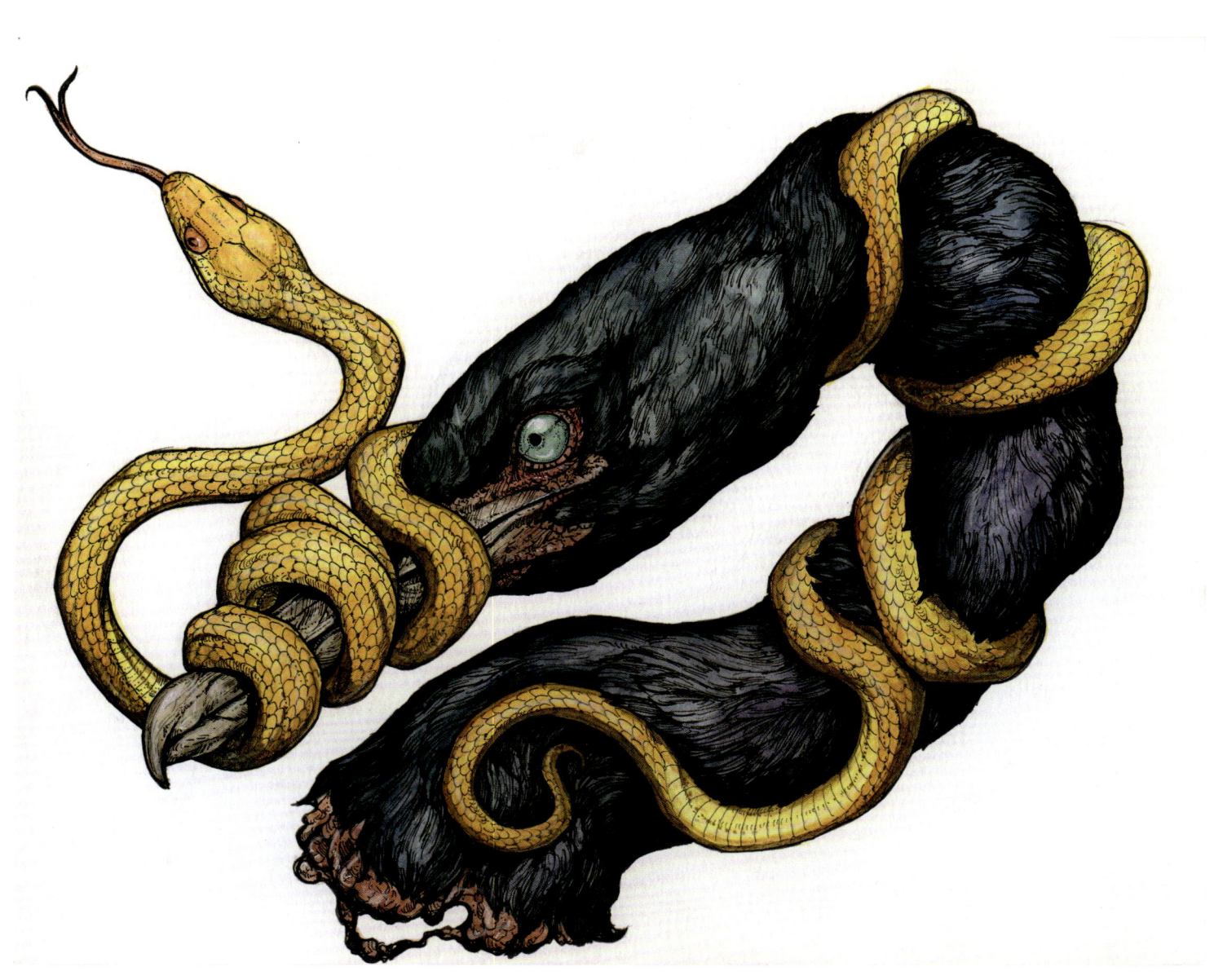

CORMORANT AND YELLOW SNAKE

10″ x 8″

Pen, watercolor, ink, gel pen, and colored pencil on paper

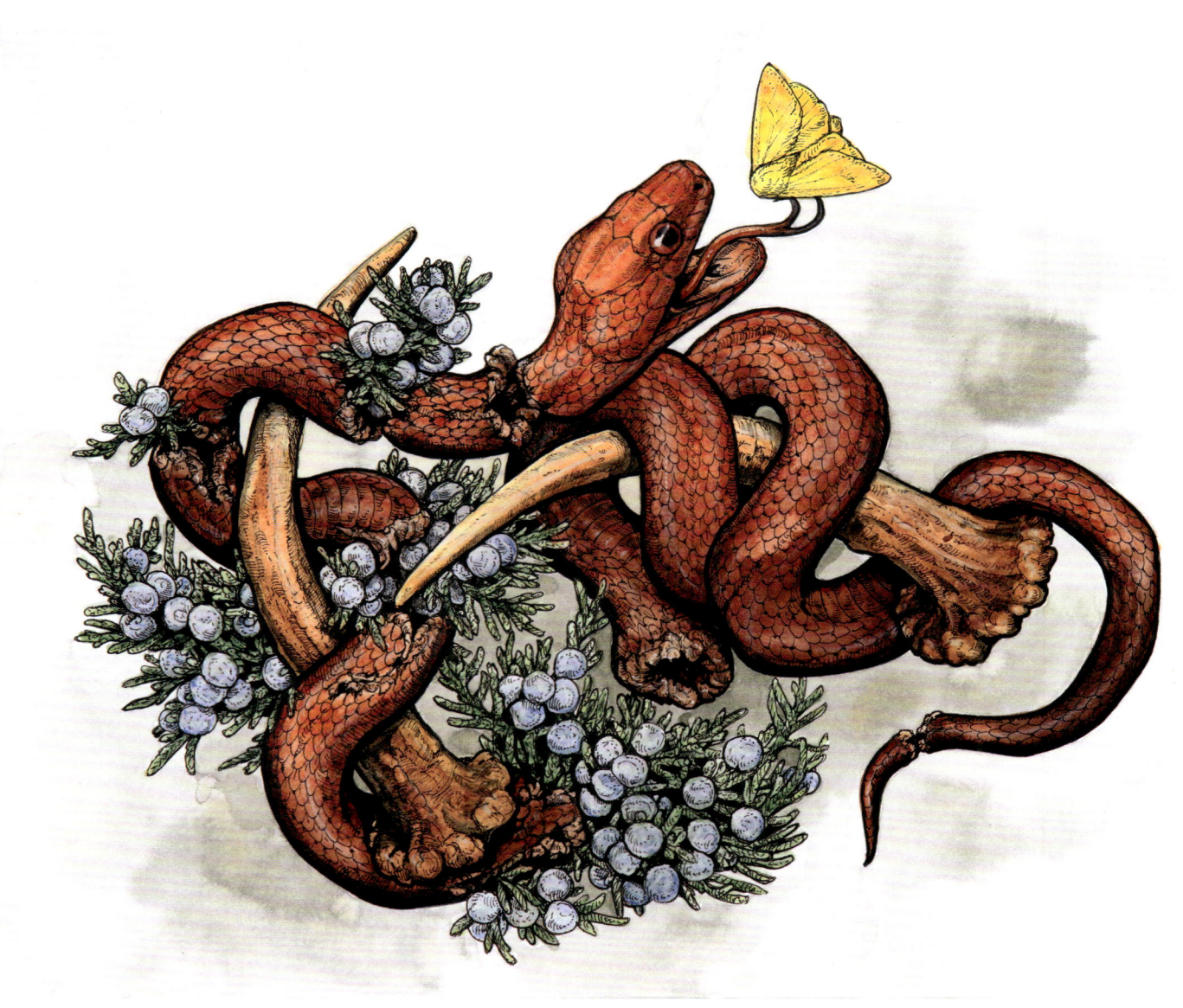

HIS ANTLERS

11″ x 8.75″

Pen, watercolor, ink, colored pencil, gel pen, and graphite on paper

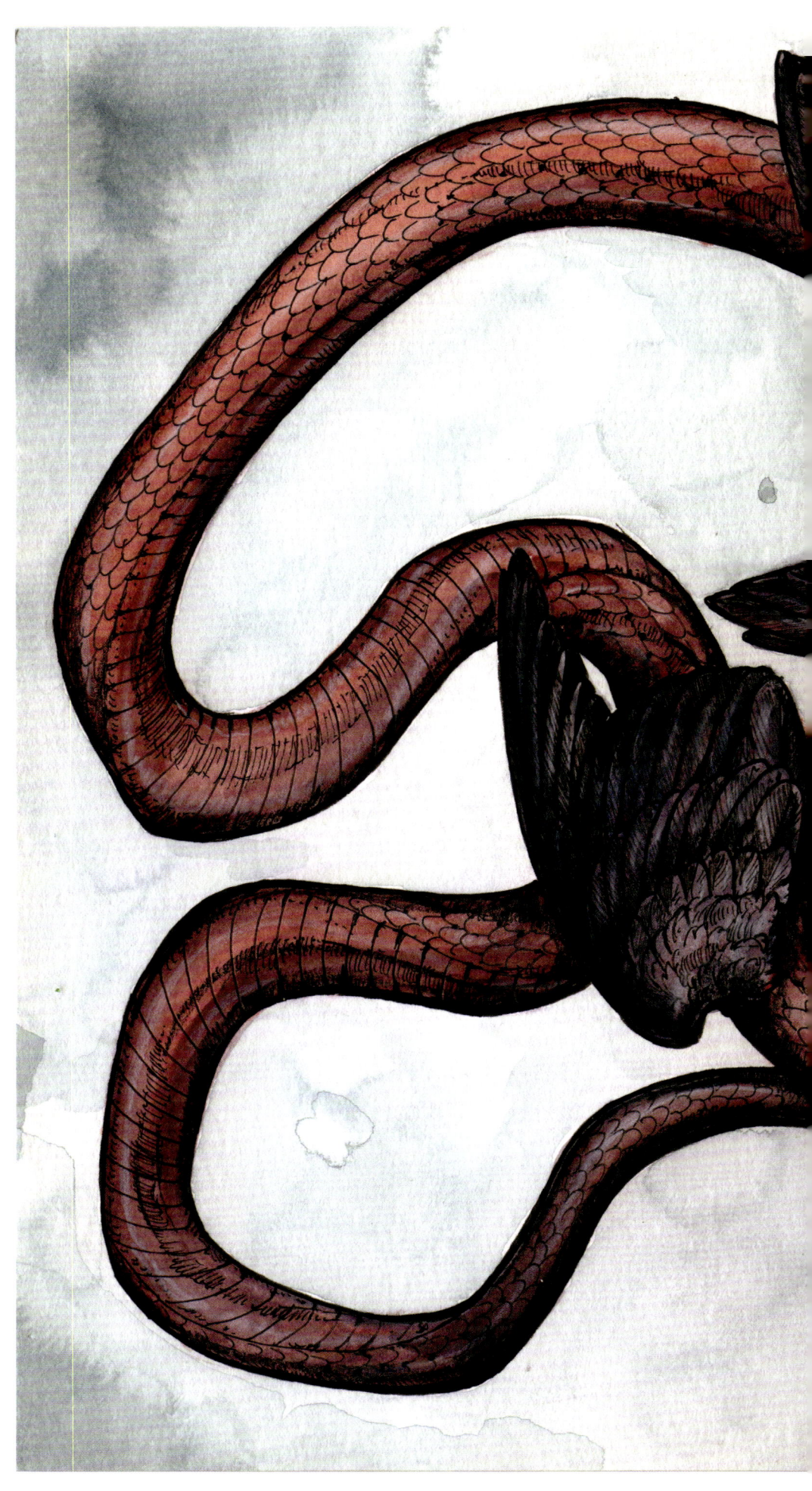

WINGED RED DEVIL

10″ x 7″

Pen, watercolor, ink, gel pen, and
colored pencil on paper

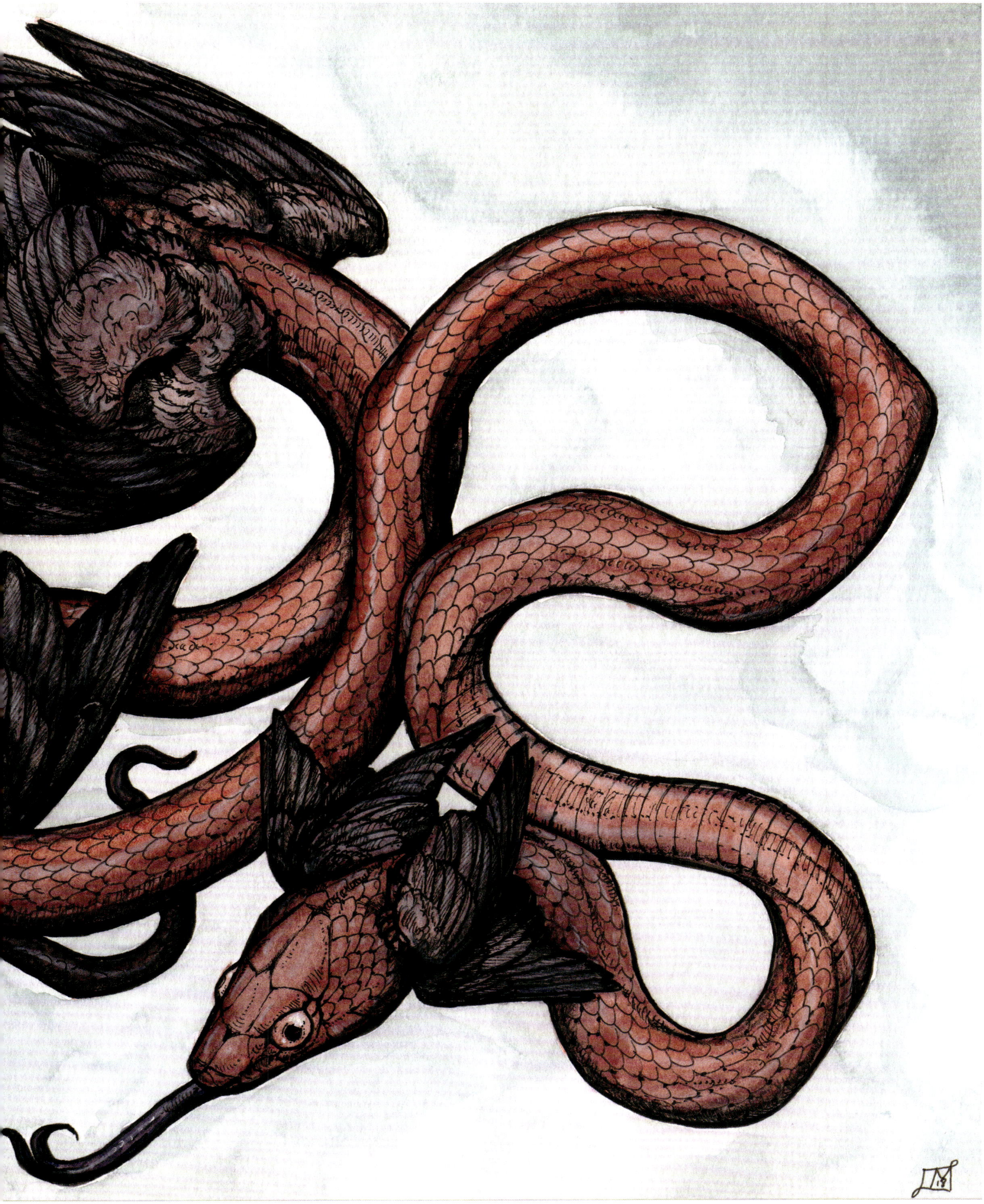

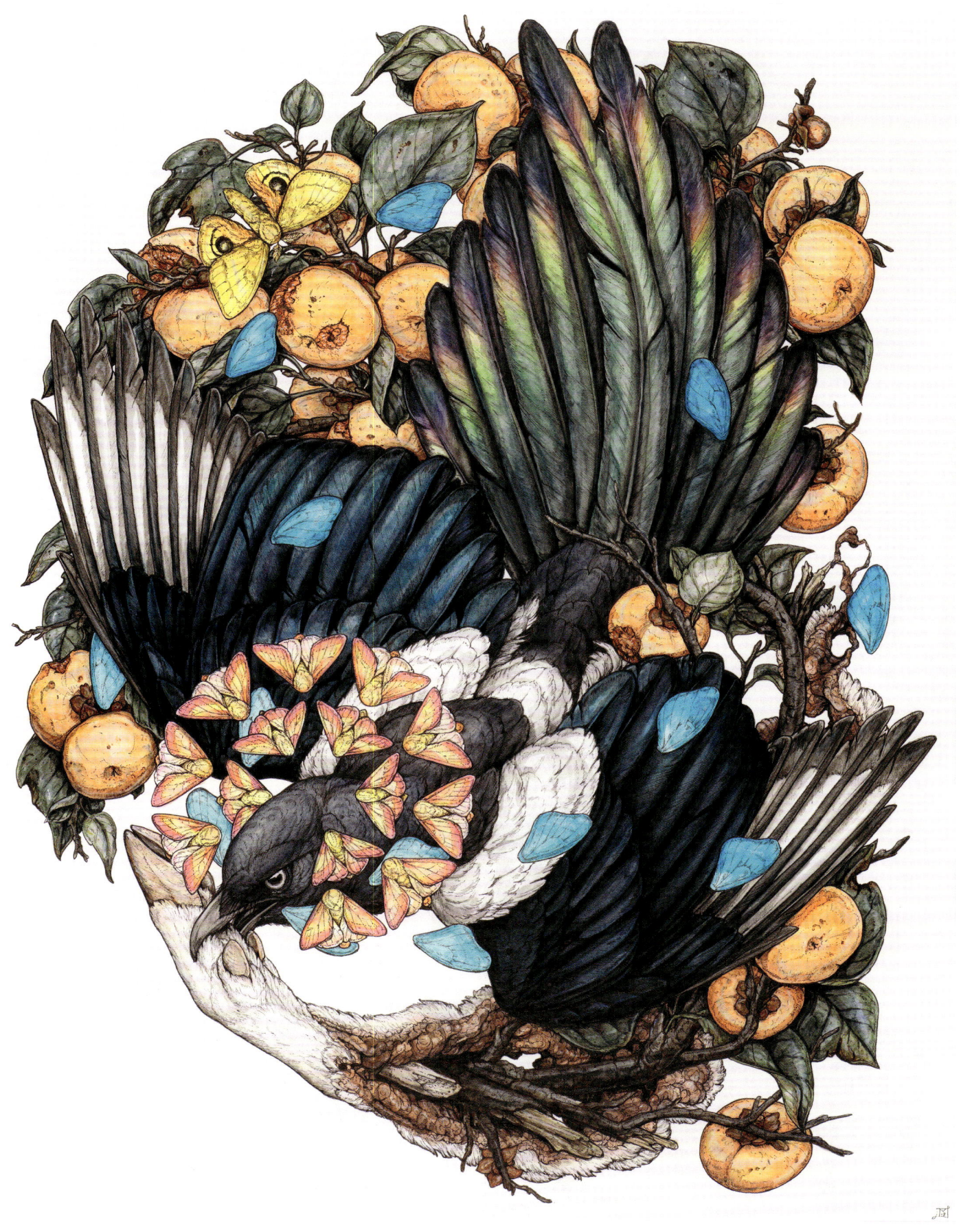

ONE FOR SORROW TAKES ONE FOR LUCK

17" x 21.75"

Pen, watercolor, ink, colored pencil, gel pen, and graphite on paper

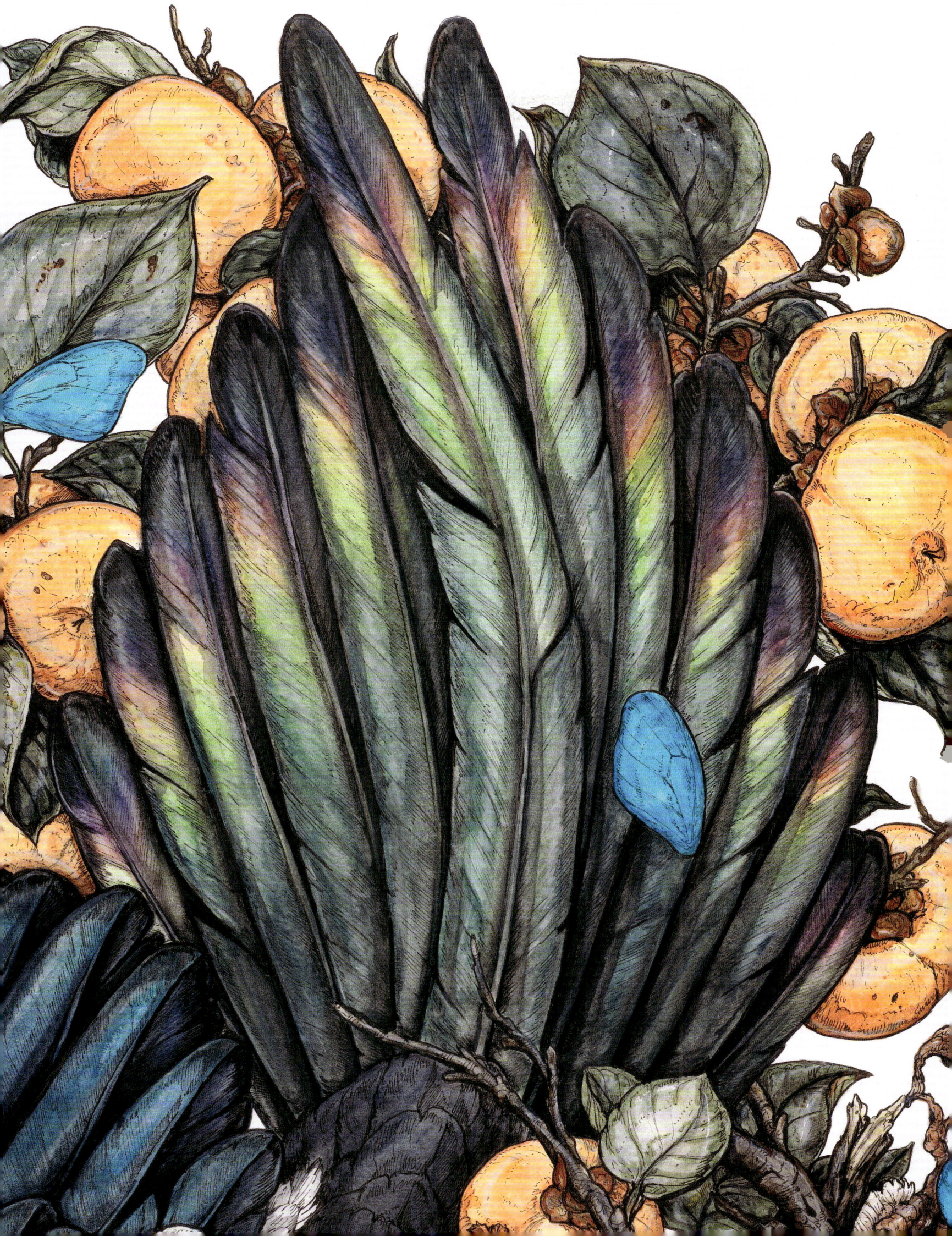

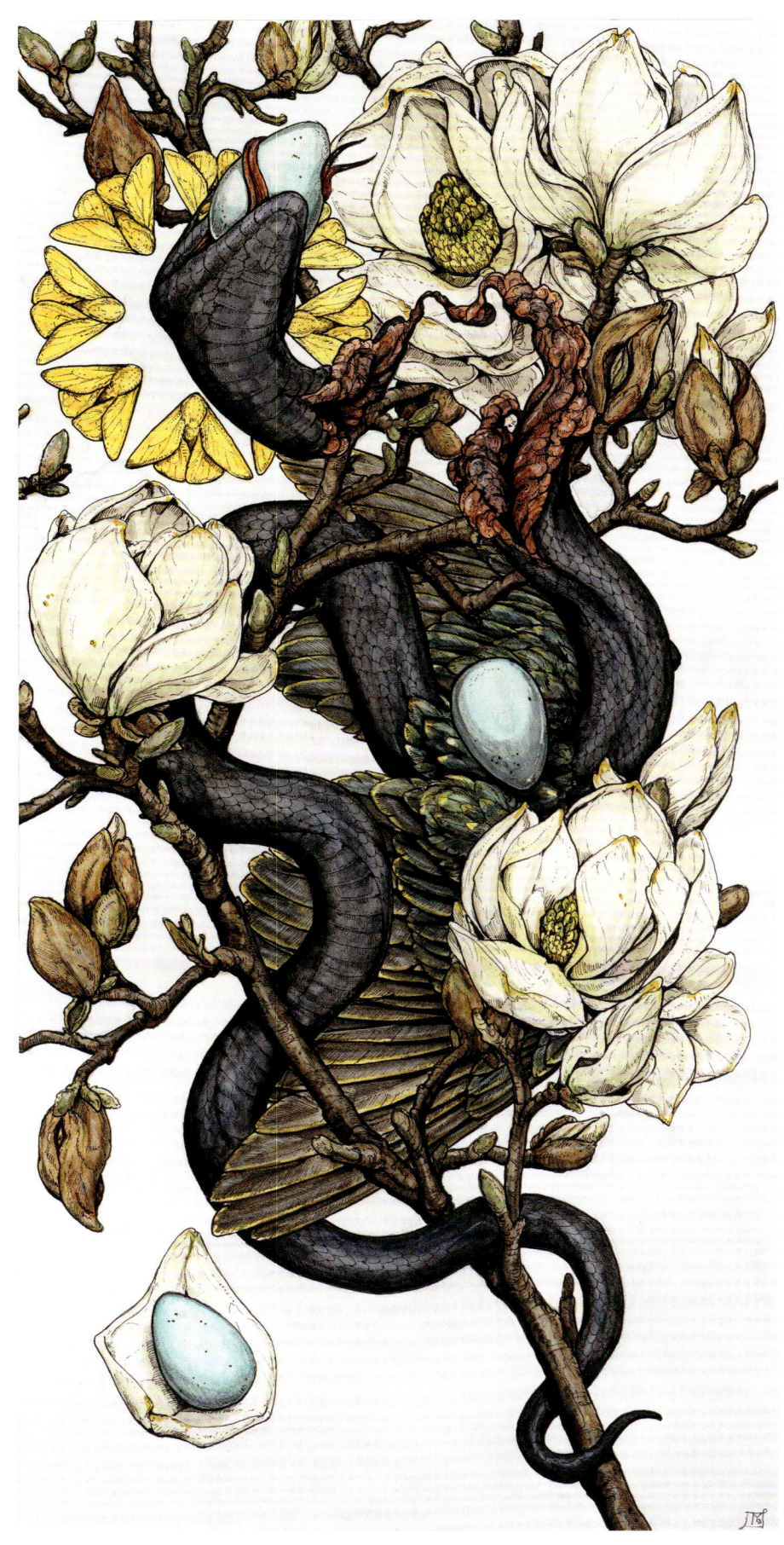

LITTLE DEVIL IN THE FLOWERS

8″ x 16″

Pen, watercolor, ink, colored pencil, gel pen, and graphite on paper

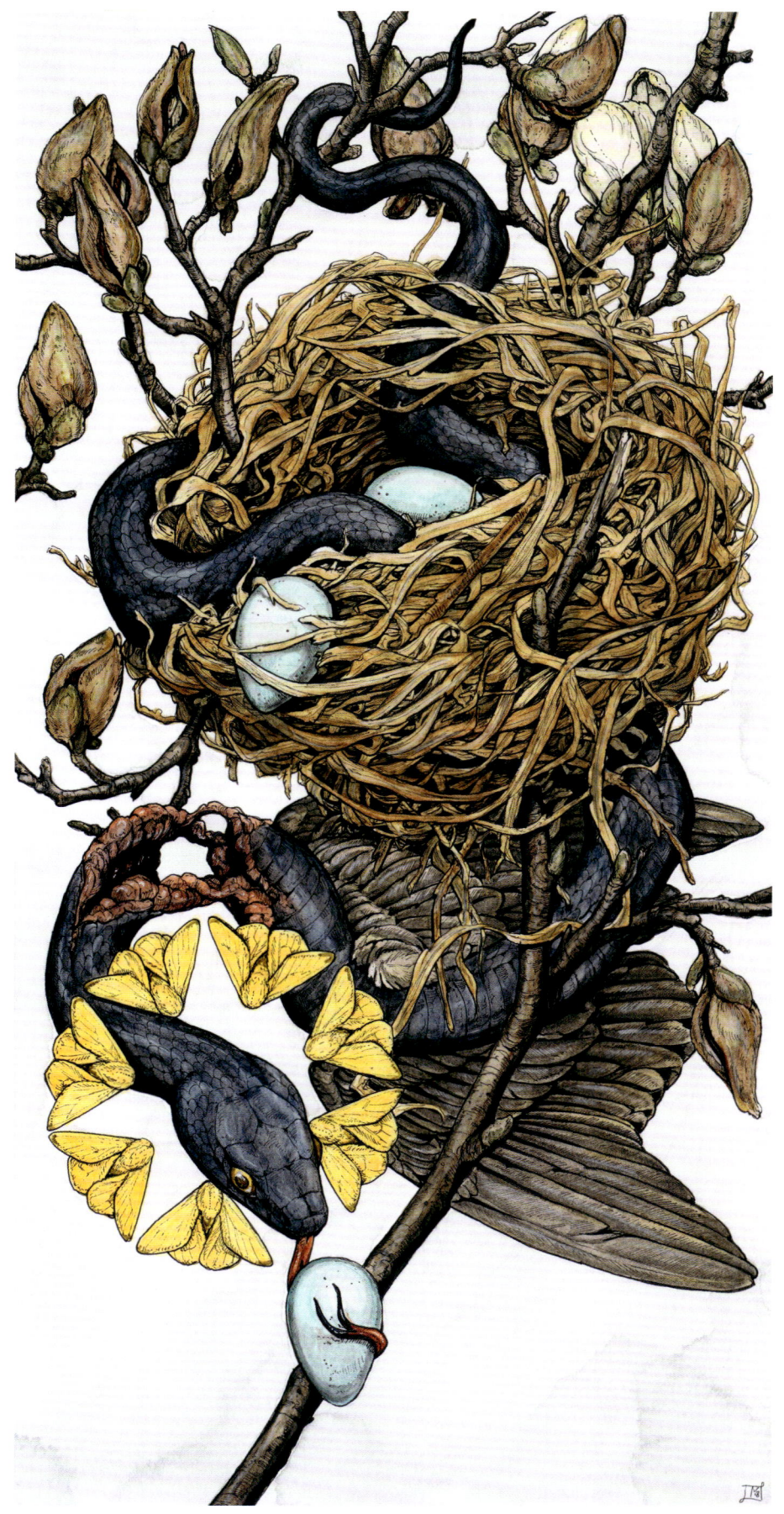

LITTLE DEVIL IN THE NEST

8″ x 16″

Pen, watercolor, ink, colored pencil, gel pen, and graphite on paper

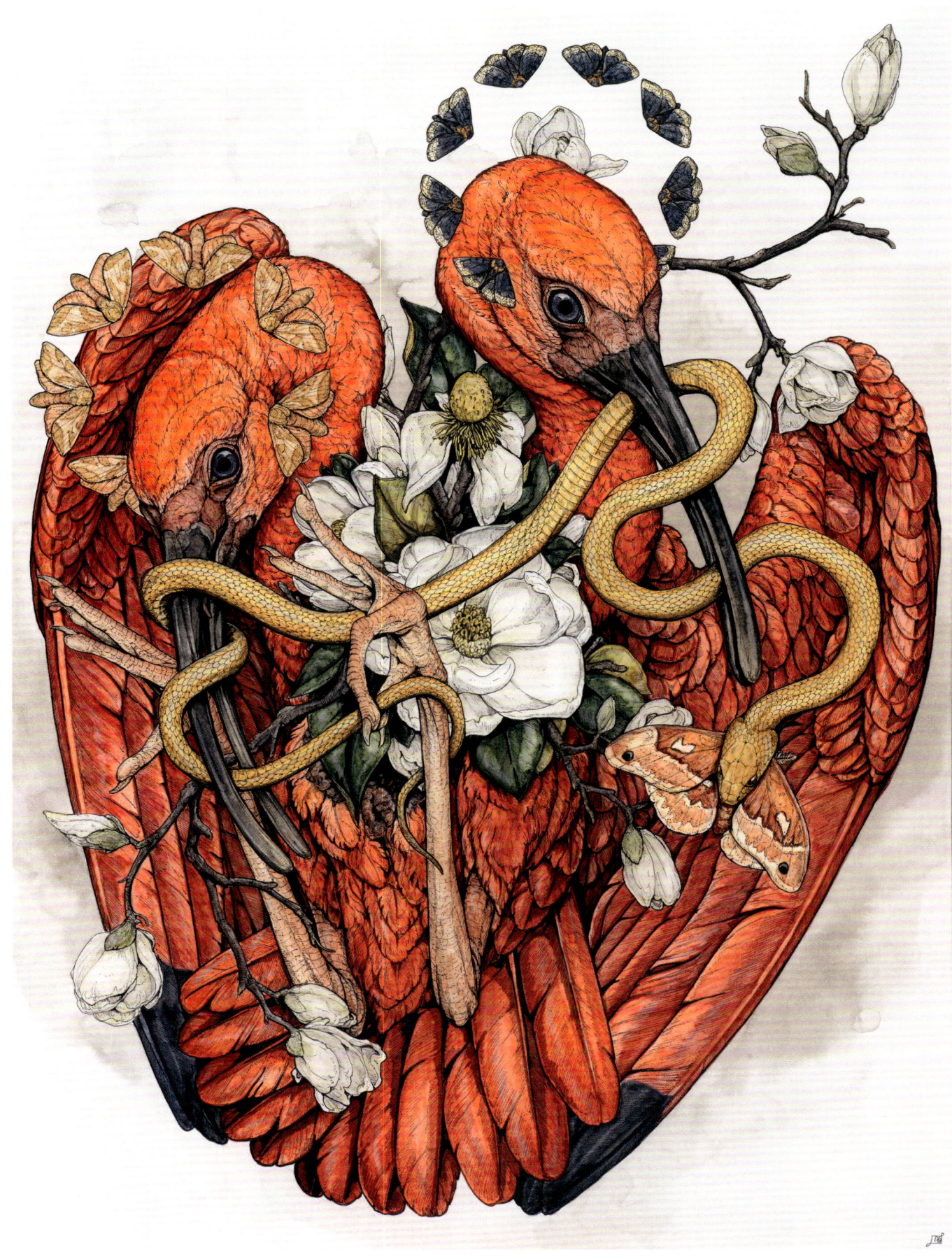

KEEPSAKE

18″ x 24″

Pen, watercolor, ink, colored pencil, gel pen, and graphite on paper

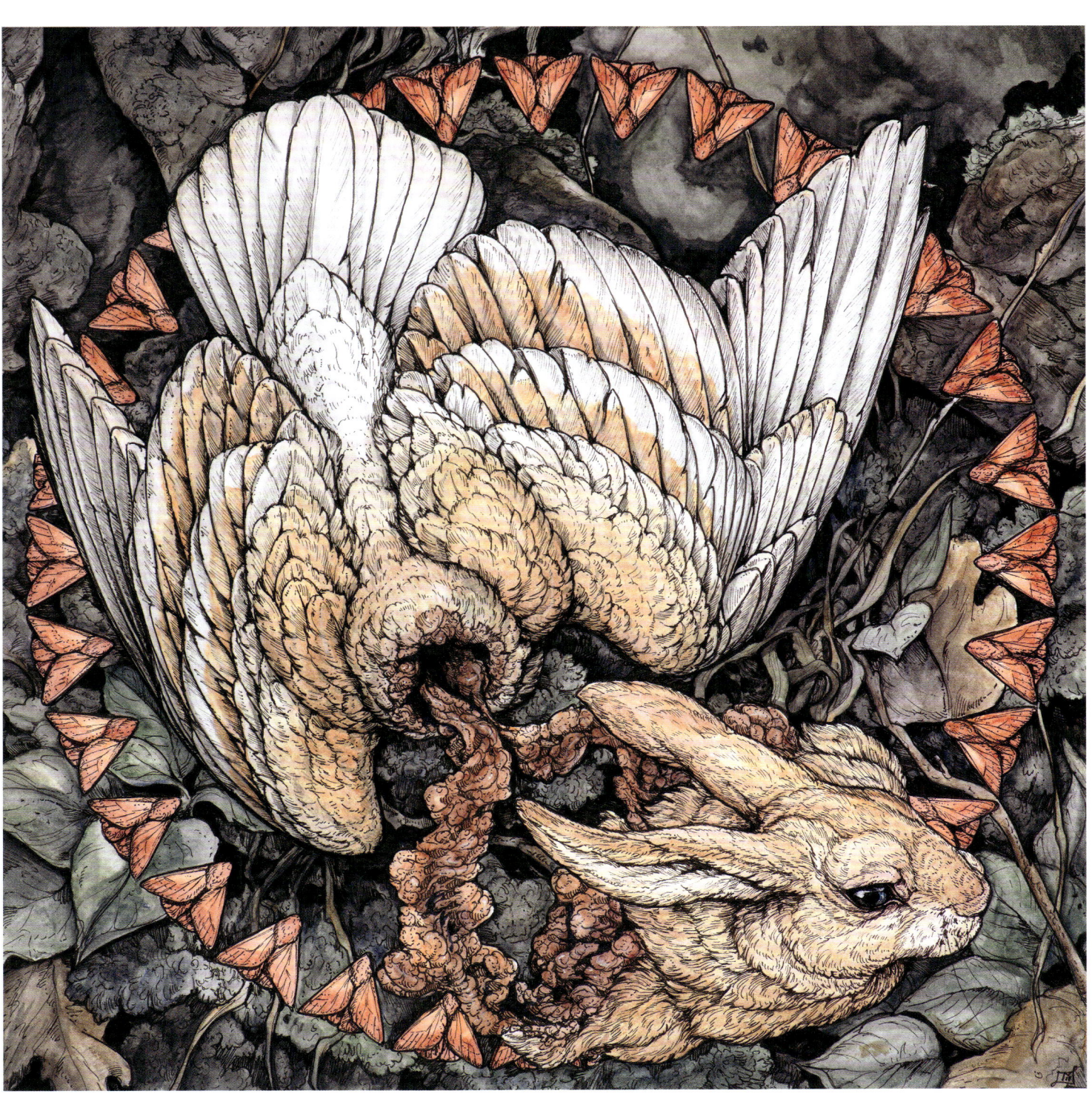

RABBIT CHIMERA

12″ × 12″

Watercolor, ink, colored pencil, gel pen, and graphite on paper

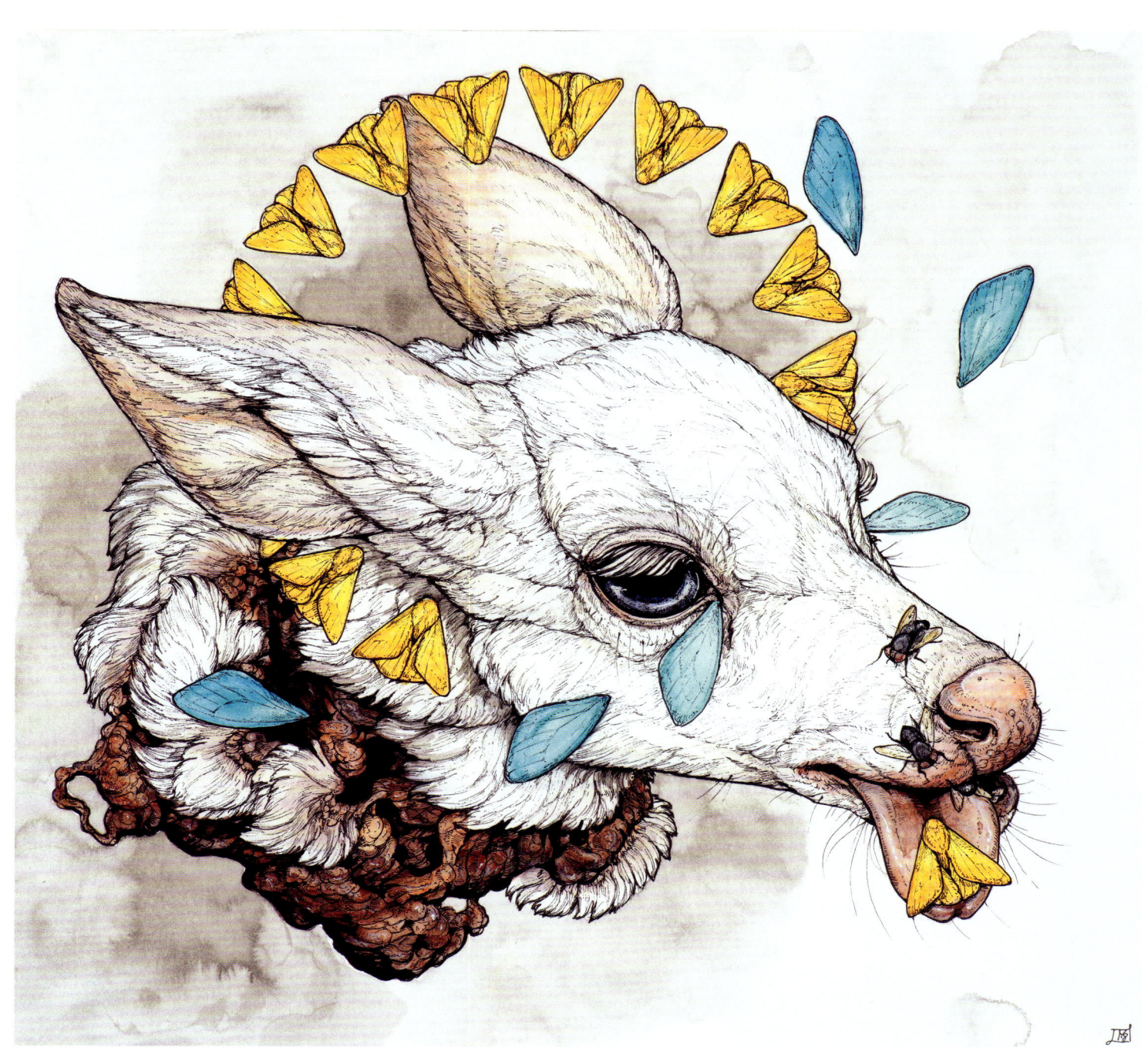

THE DECAPITATED SECOND

11.75″ x 10.75″

Pen, watercolor, ink, colored pencil, gel pen, and graphite on paper

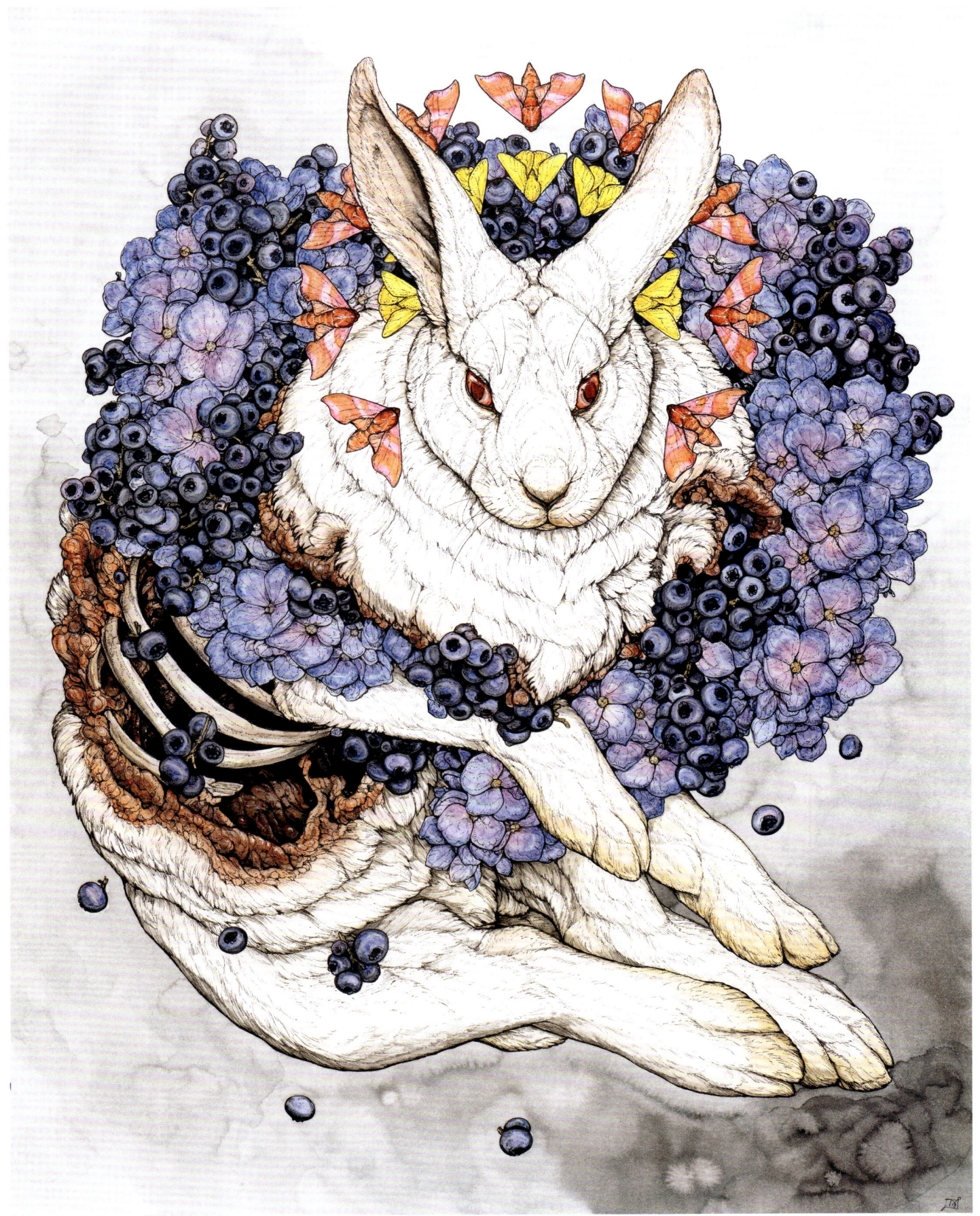

LOVELY

17.5" x 22"

Pen, watercolor, ink, colored pencil, gel pen, and graphite on paper

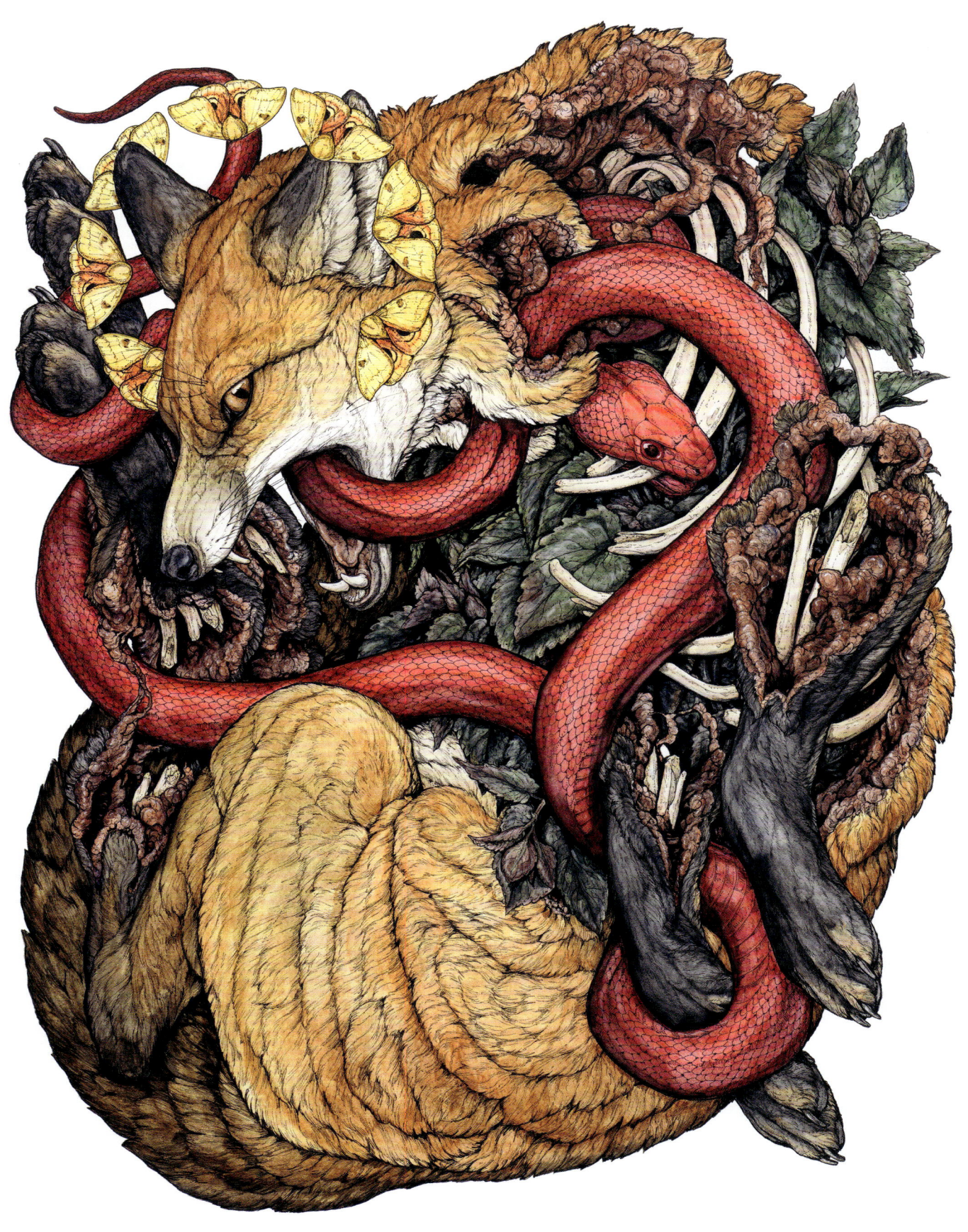

YOU KNOW JUST HOW TO HOLD ME

18″ x 23.25″

Pen, watercolor, ink, colored pencil, gel pen, and graphite on paper

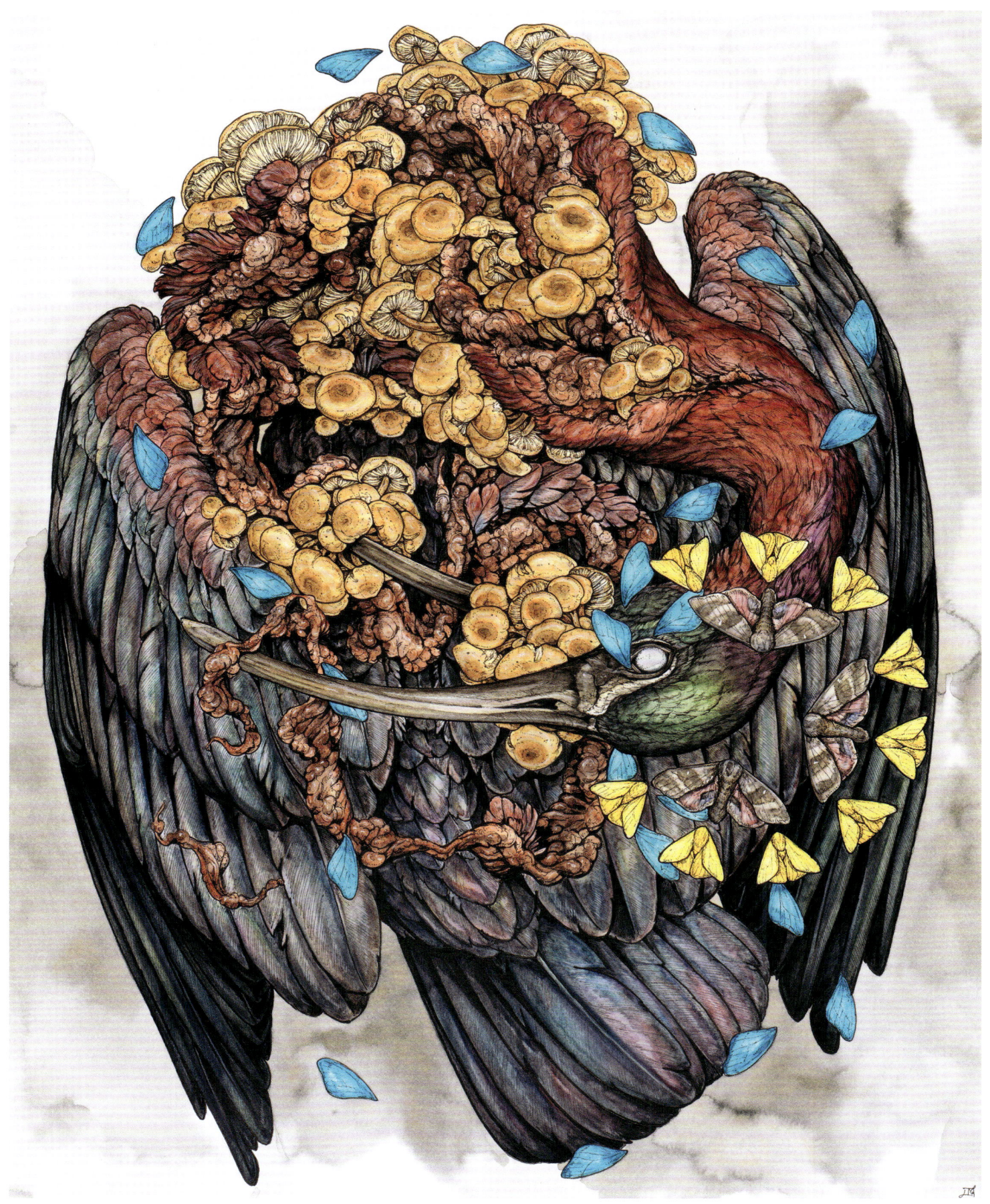

WALLOW

17" × 21"

Pen, watercolor, ink, colored pencil, gel pen, and graphite on paper

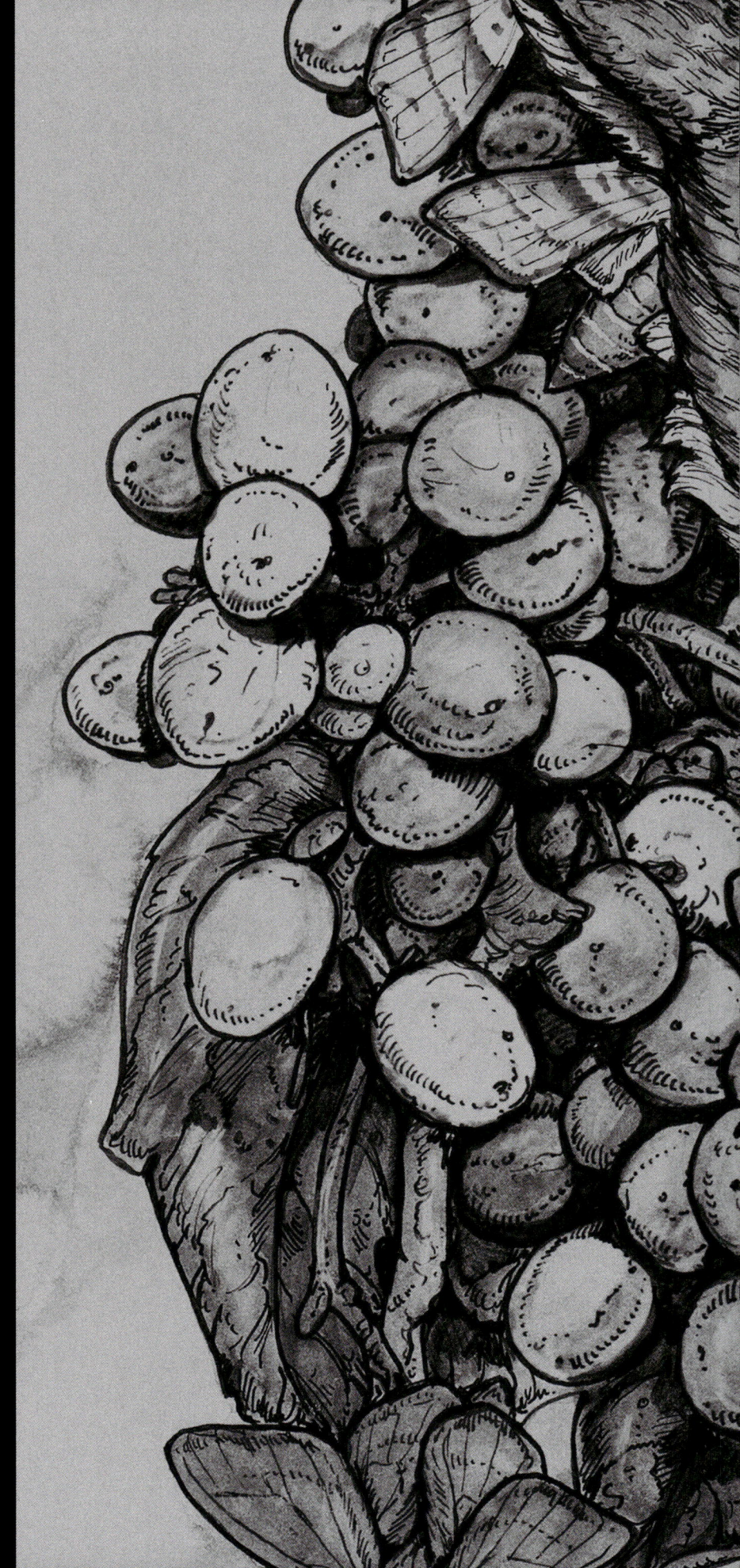

SACRED DECAY

2019

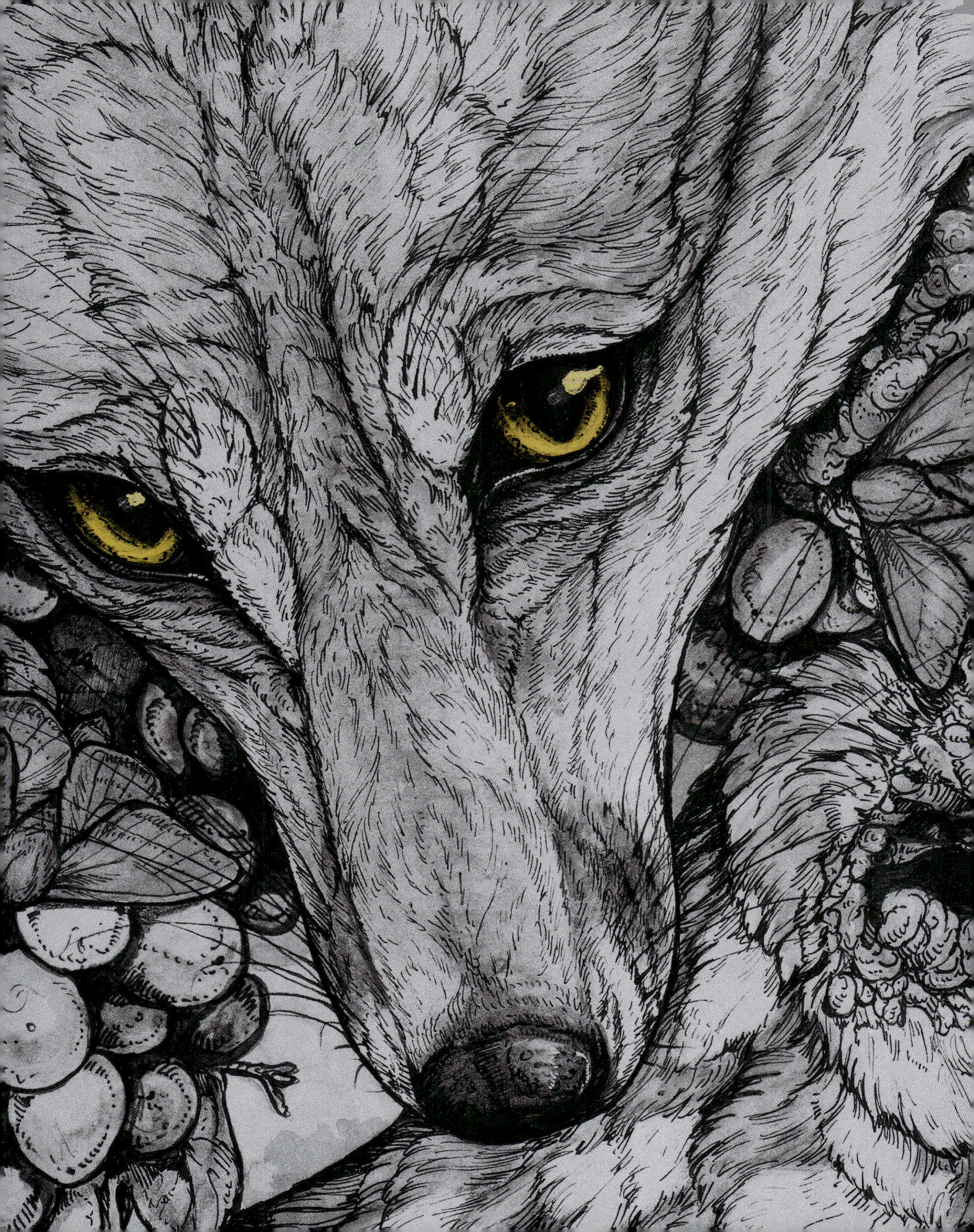

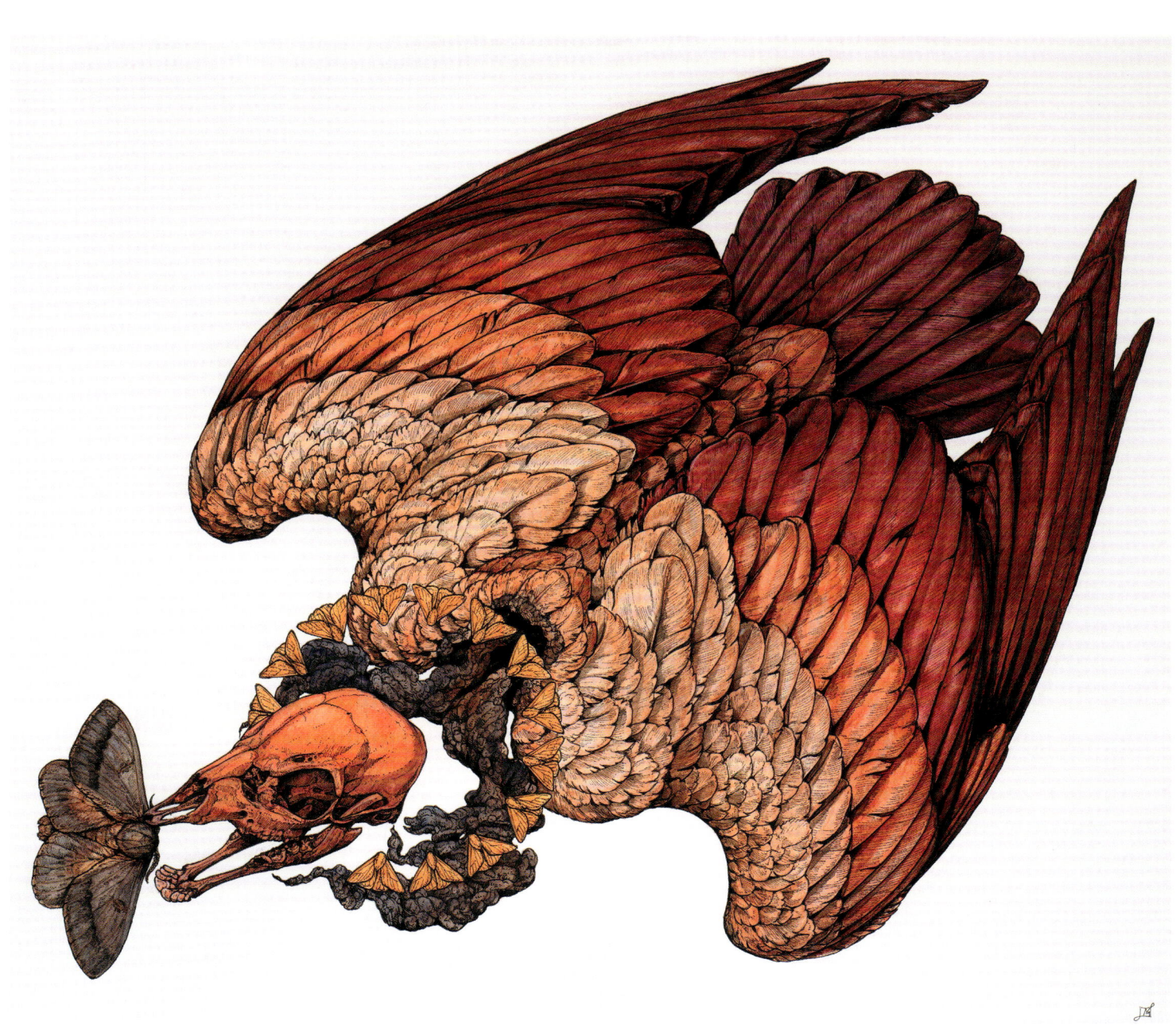

RED CHERUB

19.5″ × 17″

Pen, watercolor, ink, gel pen, and colored pencil on paper
From the exhibition "Chimera"

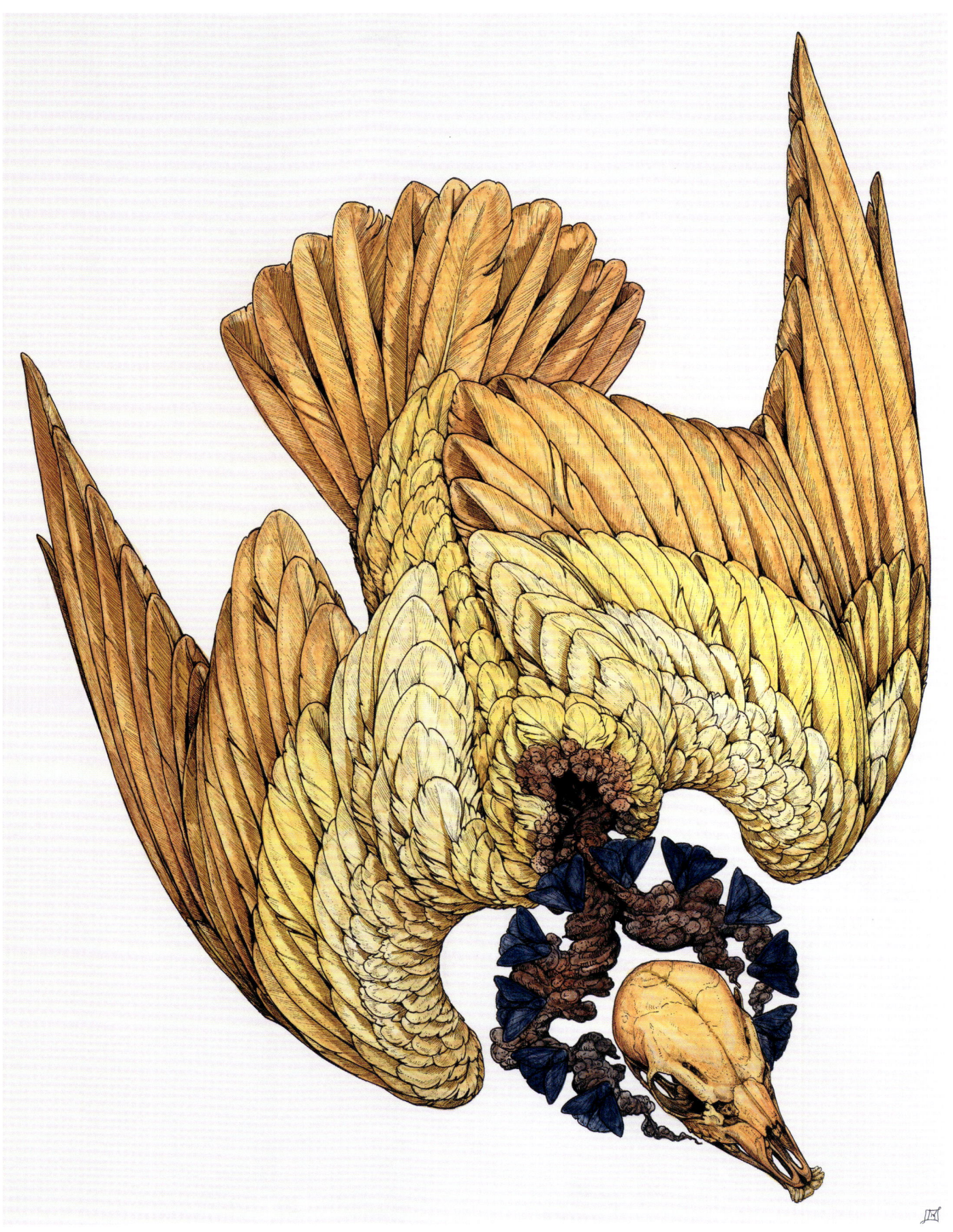

YELLOW CHERUB

16.75" x 22"

Pen, watercolor, ink, gel pen, and colored pencil on paper
From the exhibition "Chimera"

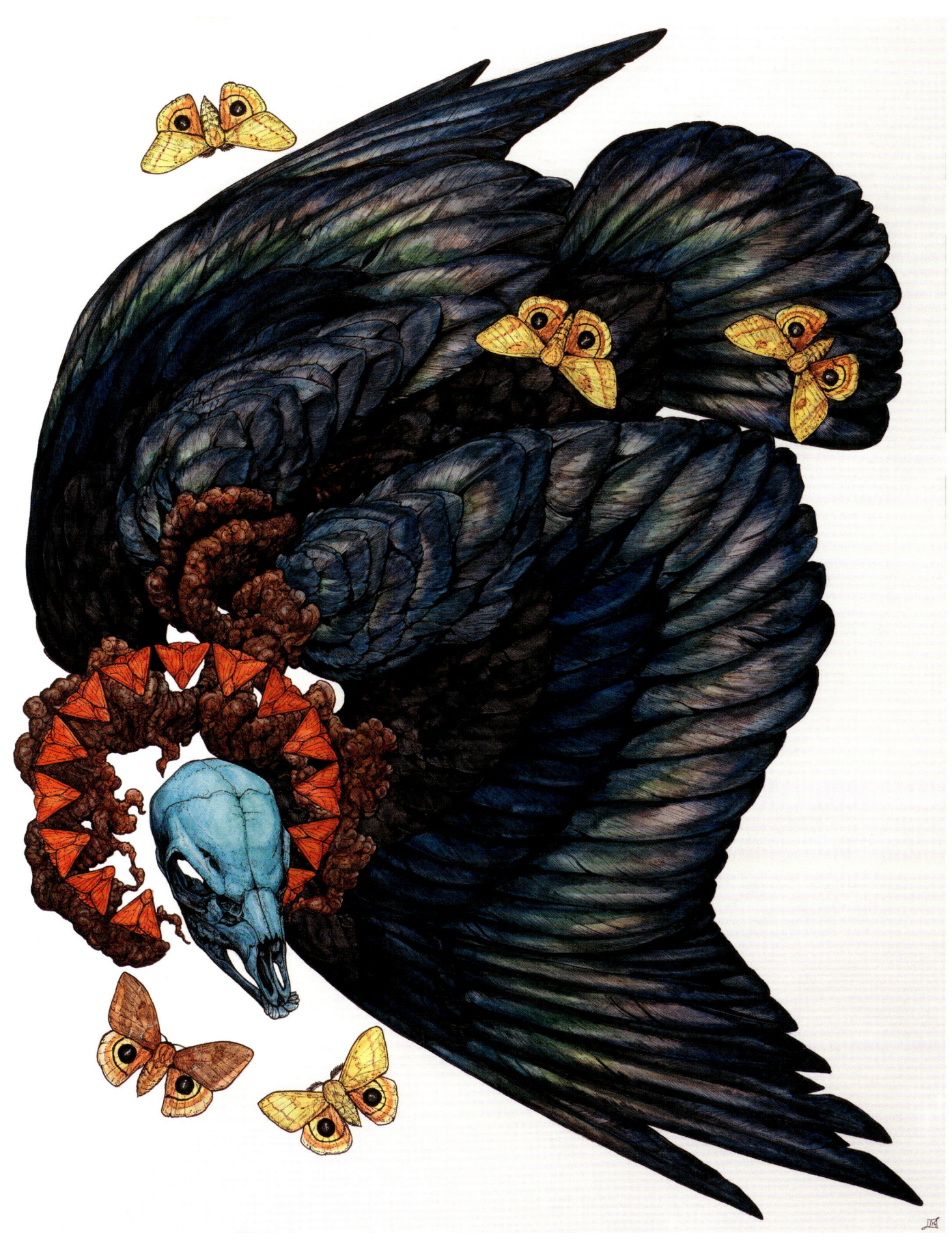

BLUE CHERUB

18" x 23.5"

Pen, watercolor, ink, gel pen, and colored pencil on paper
From the exhibition "Chimera"

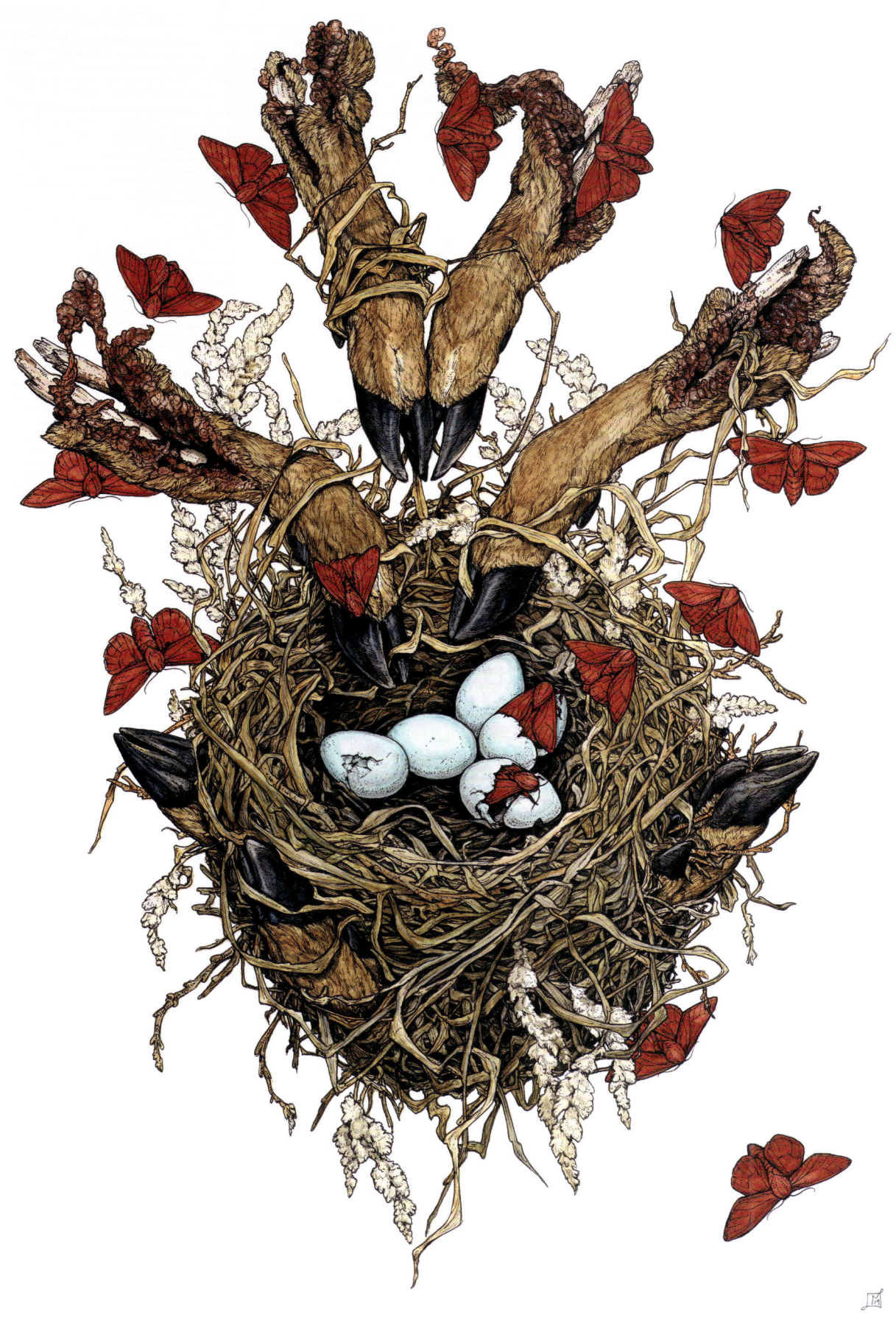

SPELL CASTING

15.5″ x 23″

Pen, watercolor, ink, gel pen, and colored pencil on paper
From the exhibition "Chimera"

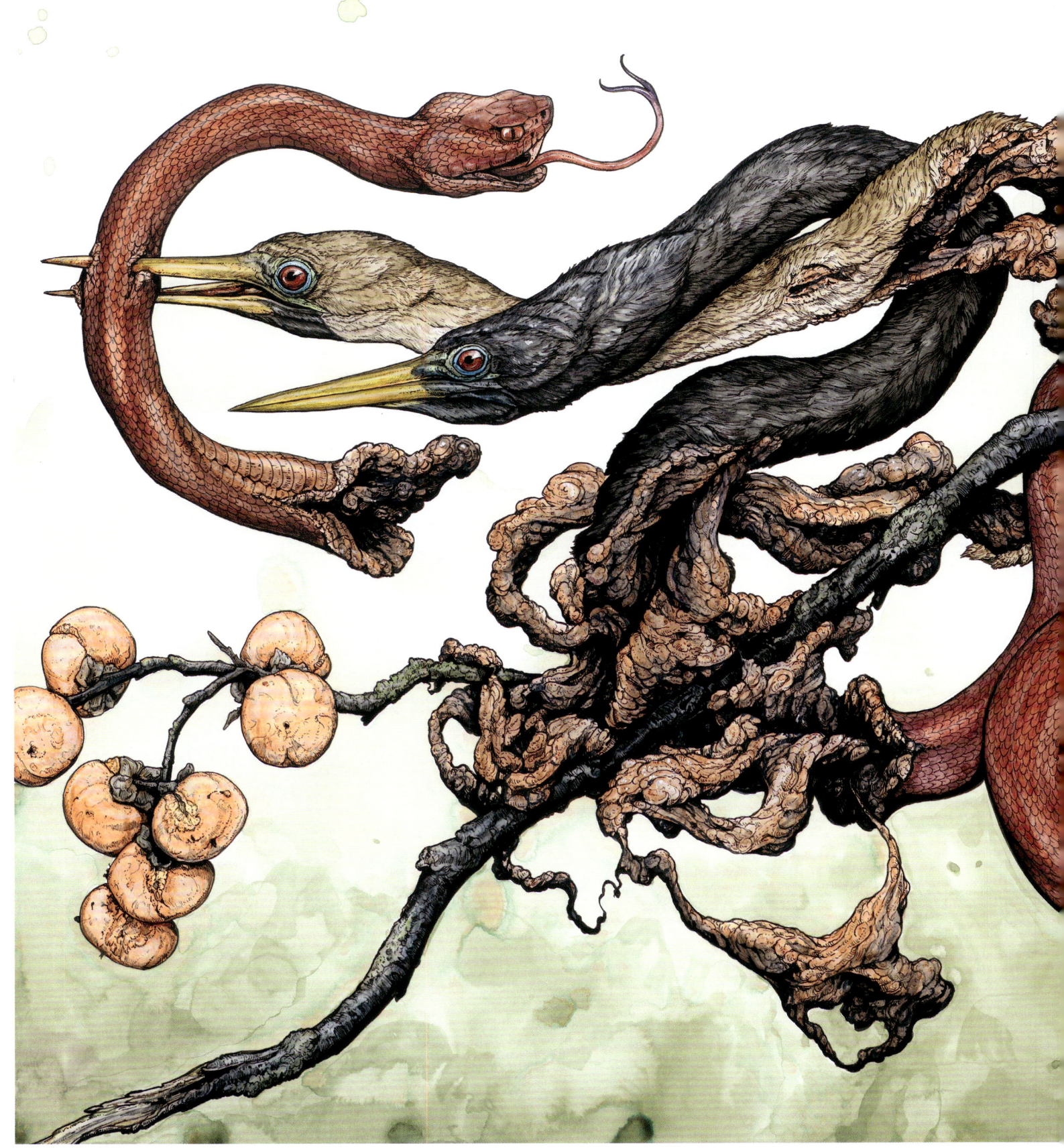

SNAKE BIRD

38" x 20"

Pen, watercolor, ink, gel pen, gouache, and colored pencil on paper
From the exhibition "Chimera"

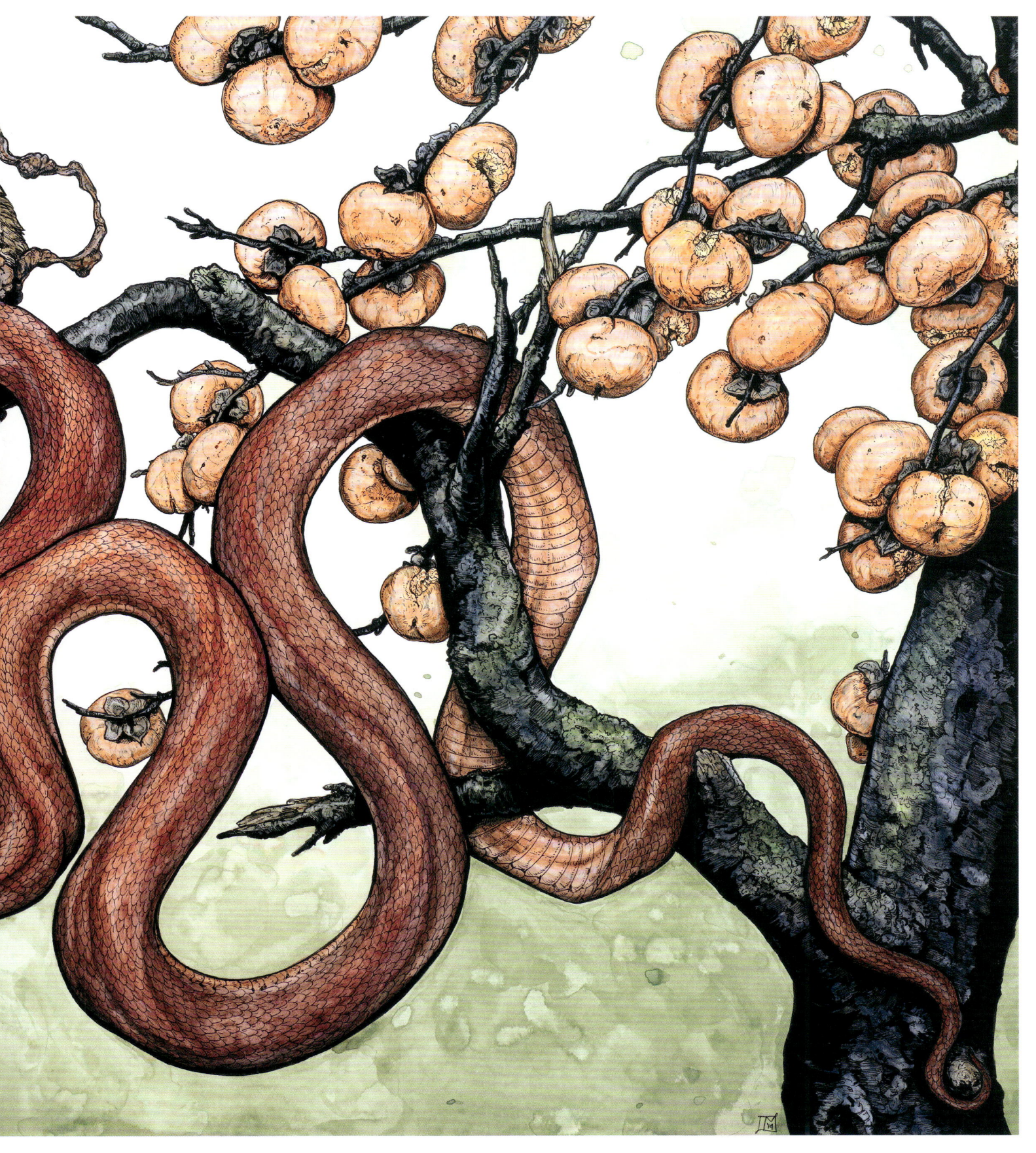

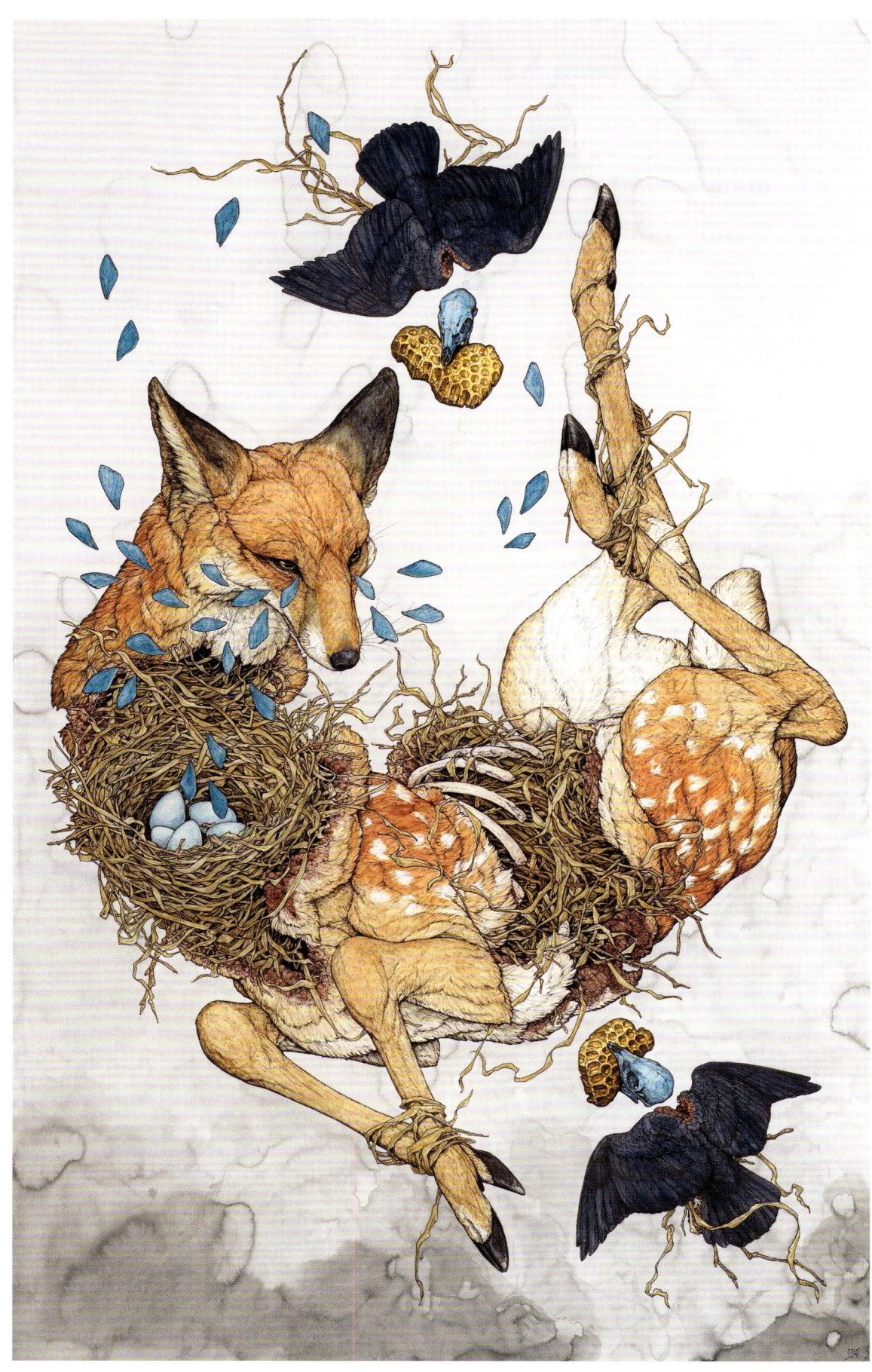

OFFERINGS

26.75" x 42.5"

Pen, watercolor, ink, gel pen, and colored pencil on paper
From the exhibition "Chimera"

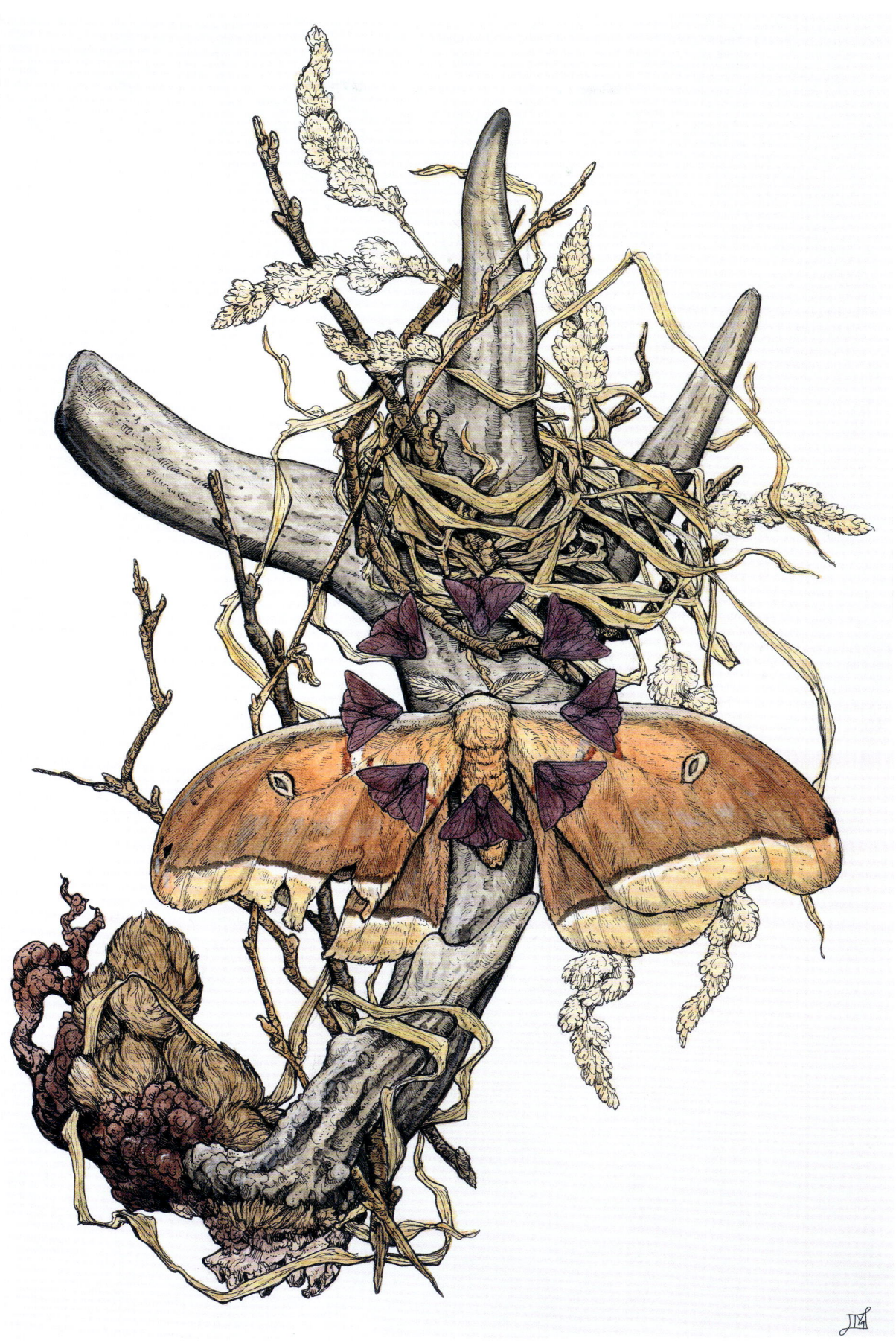

POLYPHEMUS SAINT

10" x 15"

Pen, watercolor, ink, gel pen, and colored pencil on paper
From the exhibition "Chimera"

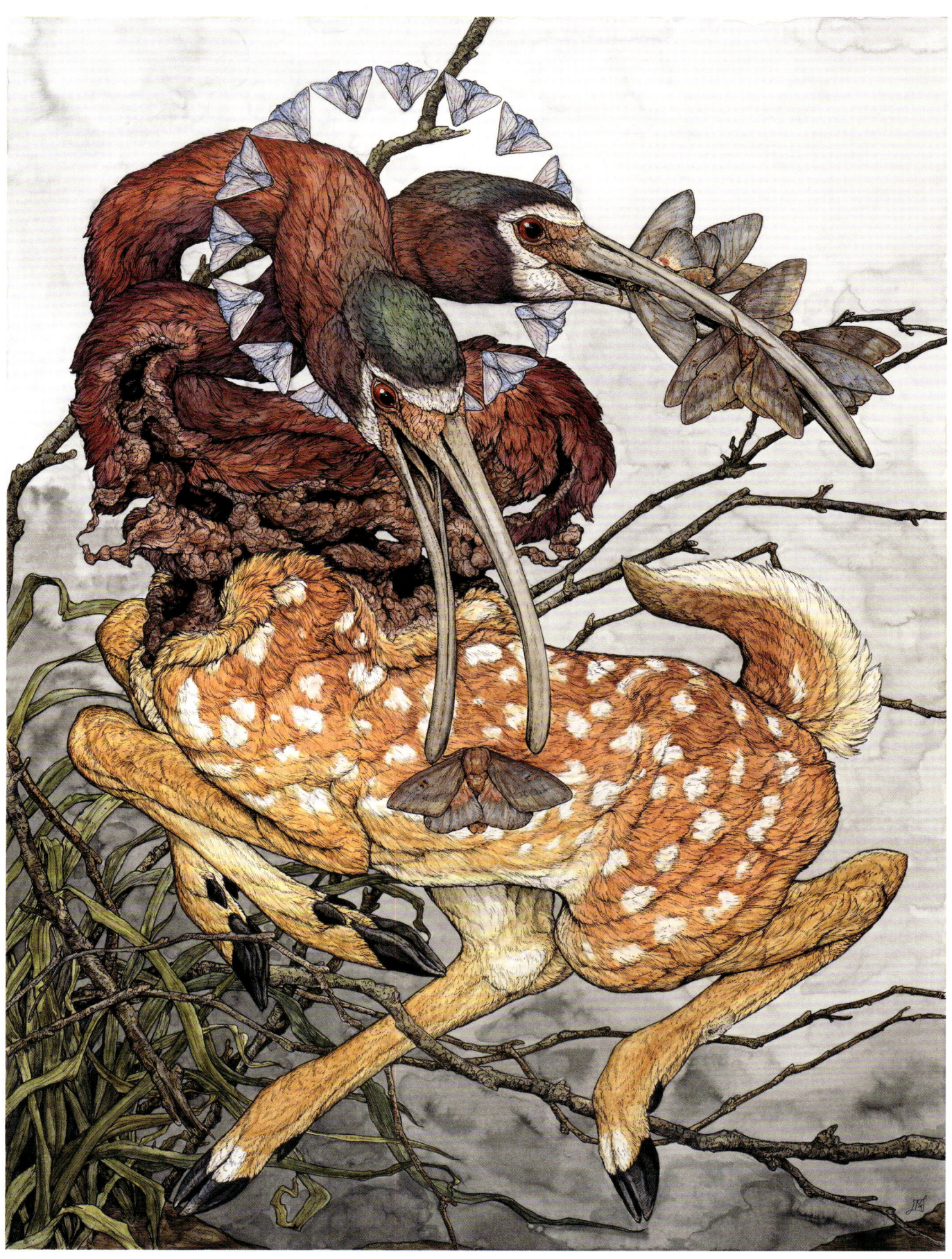

DEVIL CATCHER

18″ x 24″

Pen, watercolor, ink, gel pen, and colored pencil on paper

From the exhibition "Chimera"

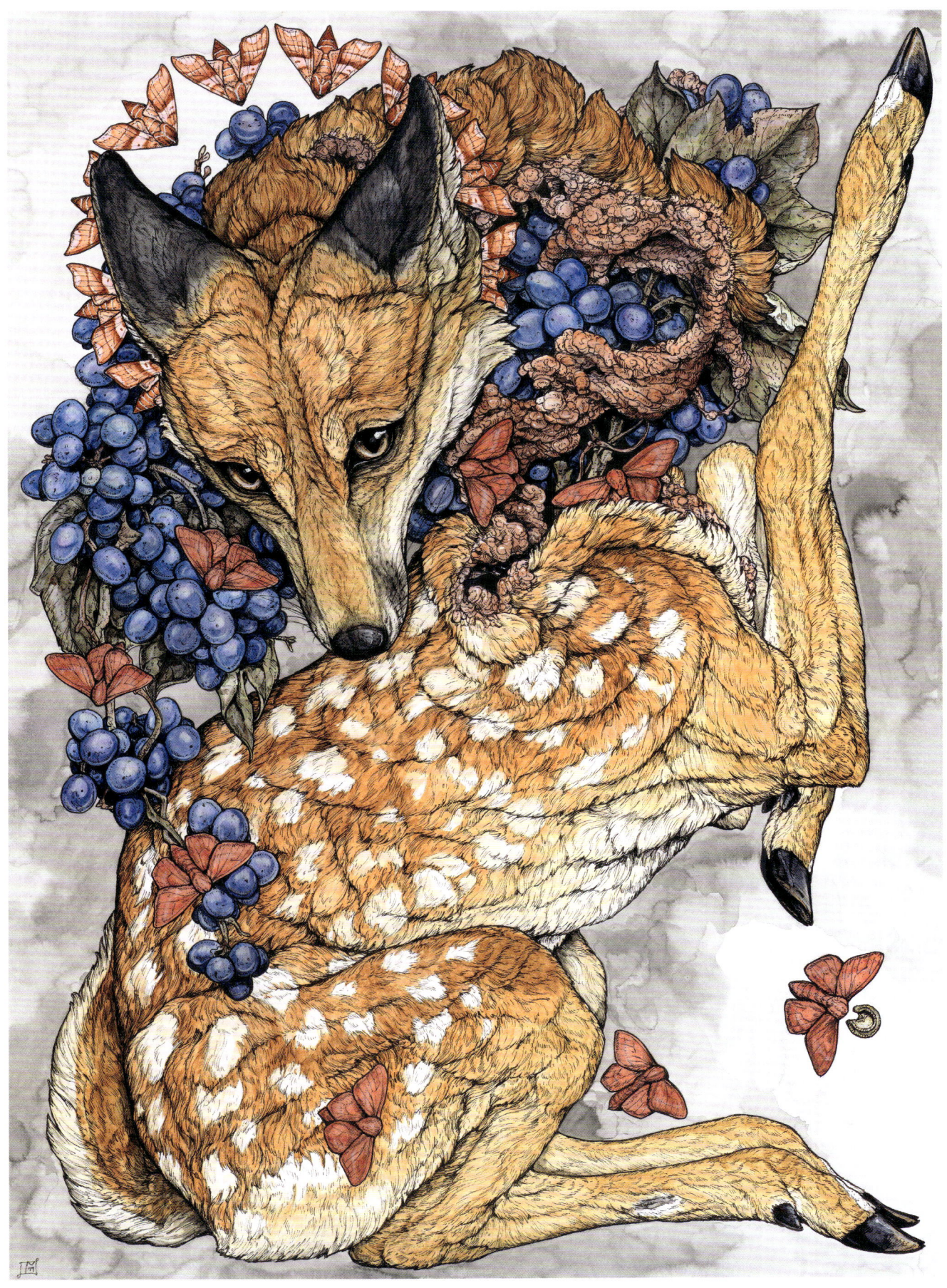

MOONSEED

16.5" x 22.75"

Pen, watercolor, ink, gel pen, and colored pencil on paper
From the exhibition "Chimera"

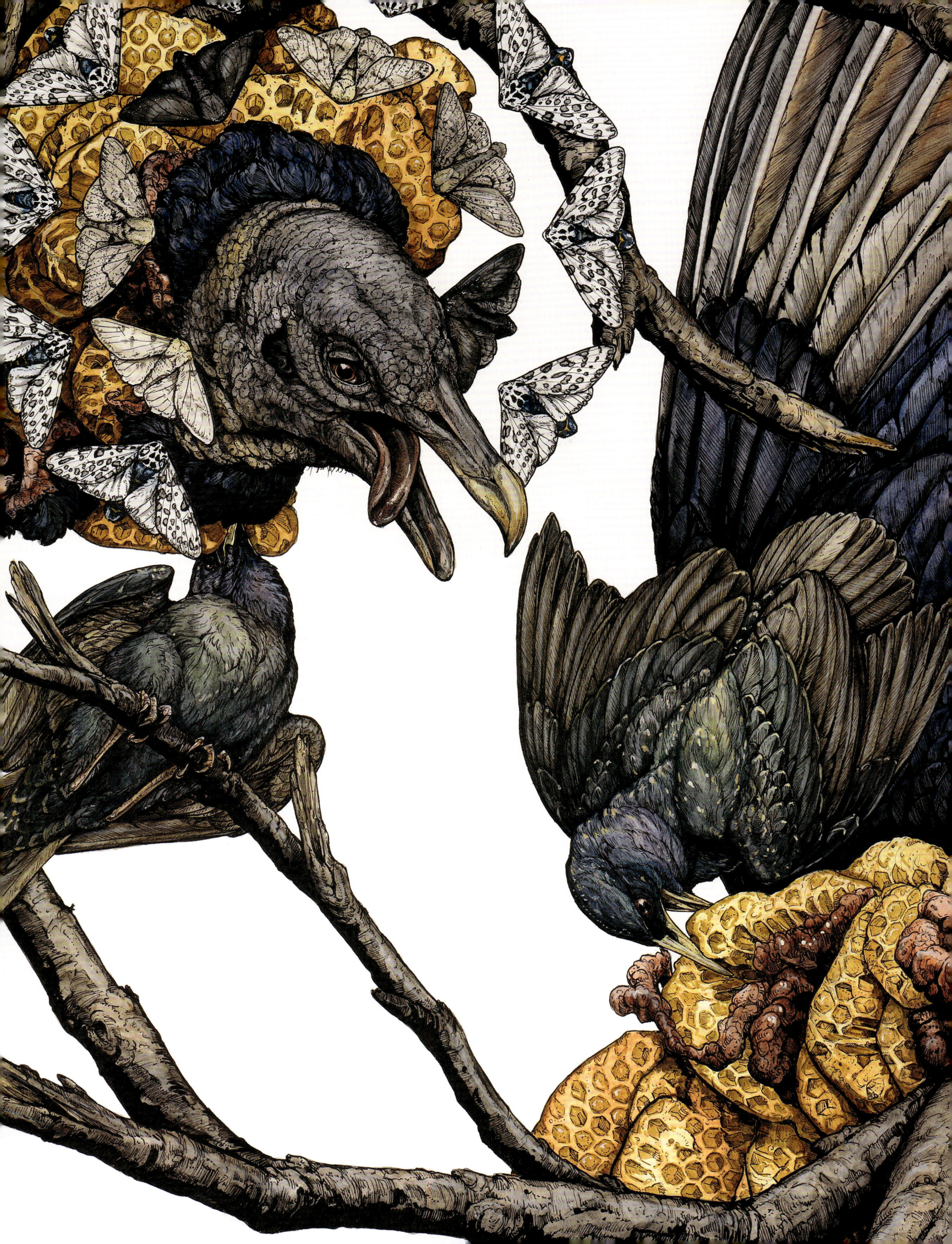

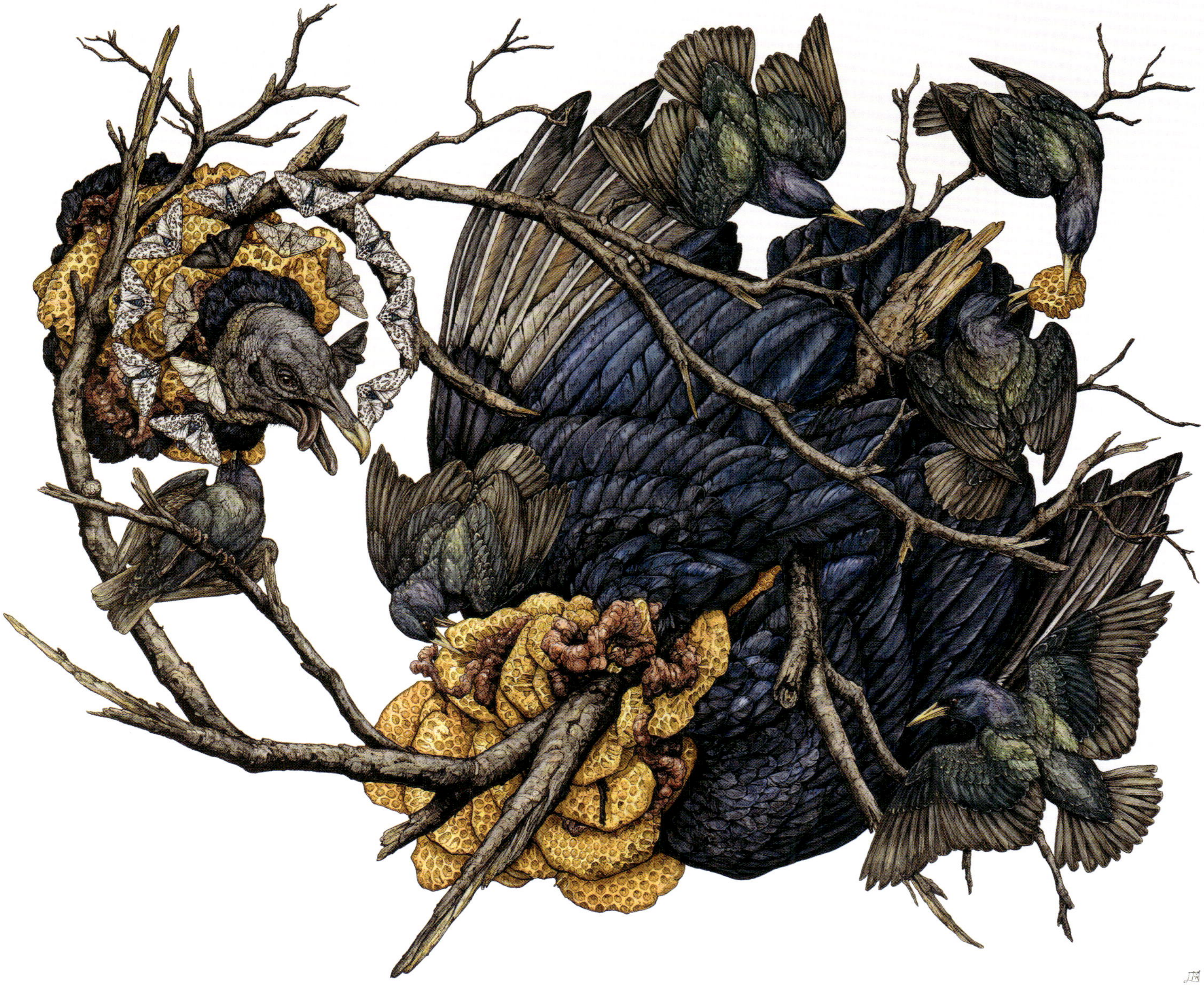

HONEY

37.25″ x 31″

Pen, watercolor, ink, gel pen, gouache, and colored pencil on paper
From the exhibition "Chimera"

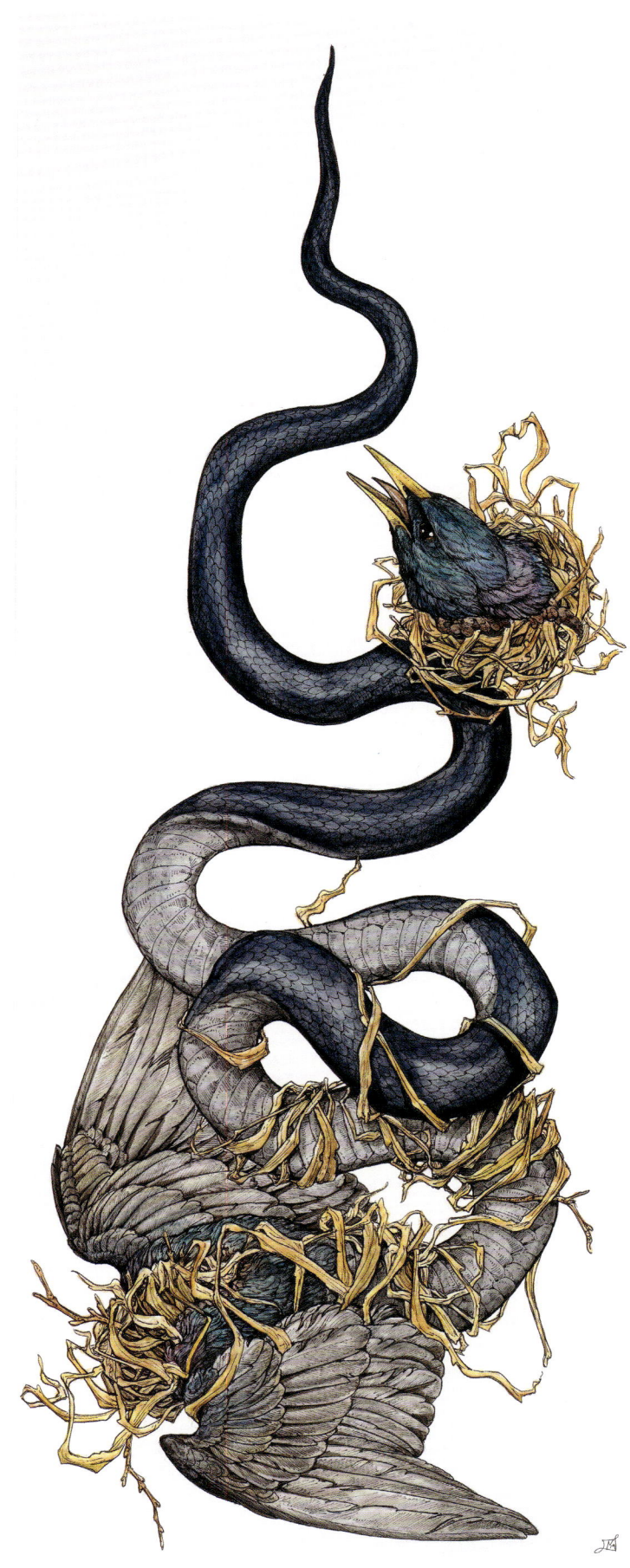

ENTANGLED

9″ x 22.5″

Pen, watercolor, ink, gel pen, and colored pencil on paper
From the exhibition "Chimera"

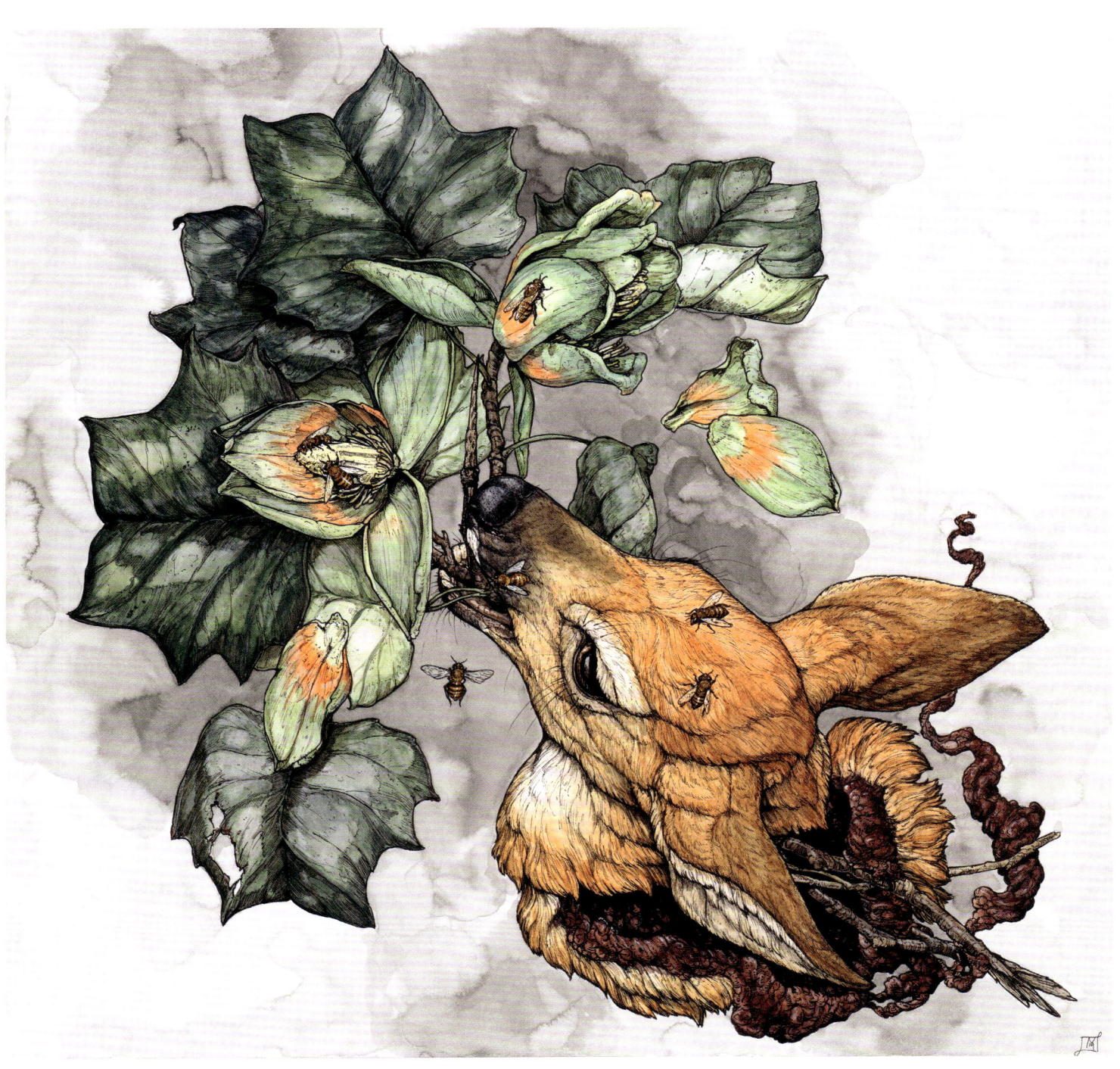

SWEETS

17.75" x 17"

Pen, watercolor, ink, gel pen, and colored pencil on paper
From the exhibition "Chimera"

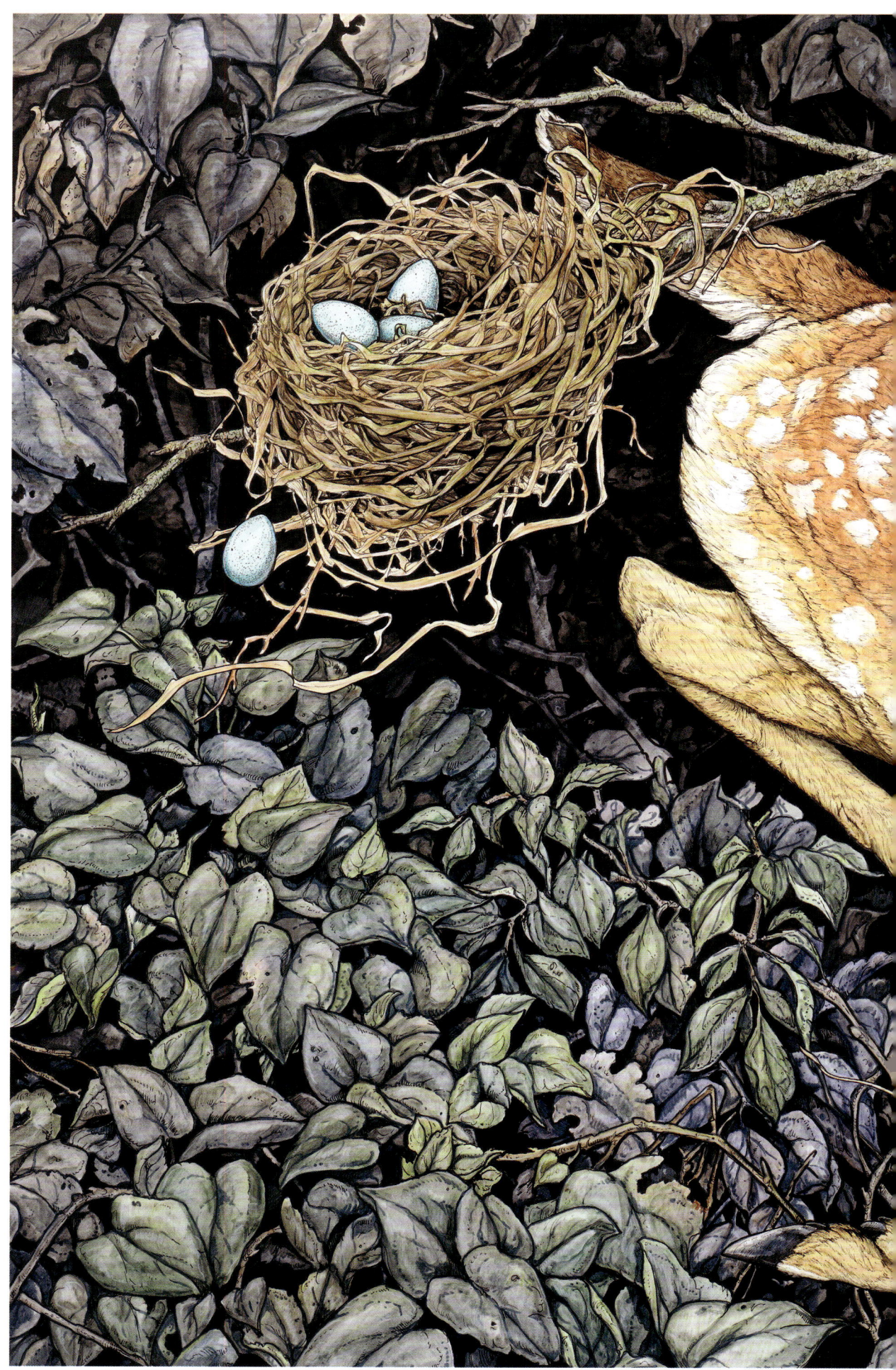

NESTED FAWN

40″ x 25.75″

Pen, watercolor, ink, gel pen, and
colored pencil on paper
From the exhibition "Chimera"

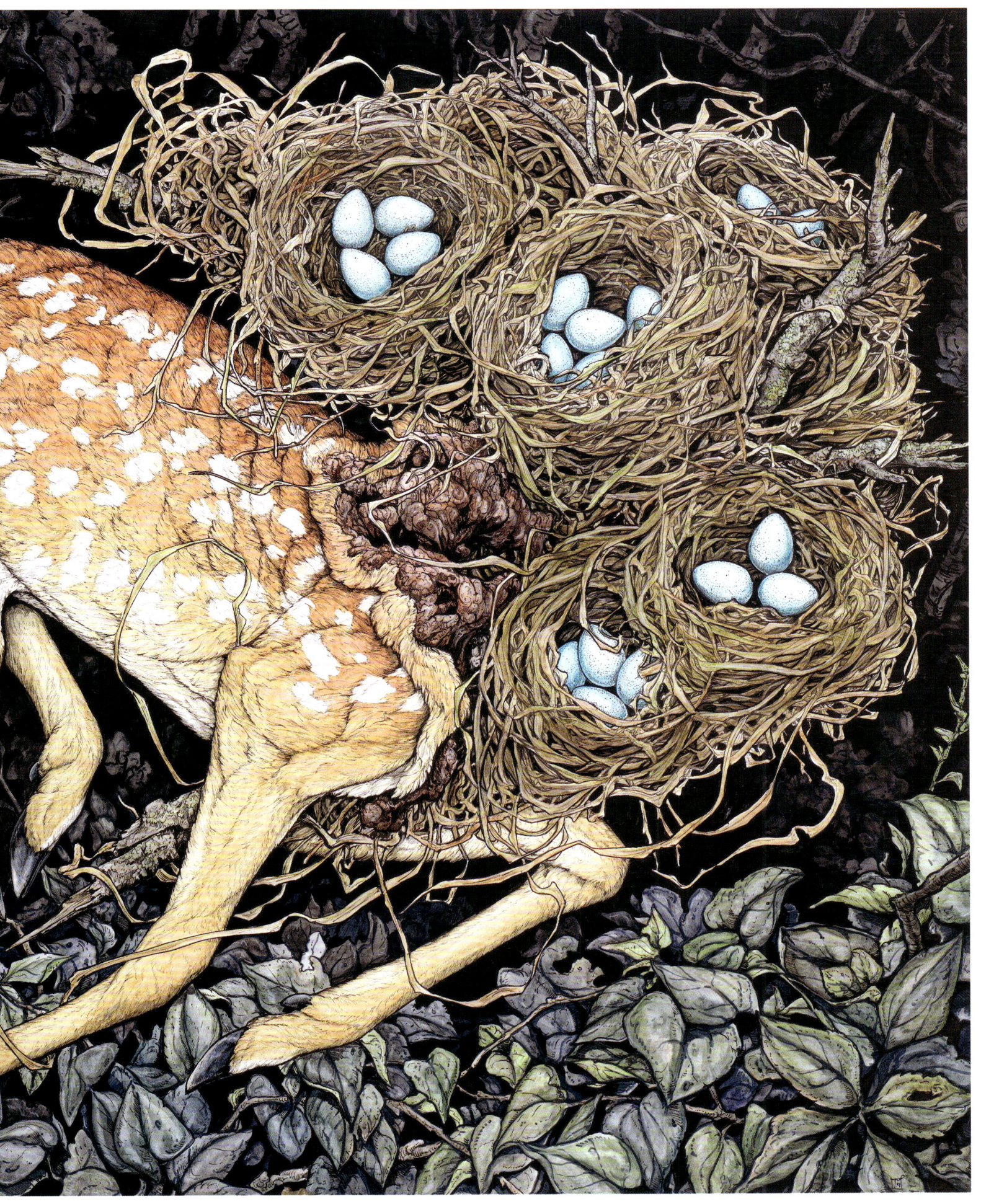

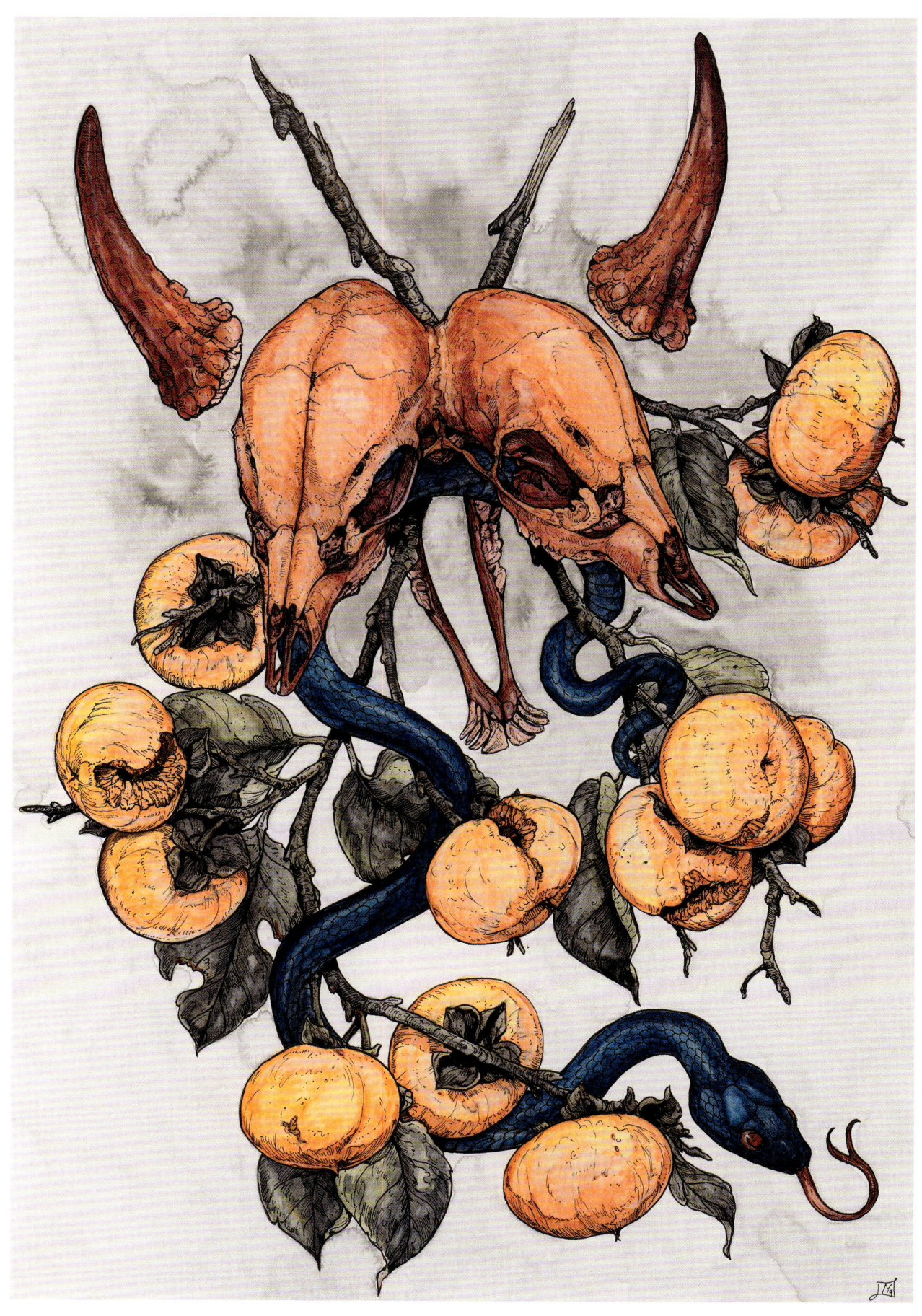

TEMPTATION

11" x 15.75"

Pen, watercolor, ink, gel pen, and colored pencil on paper
From the exhibition "Chimera"

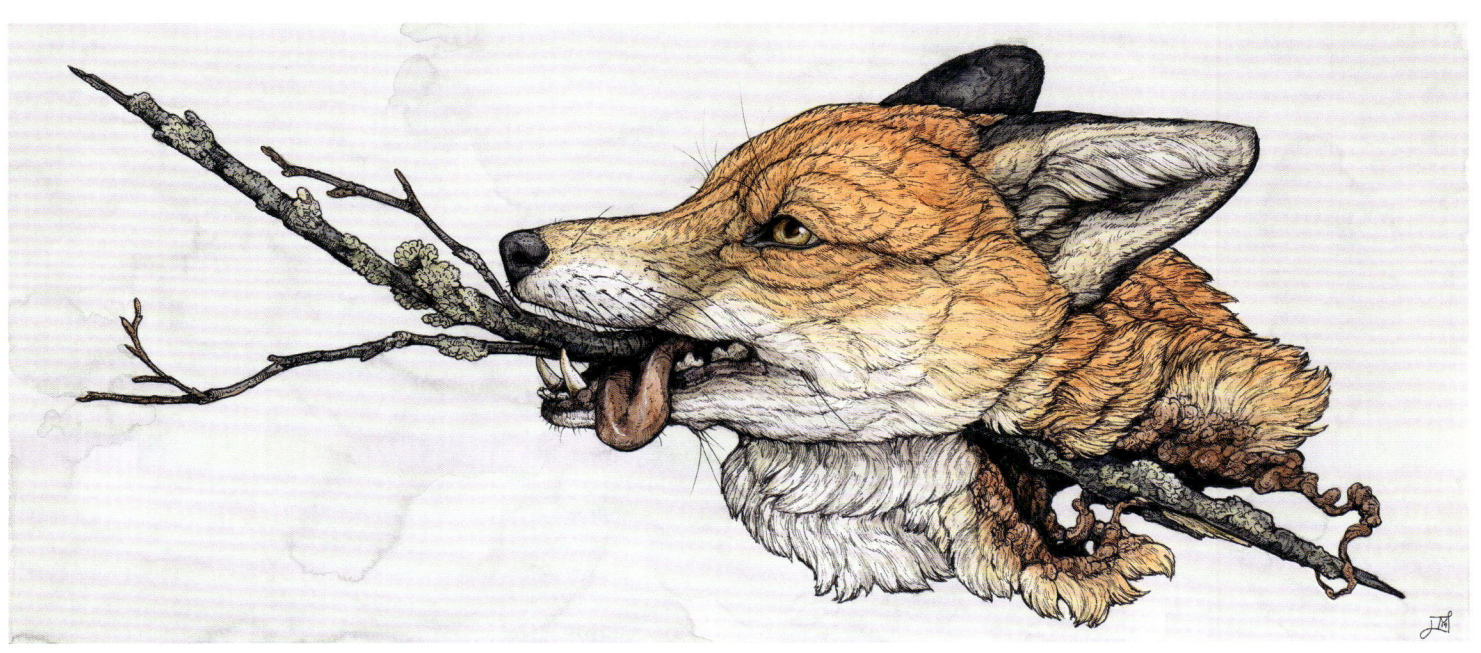

RED FOX AND LICHEN

18″ x 7.75″

Pen, watercolor, ink, gel pen, and colored pencil on paper
From the exhibition "Chimera"

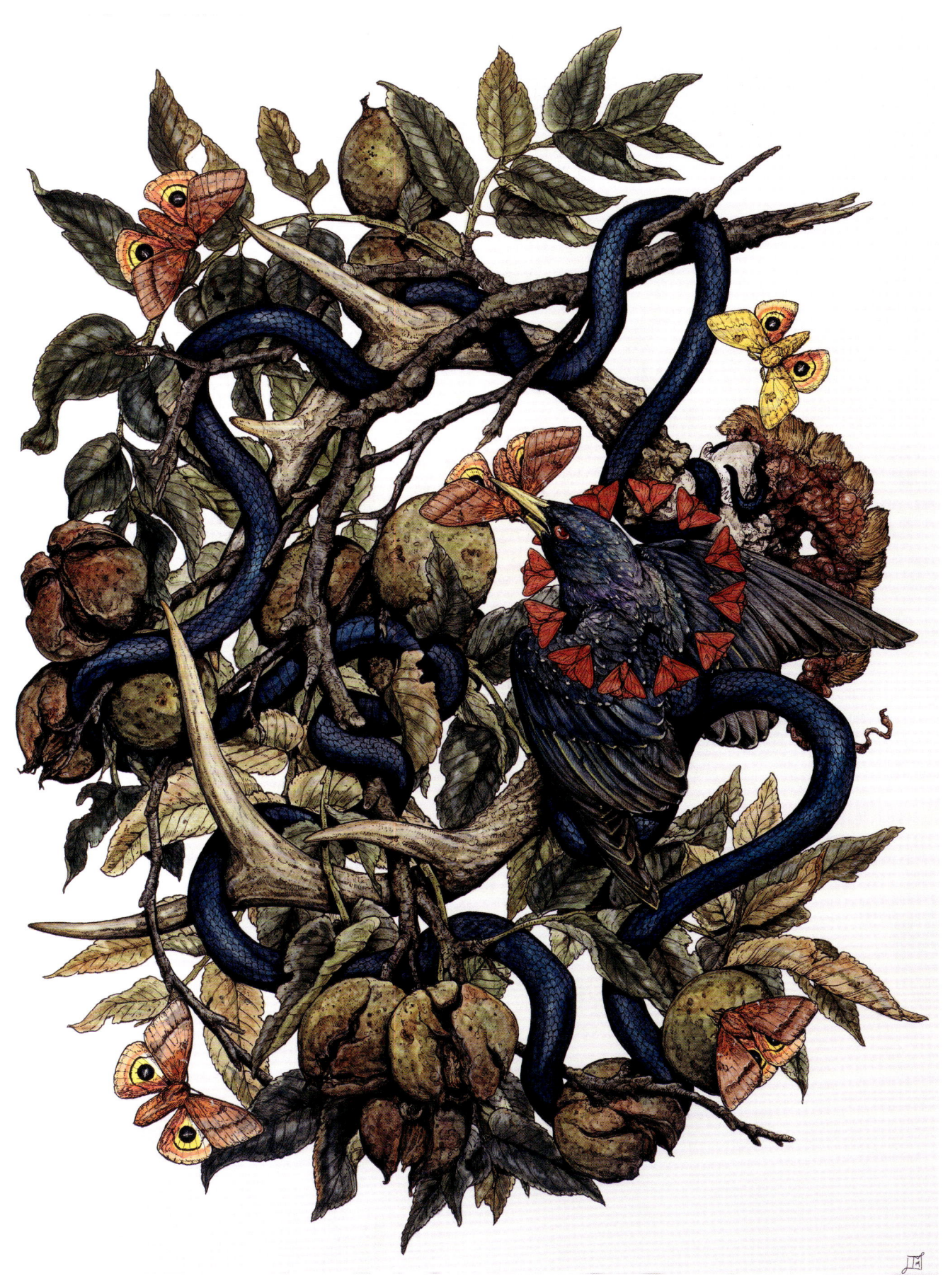

THE SERPENT OF MISSOURI

17" x 23.25"

Pen, watercolor, ink, gel pen, and colored pencil on paper
From the exhibition "Chimera"

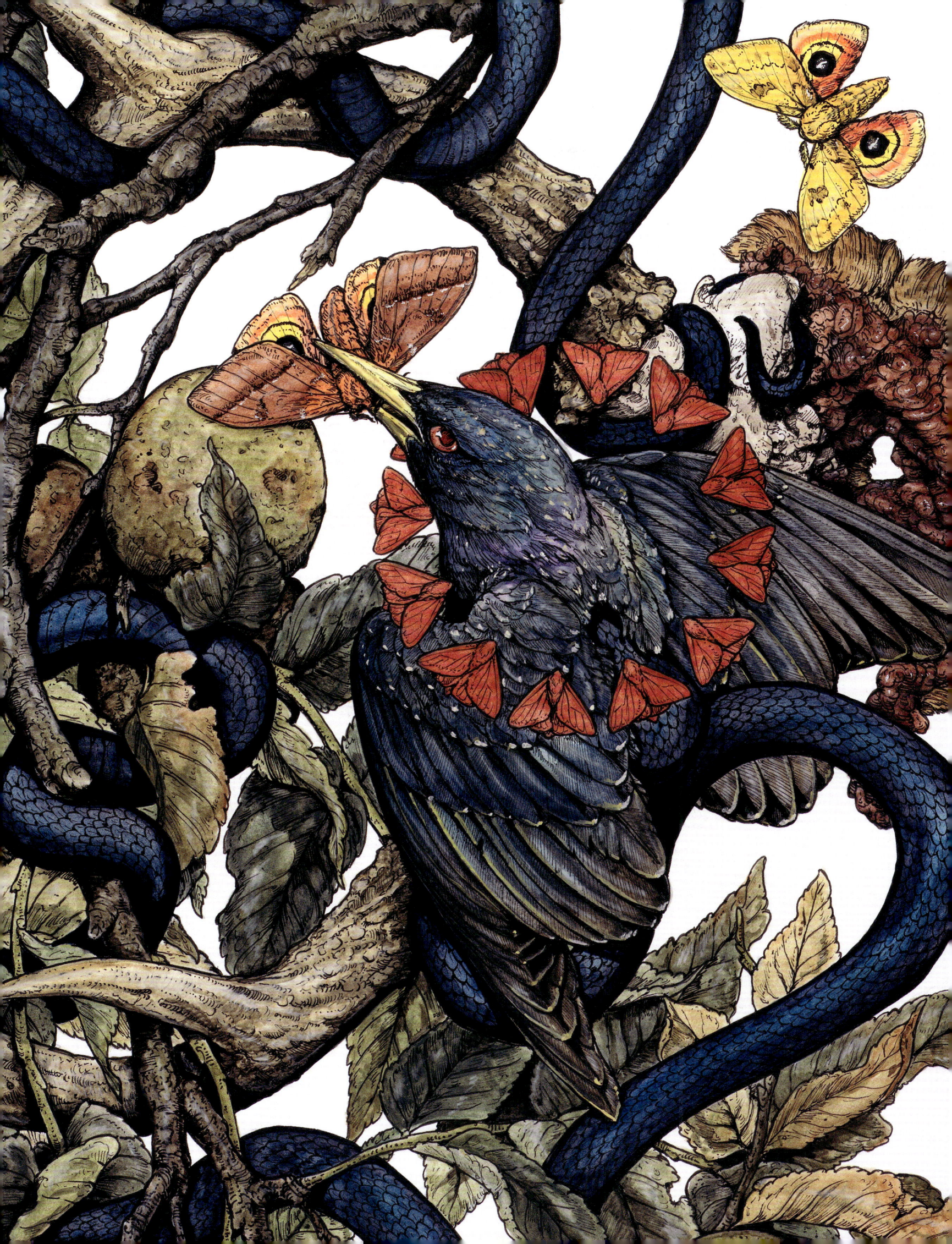

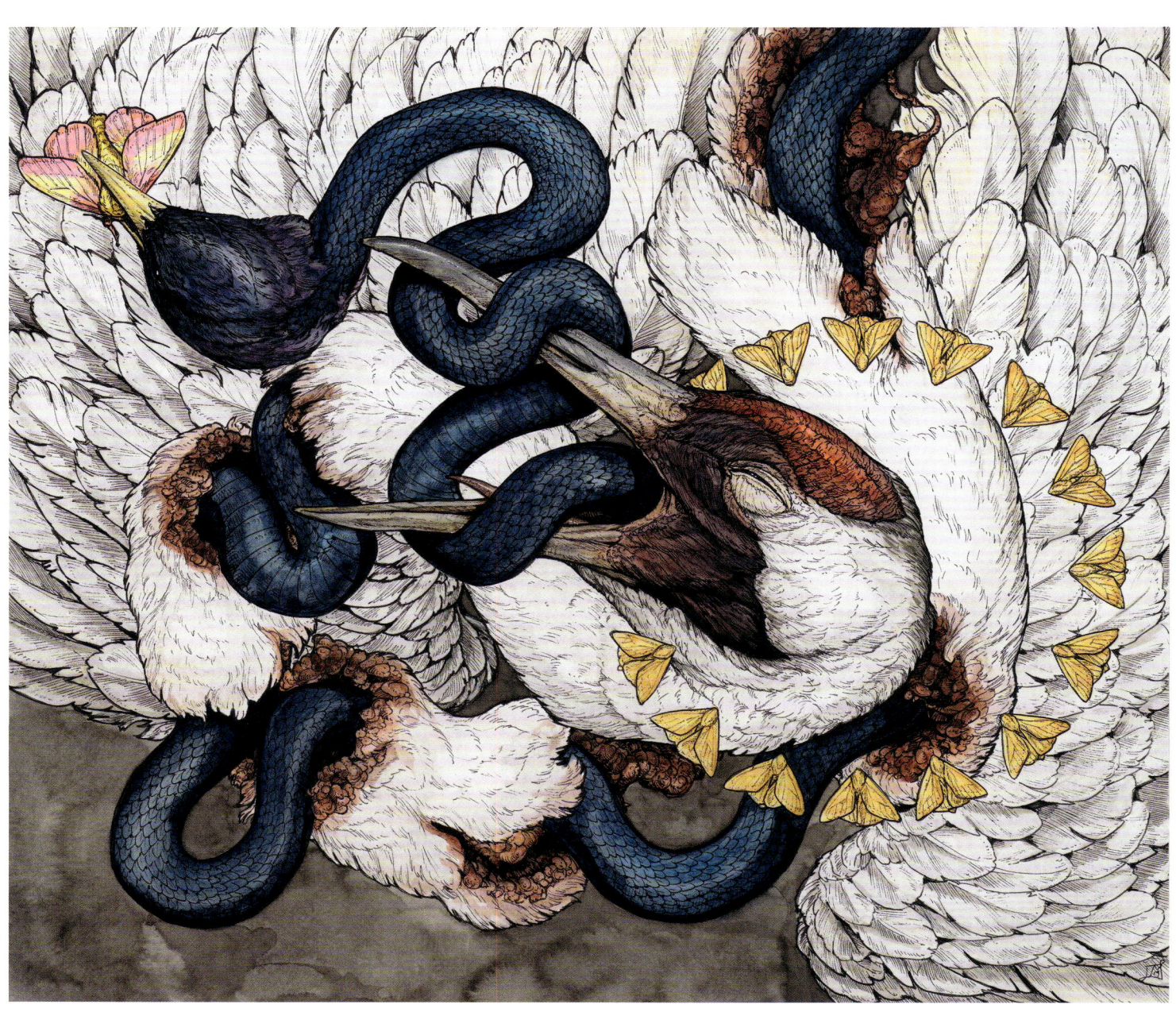

SIN SPEAK

14″ x 12″

Pen, watercolor, ink, gel pen, and colored pencil on paper
From the exhibition "Chimera"

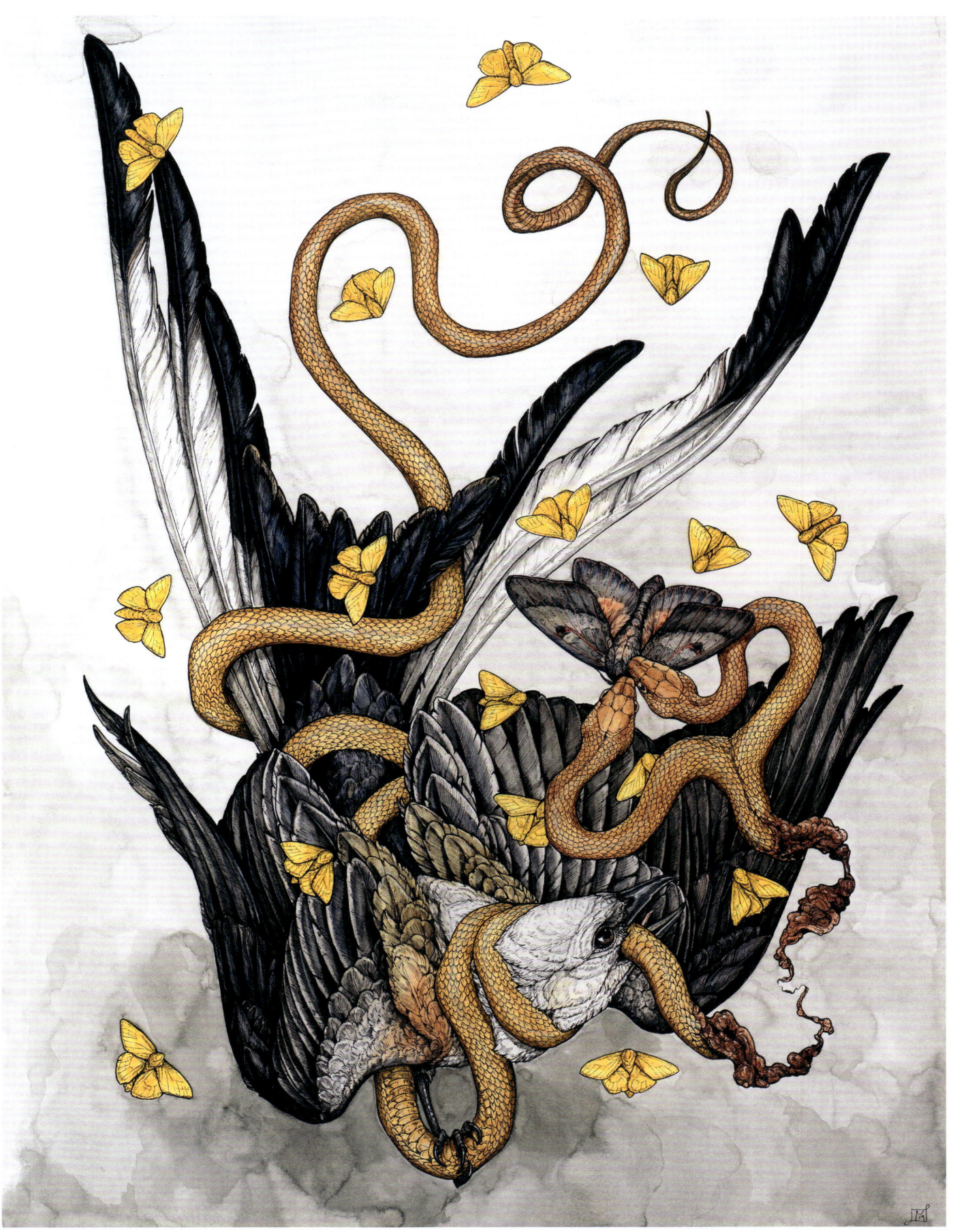

SCISSOR-TAILED FLYCATCHER

17.75" x 23"

Pen, watercolor, ink, gel pen, and colored pencil on paper
From the exhibition "Chimera"

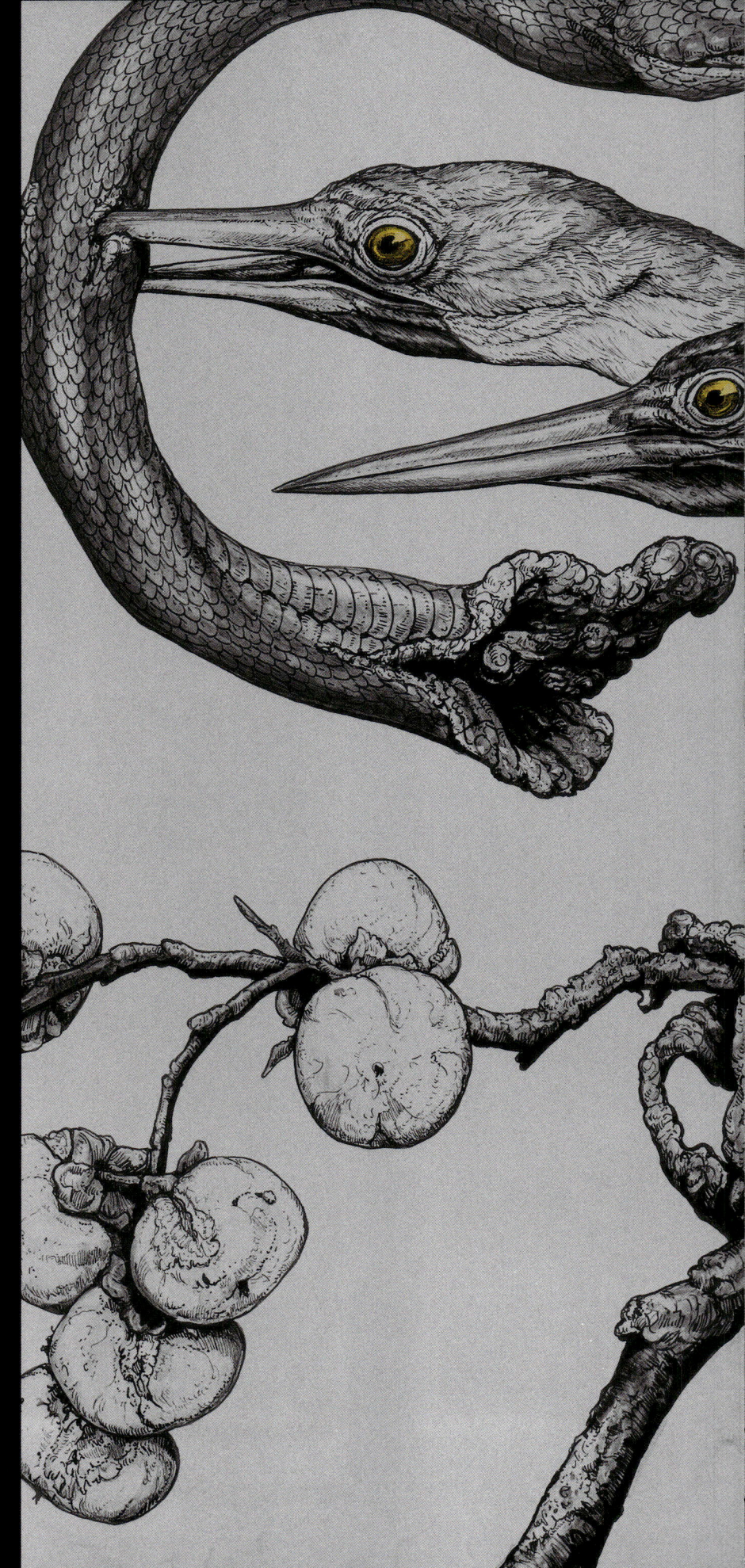

SACRED DECAY

SKETCHBOOK

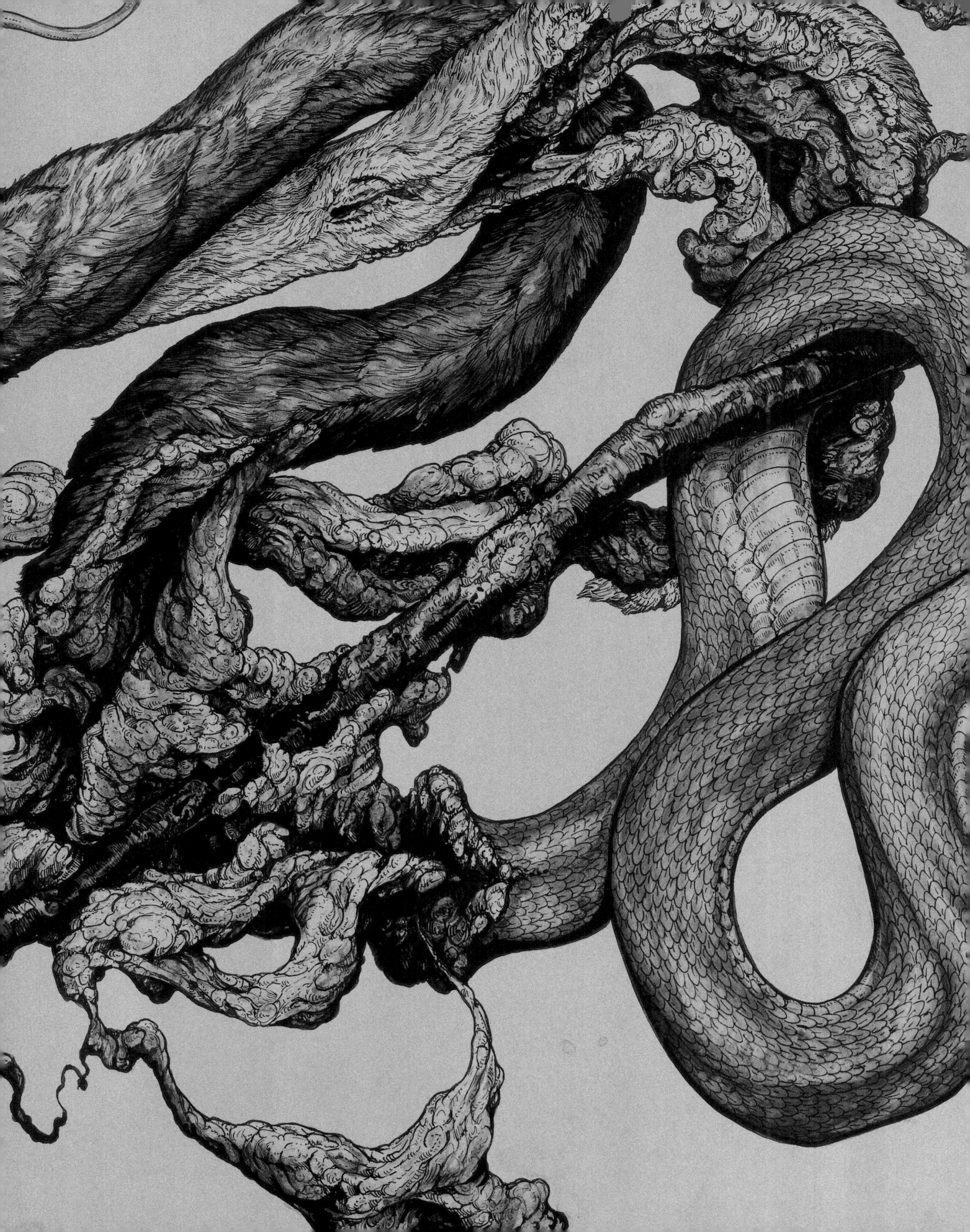

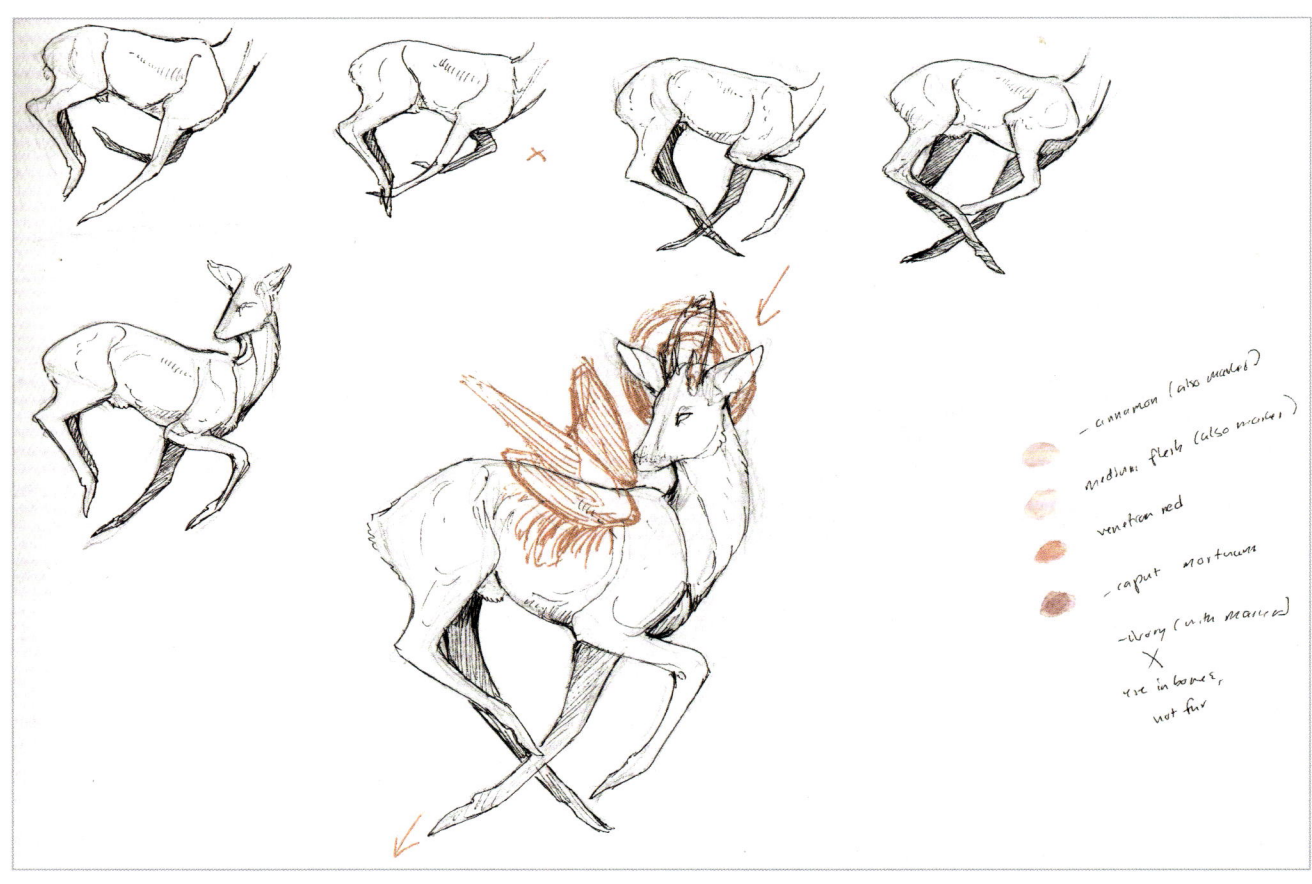

Color swatches (right side):
- cinnamon (also modern?)
- medium flesh (also modern)
- venetian red
- caput mortuum
- ivory (with maroon)
  X
  roe in bones, not fur

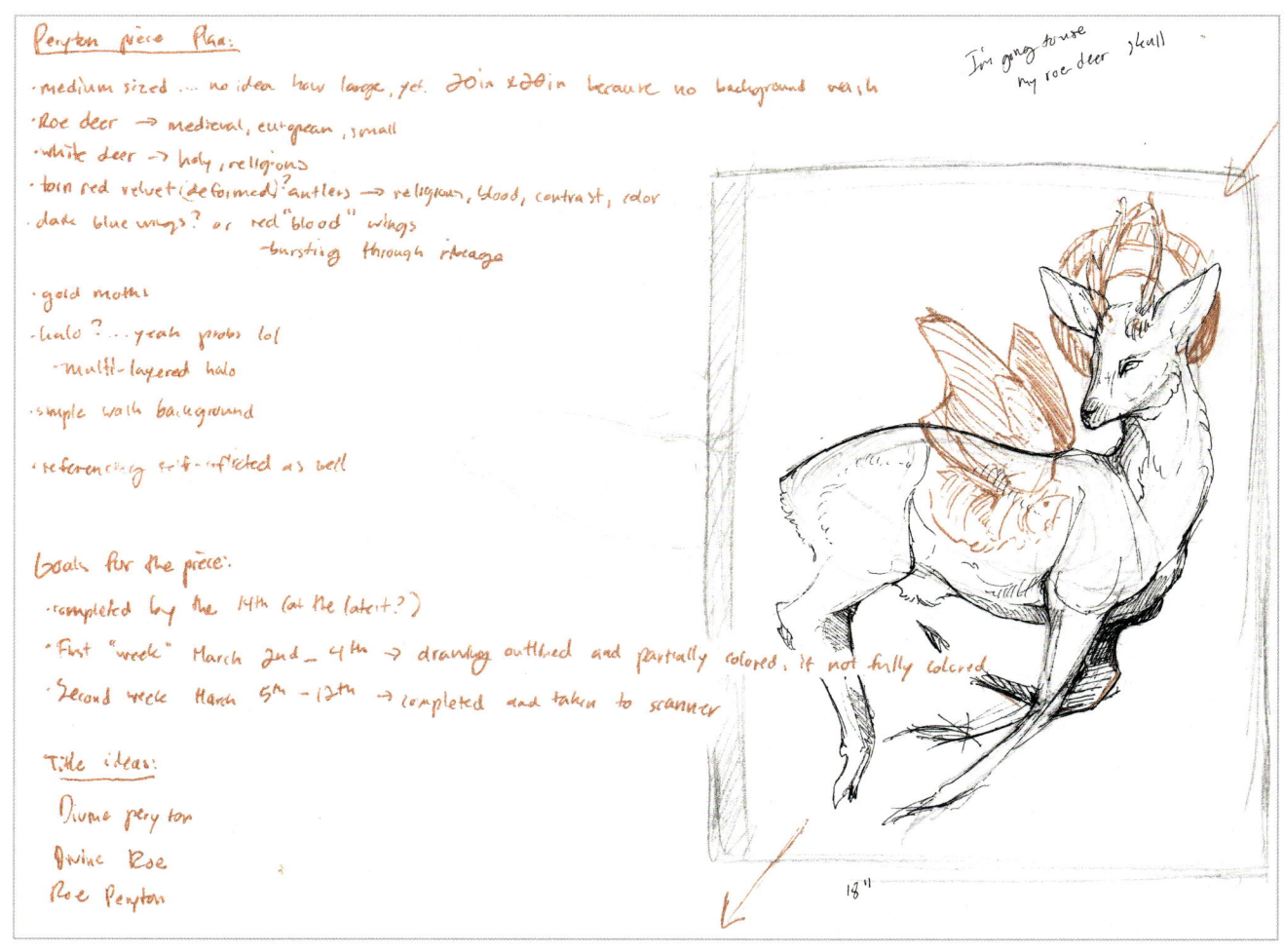

Peryton piece Plan:

- medium sized ... no idea how large, yet. 20in x 28in because no background wash
- Roe deer → medieval, european, small
- white deer → holy, religions
- torn red velvet (deformed?) antlers → religious, blood, contrast, color
- dark blue wings? or red "blood" wings
                  → bursting through ribcage

- gold moths
- halo? ...yeah probs lol
  - multi-layered halo
- simple wash background

- referencing self-inflicted as well

Goals for the piece:

- completed by the 14th (at the latest?)
- First "week" March 2nd - 4th → drawing outlined and partially colored, if not fully colored
- Second week March 5th - 12th → completed and taken to scanner

Title ideas:

Divine peryton
Divine Roe
Roe Peryton

I'm going to use my roe deer skull

18"

132

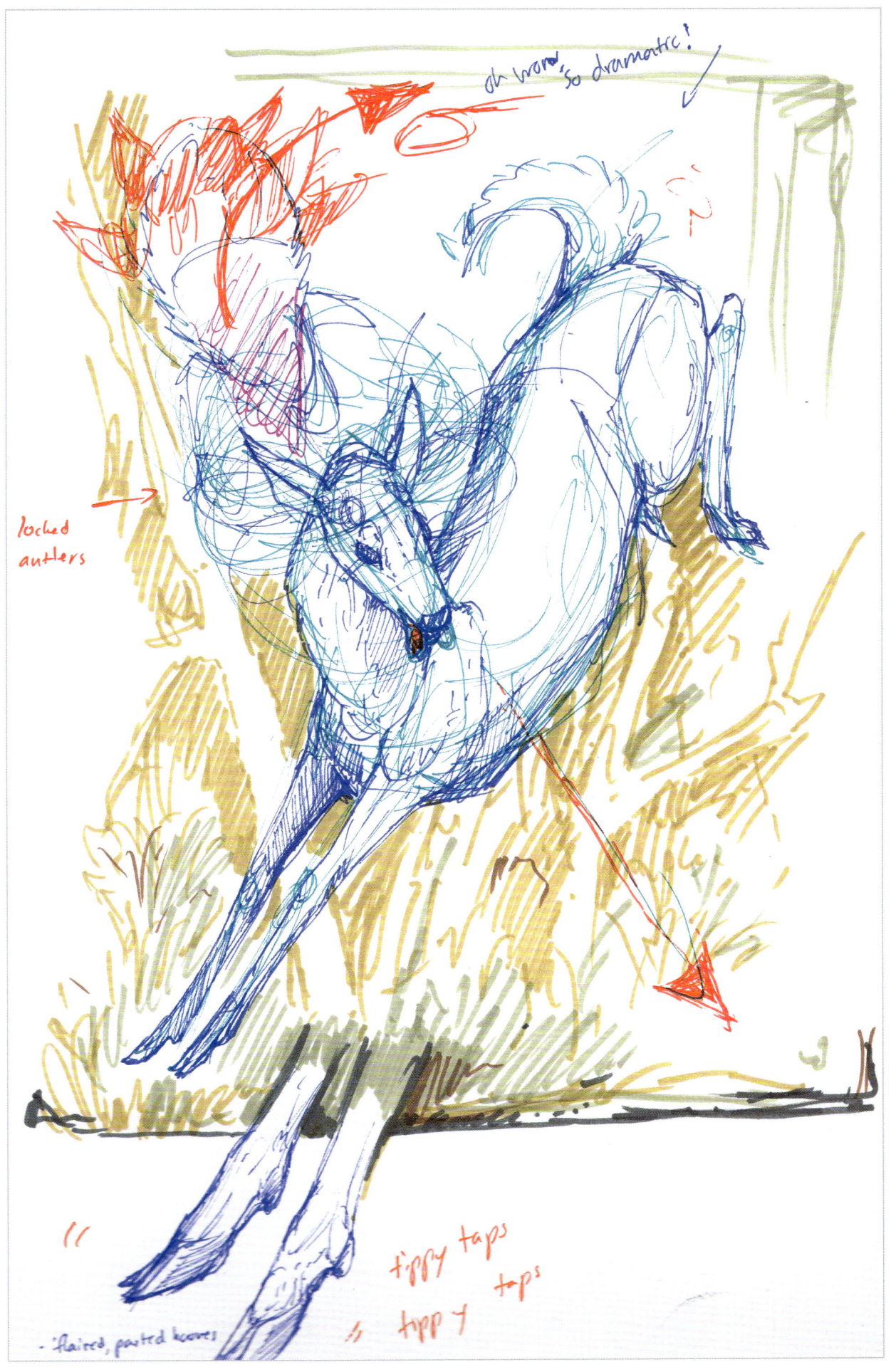

133

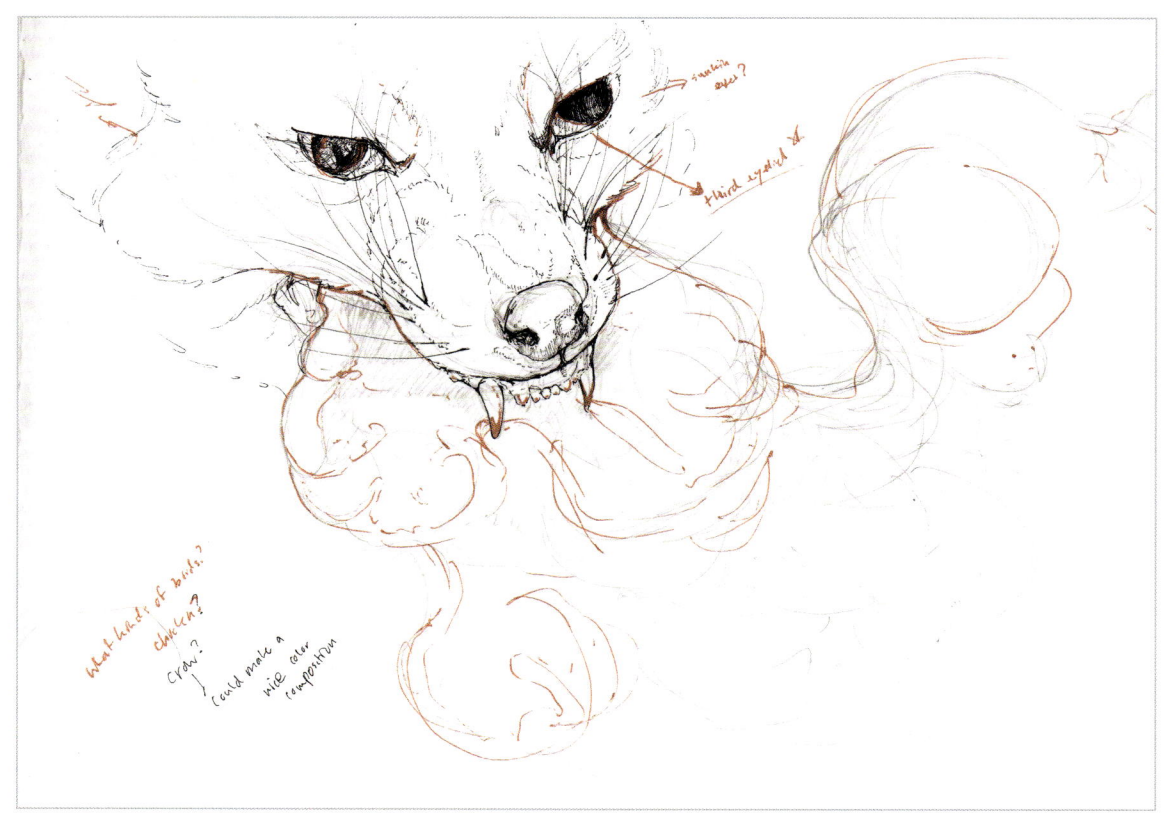

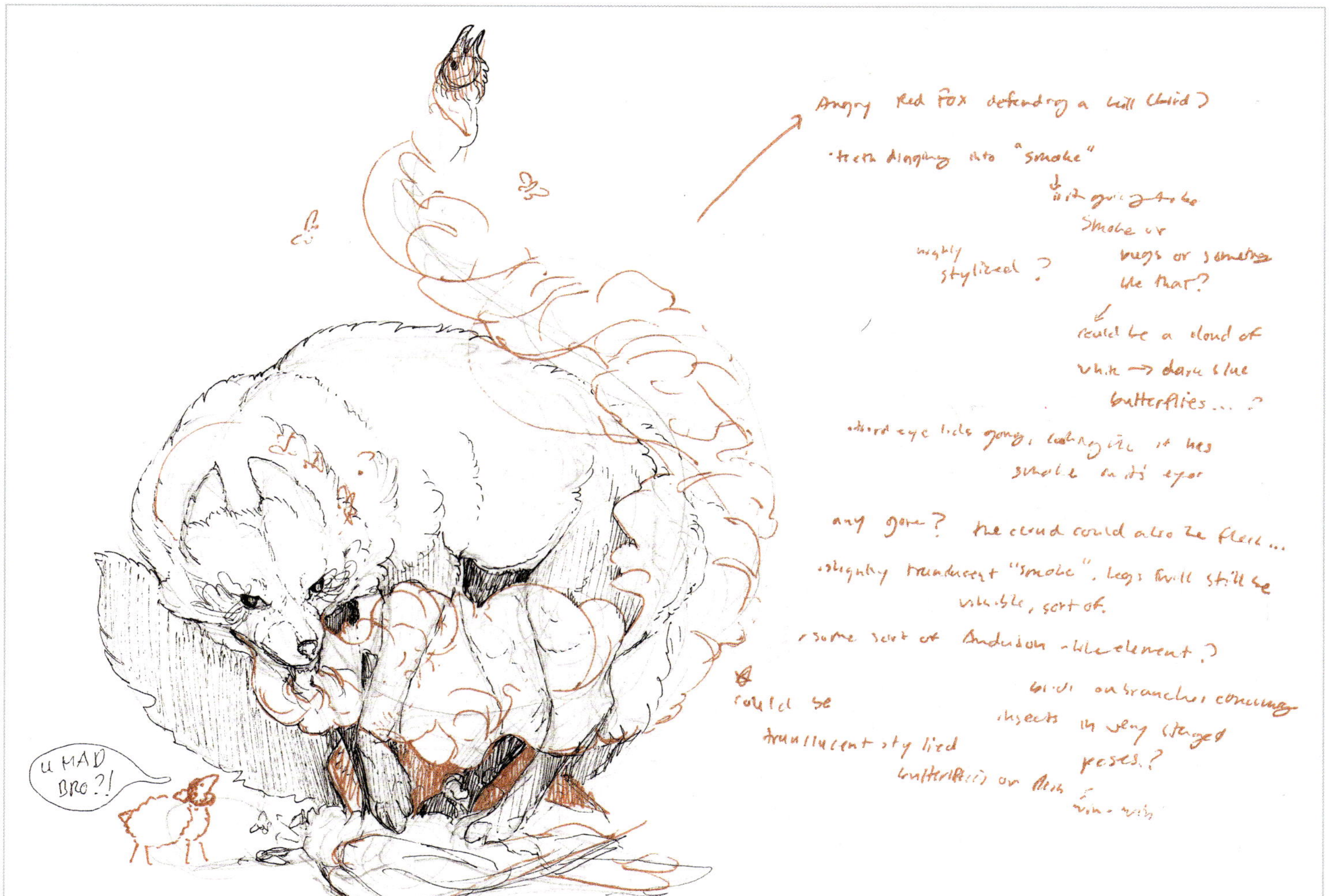

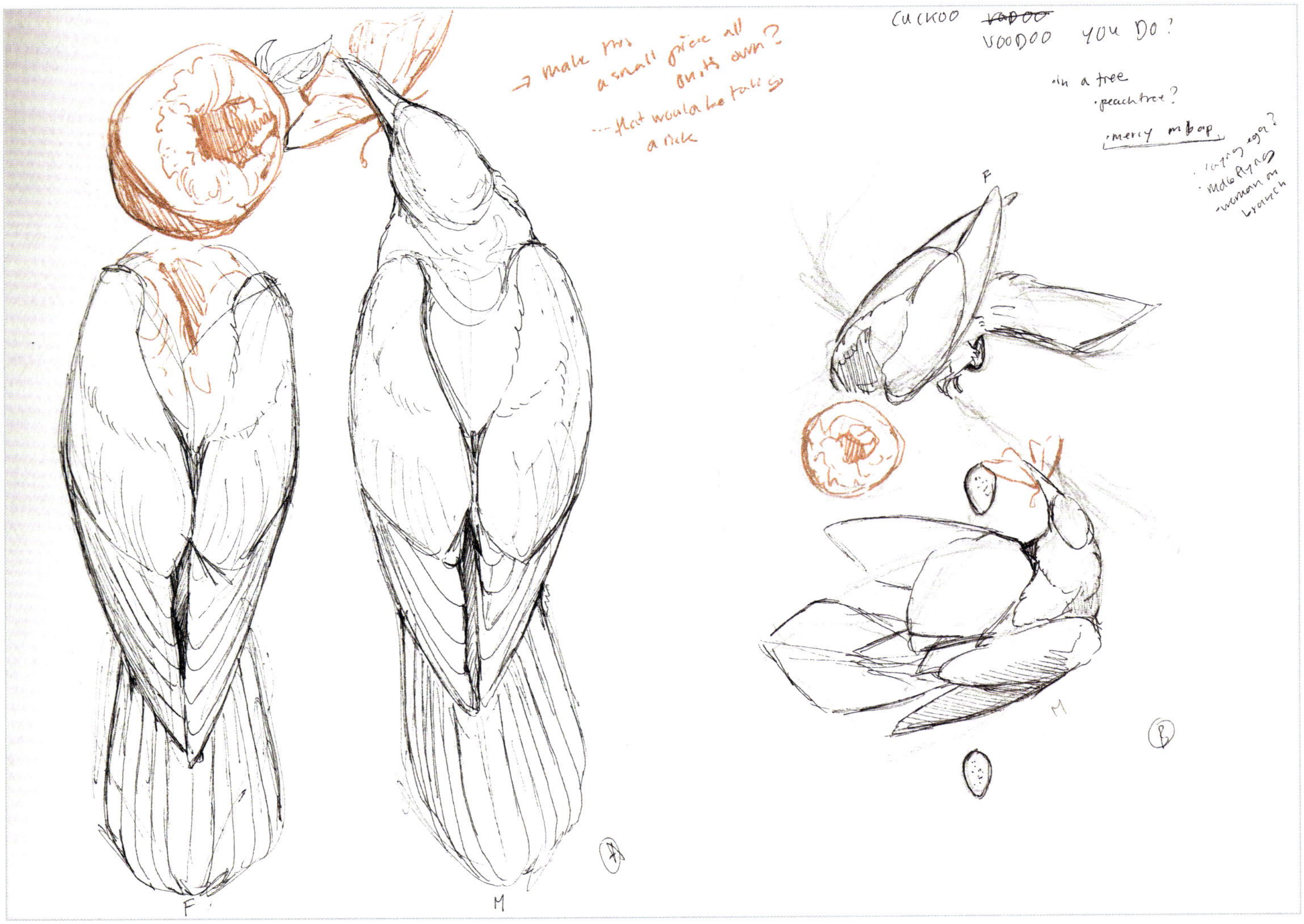

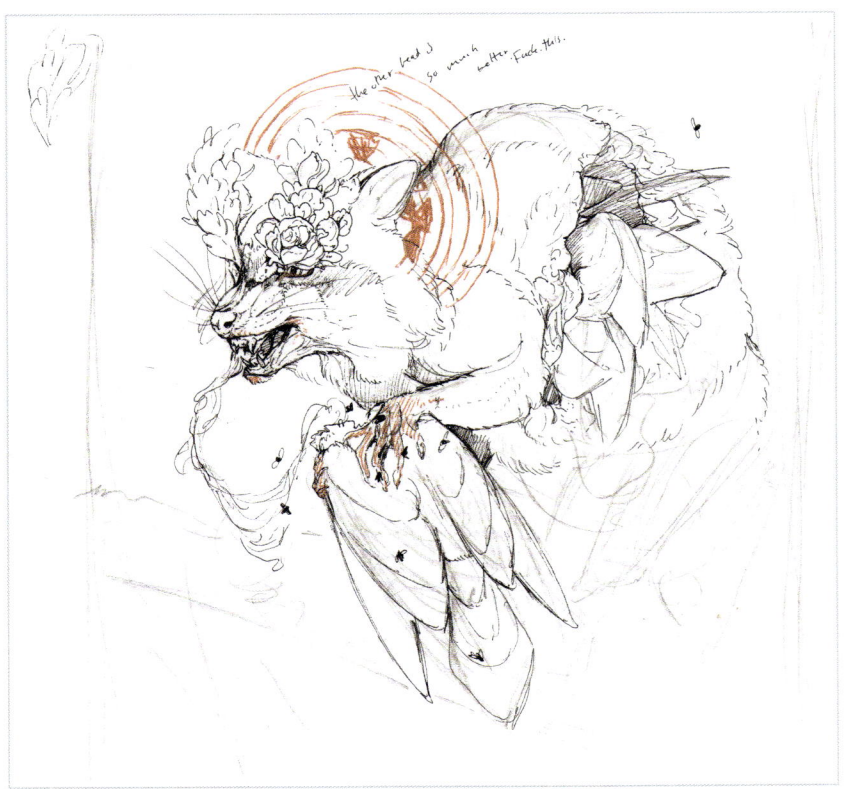
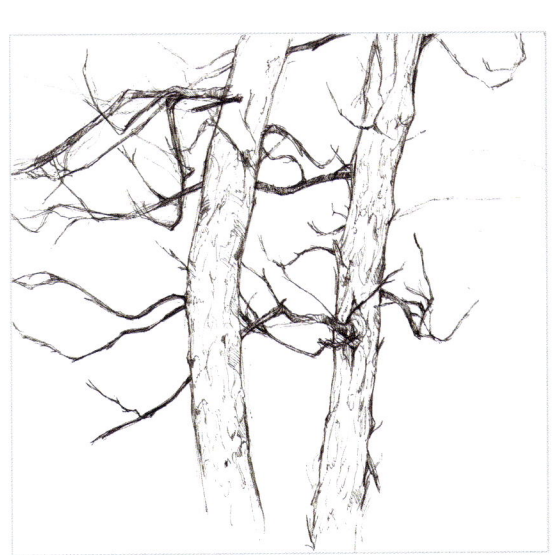

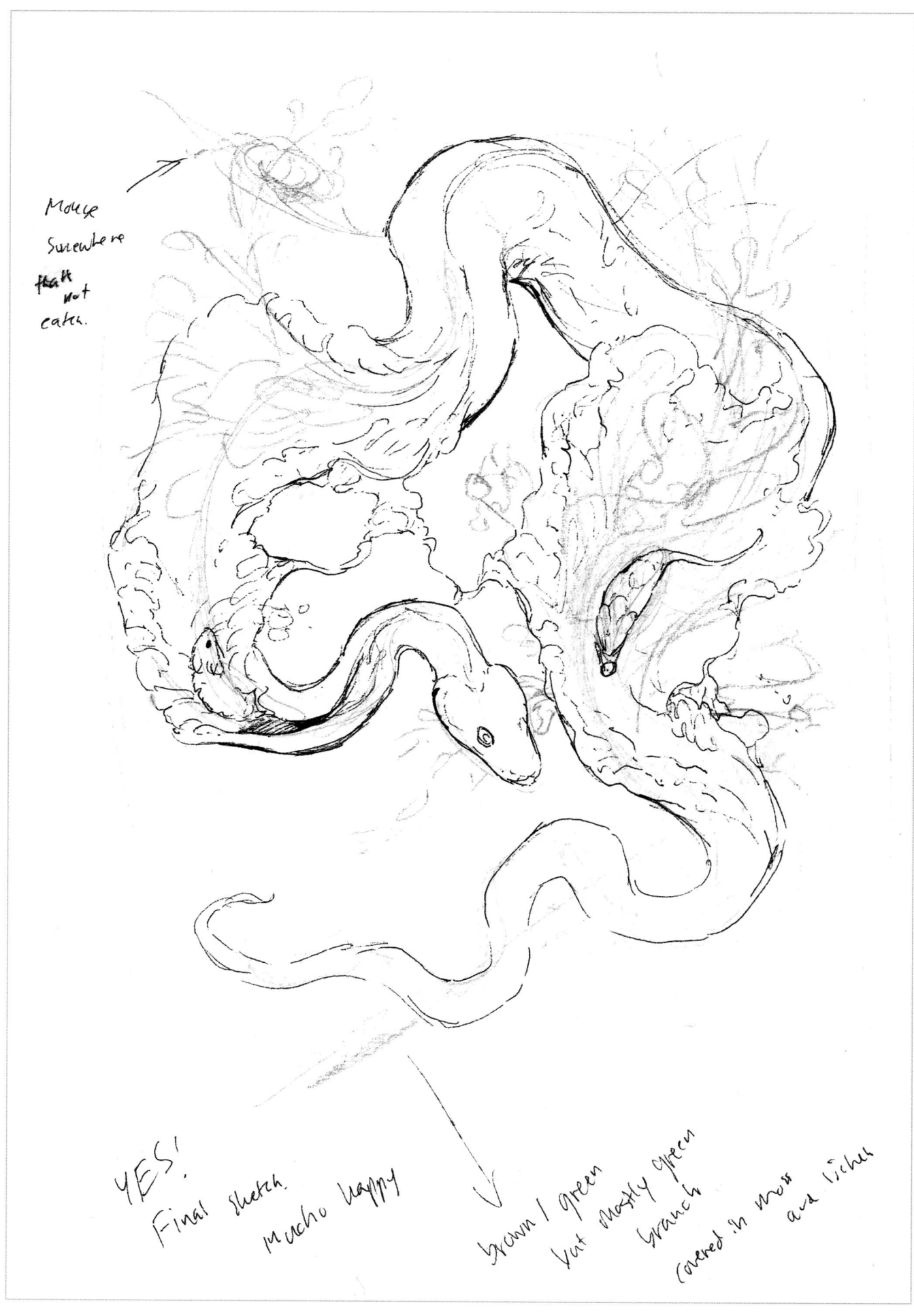

Mouse
Somewhere
that not
eaten.

YES!
Final sketch.
mucho happy

brown / green
but mostly green
branch
covered in moss
and lichen

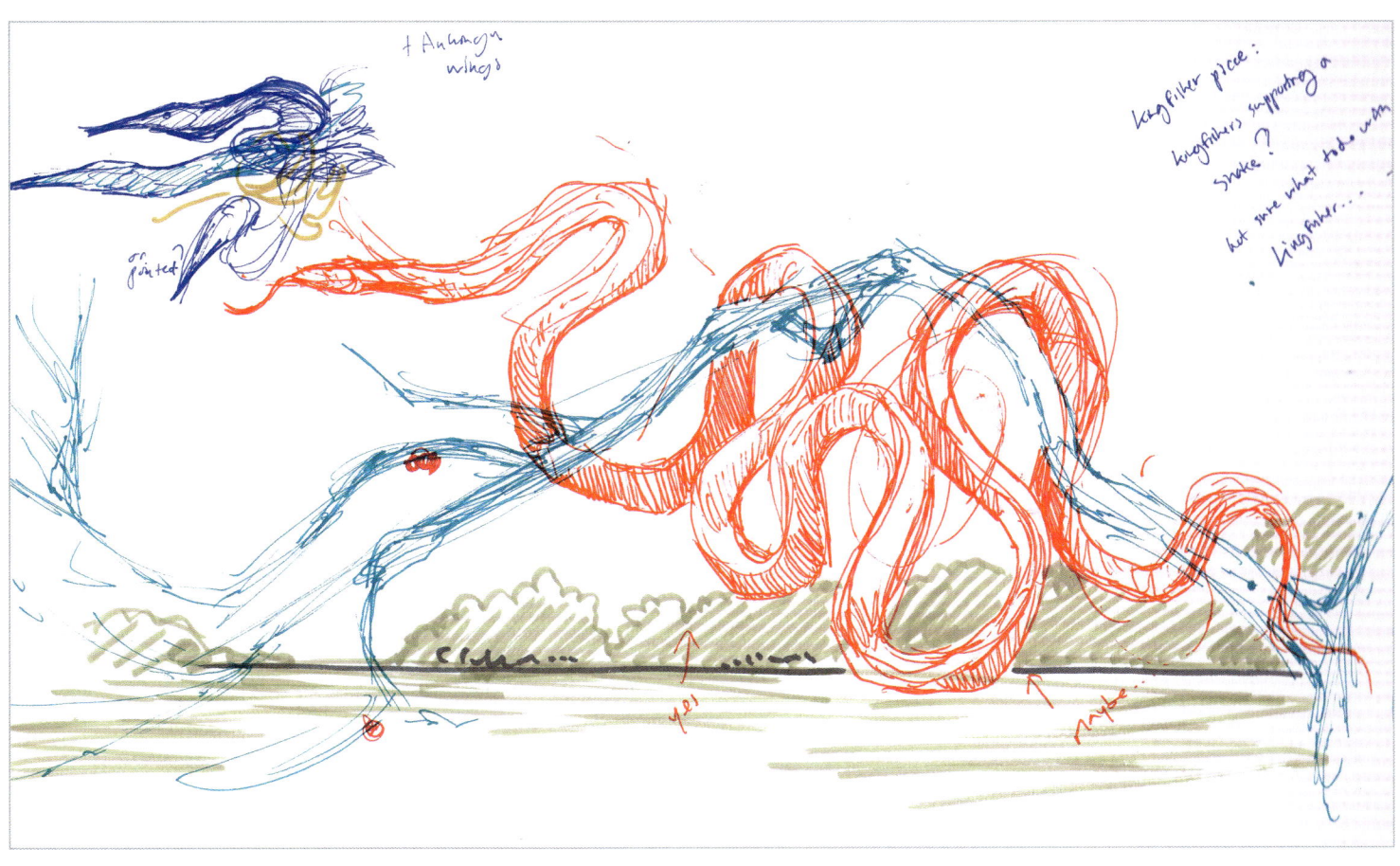

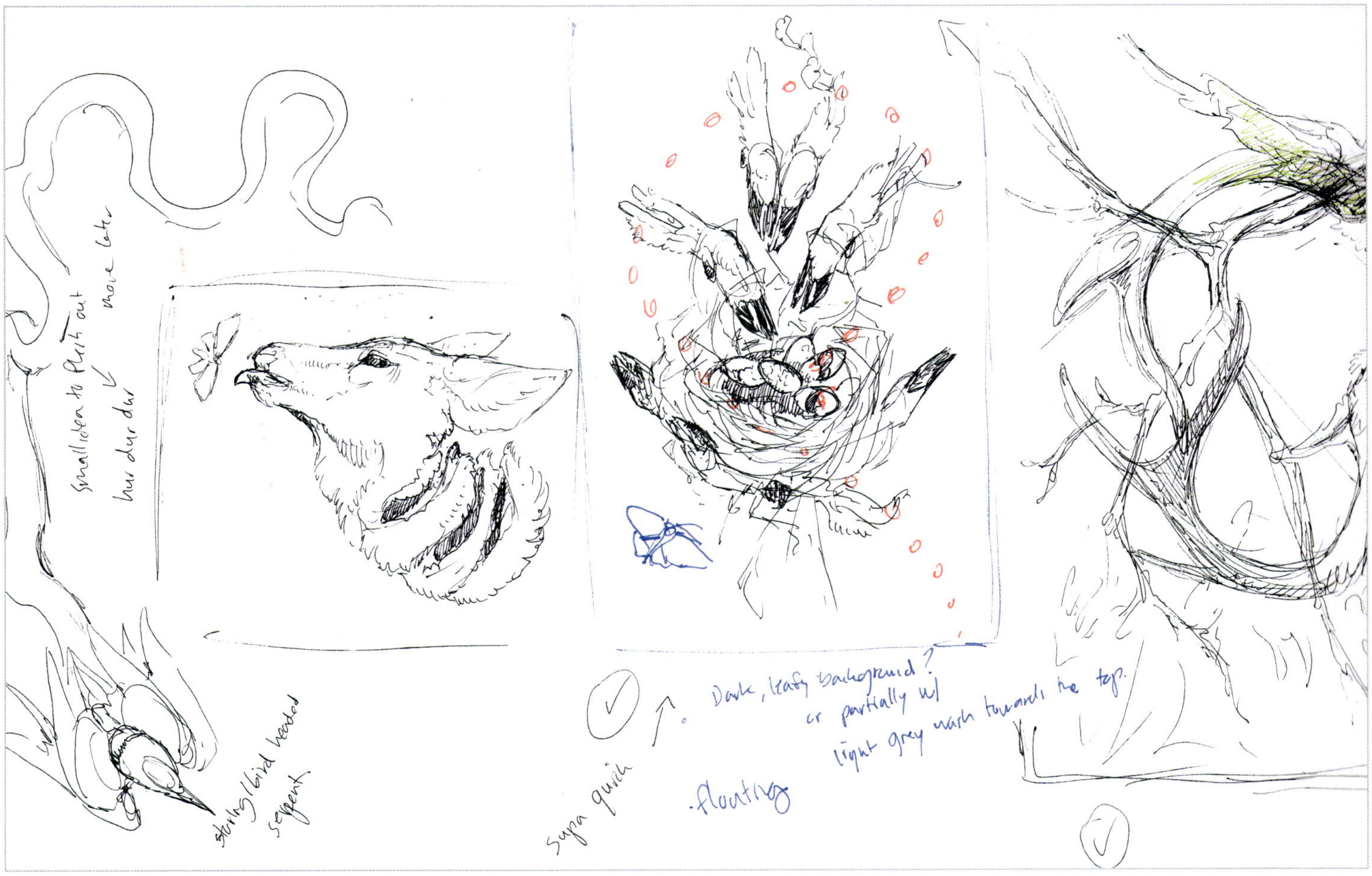

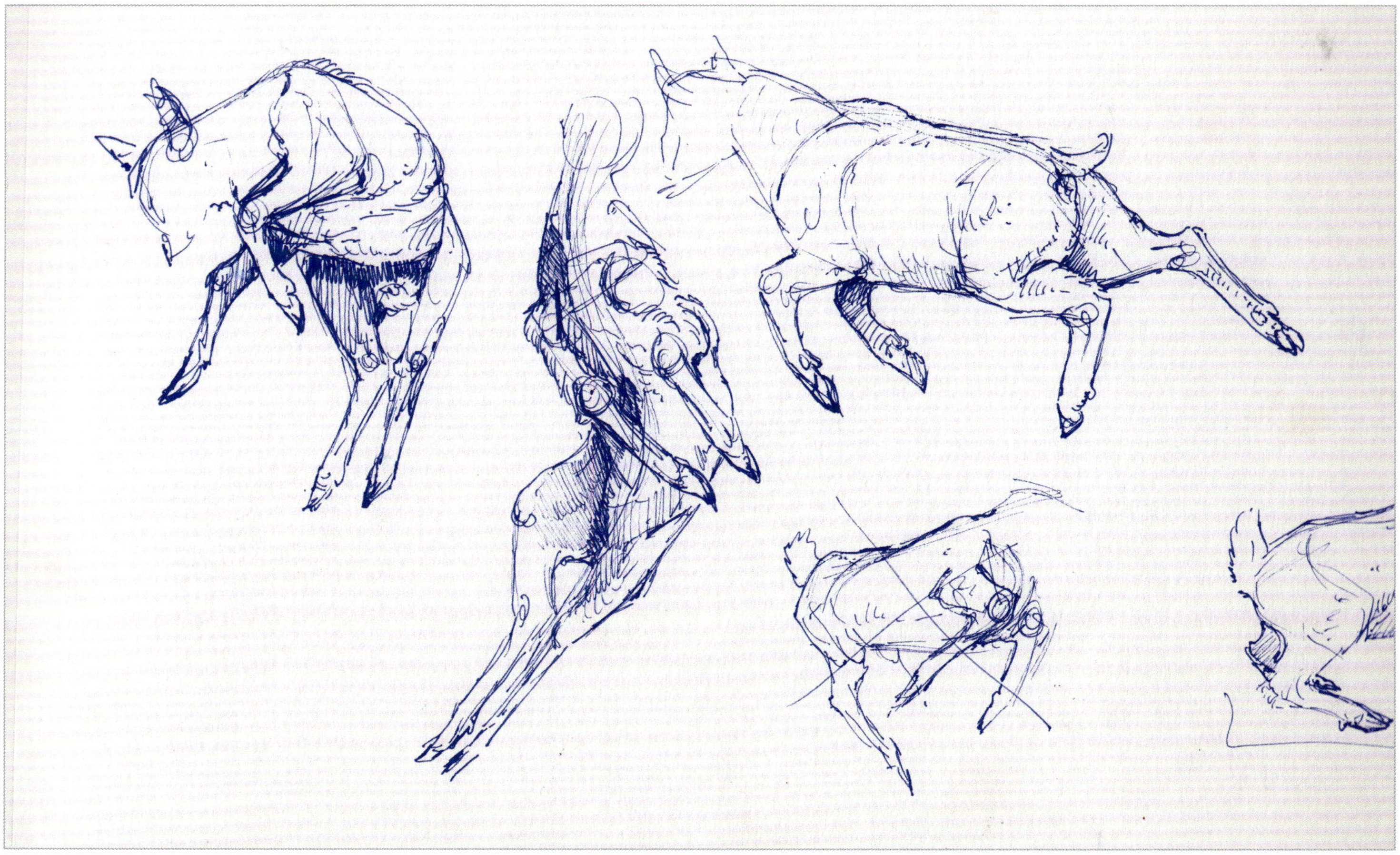

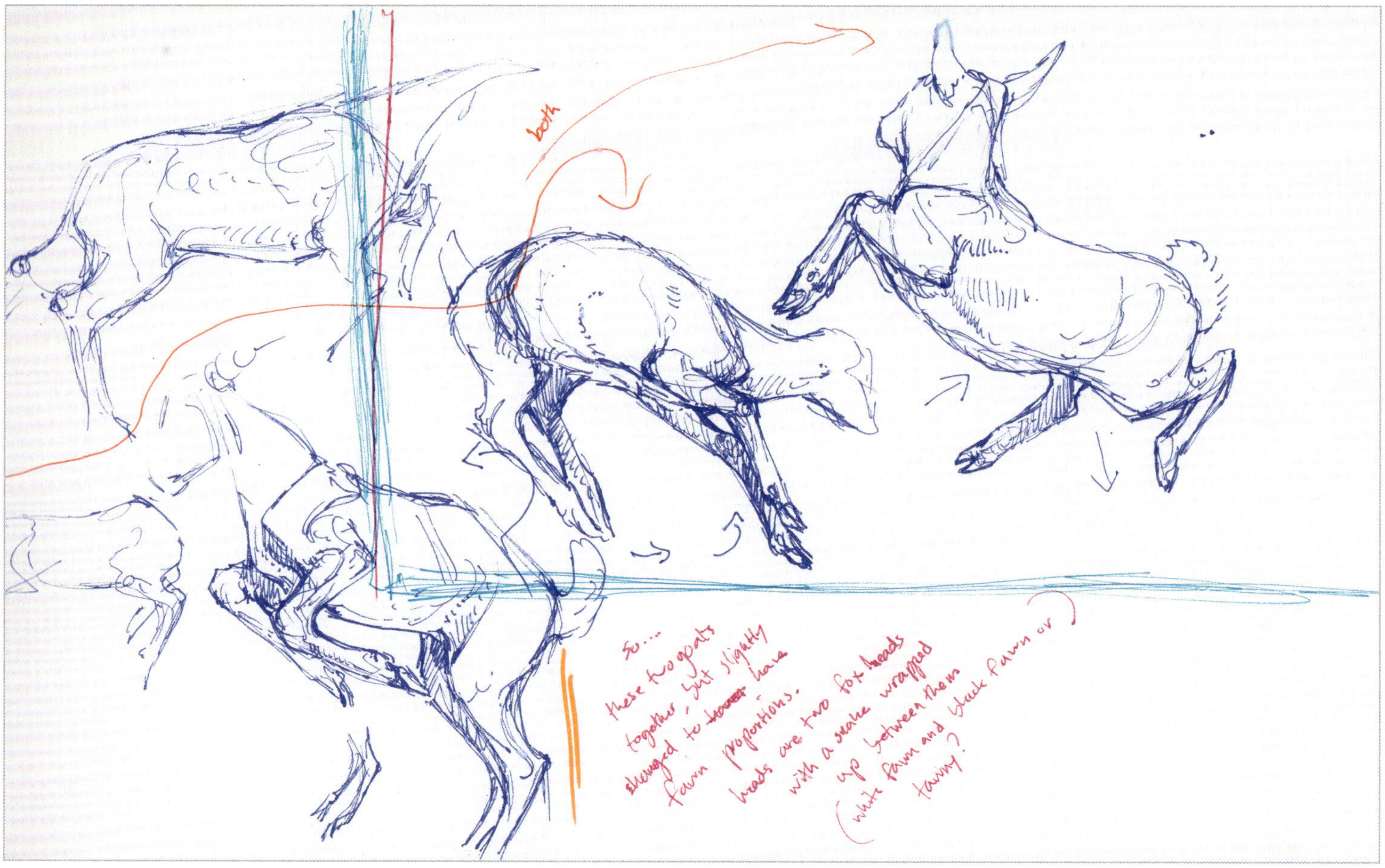

So...
these two goats
together, but slightly
skewed to be a have
fawn proportions.
heads are two fox heads
with a seam wrapped
up between them
(white fawn and black fawn or)
tawny?

"Love" : white rabbit with fawn skull entangeled in it   (large)

Things to include:
- chemical makeup of Dopamine
- white rabbit
- love colors: pinks, reds, teals, "soft" blues
    - VIBRANT.
- chantrelles : Contemplation of Lepus
- lush as fuck
- european starling

dopamine if possible
or some sort of "love drug"

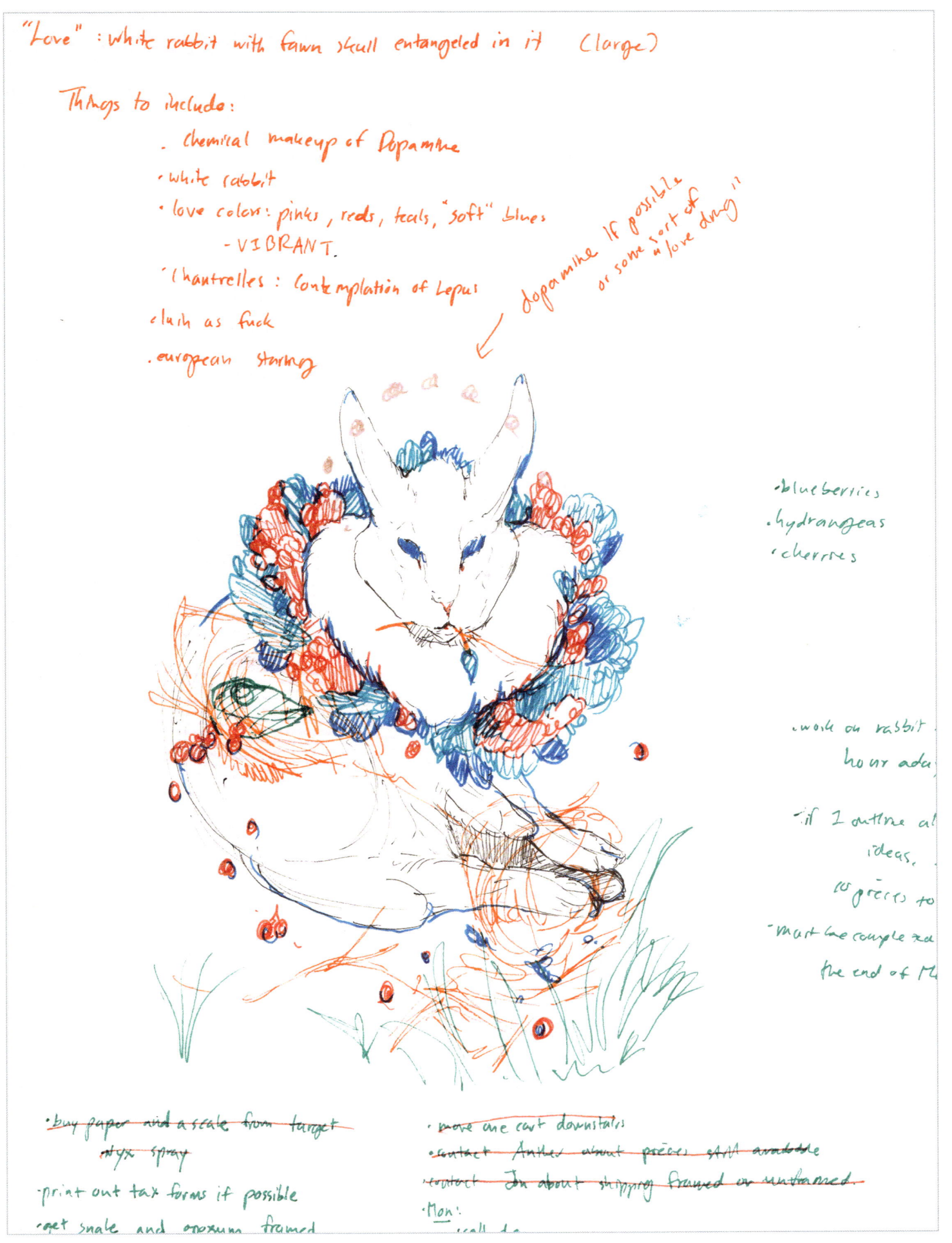

- blueberries
- hydrangeas
- cherries

- work on rabbit
    hour ada_
- if I outline al
    ideas,
    10 pieces to
- must be couple za_
    the end of M_

- buy paper ~~and a scale from target~~
    ~~Nyx spray~~
- print out tax forms if possible
- get snale and opossum framed

- ~~move one cart downstairs~~
- ~~contact Amber about pieces still available~~
- ~~contact Jon about shipping framed or unframed~~
- Mon:
    - call to

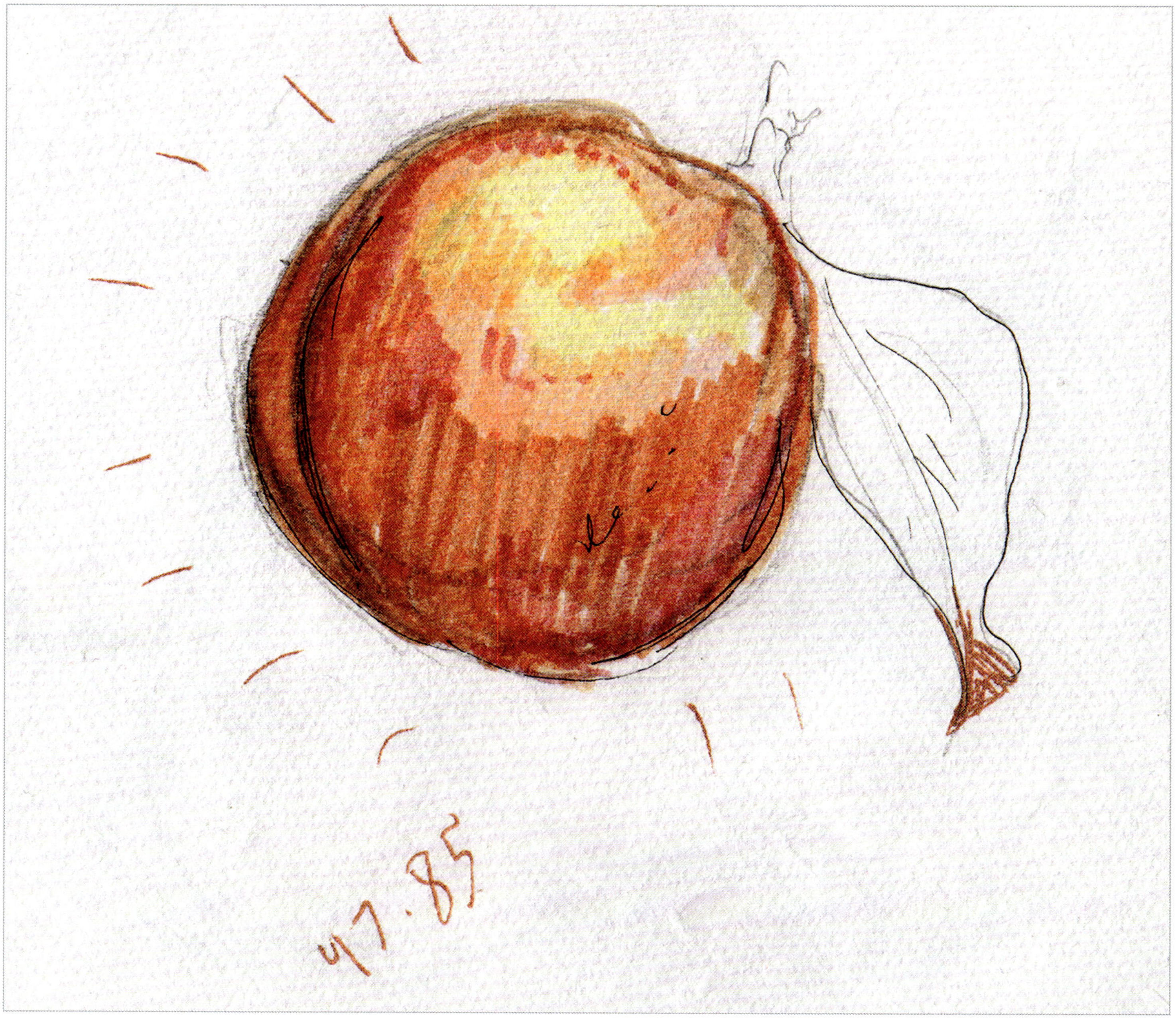

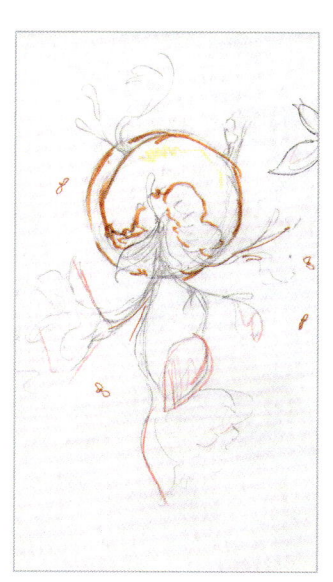

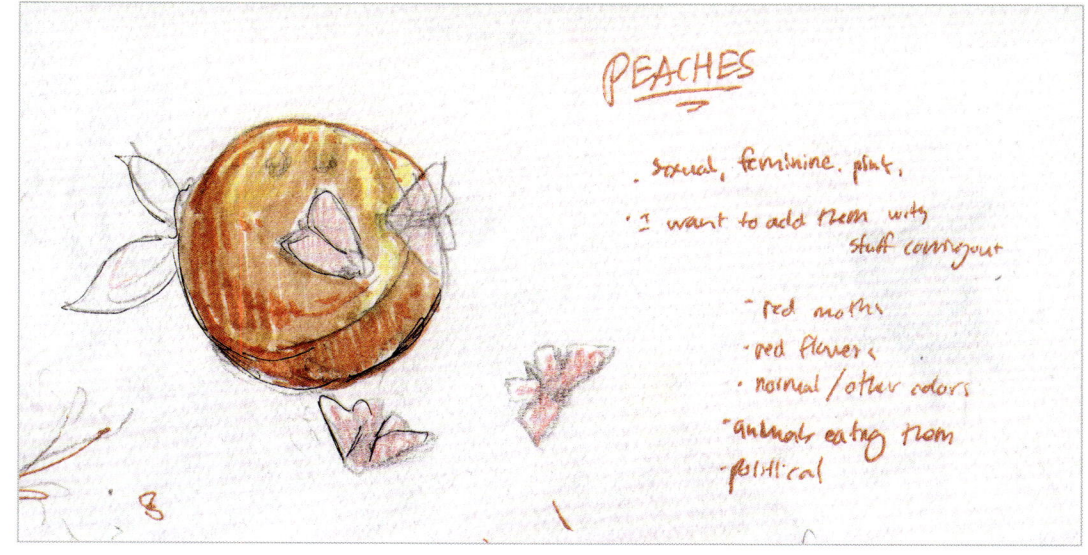

47.85

PEACHES

· sexual, feminine, pink.

· I want to add them with
                    stuff coming out

   · red moths
   · red flowers
   · normal / other colors
· animals eating from
· political

140

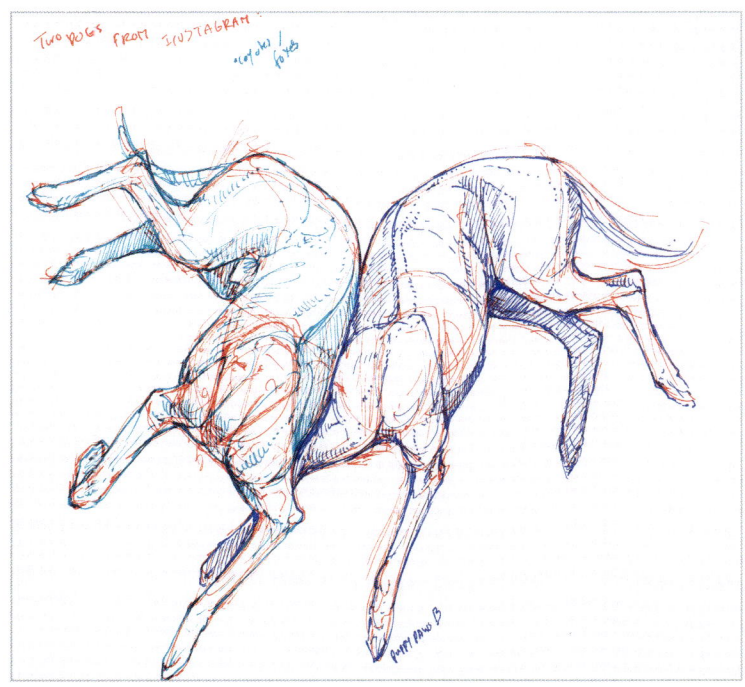

TWO DOGS FROM INSTAGRAM

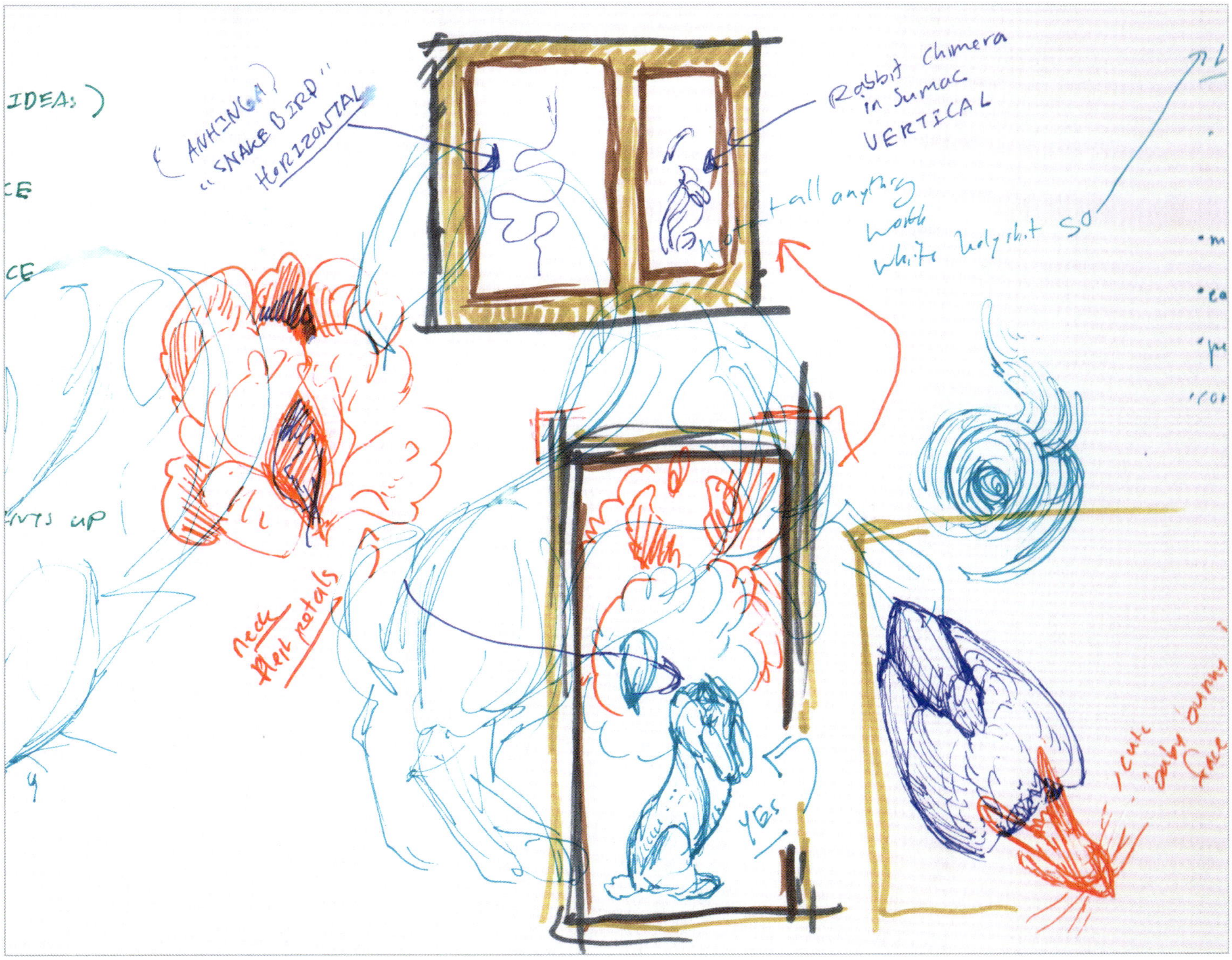

POMMPAW B

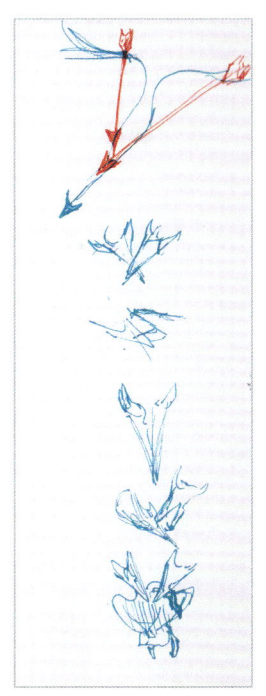

(IDEAS)

CE

CE

(ANHINGA)
"SNAKE BIRD"
HORIZONTAL

Rabbit Chimera
in Sumac
VERTICAL

Rabbit — all anything
with
white body shit SO

NTS UP

need
feet metals

cute
baby bunny
face

YES

141

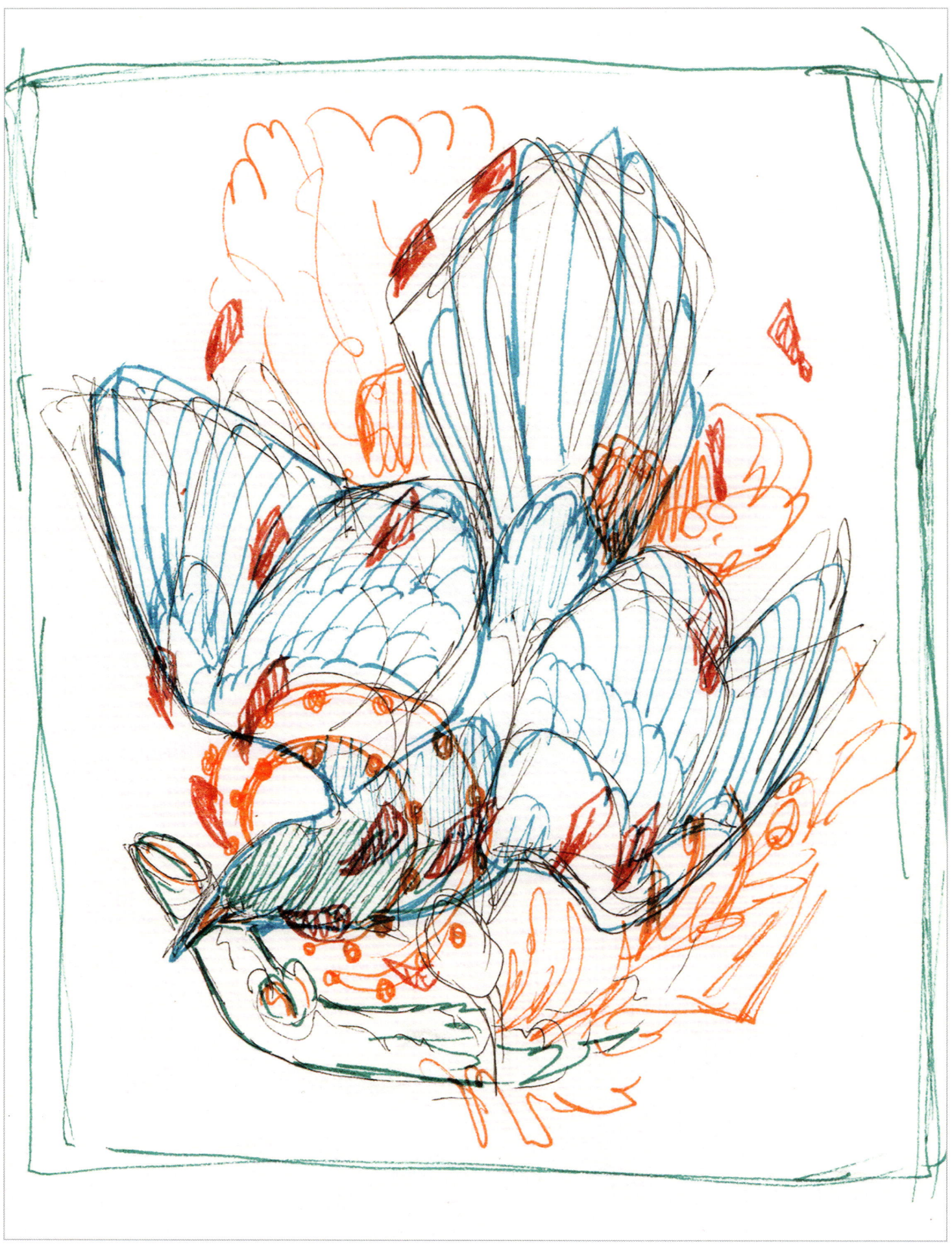

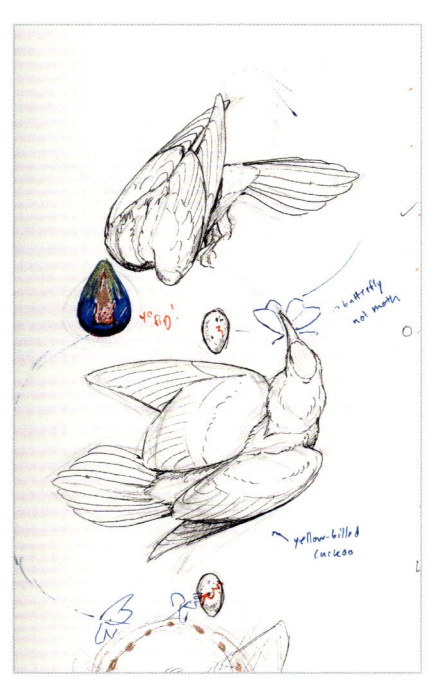

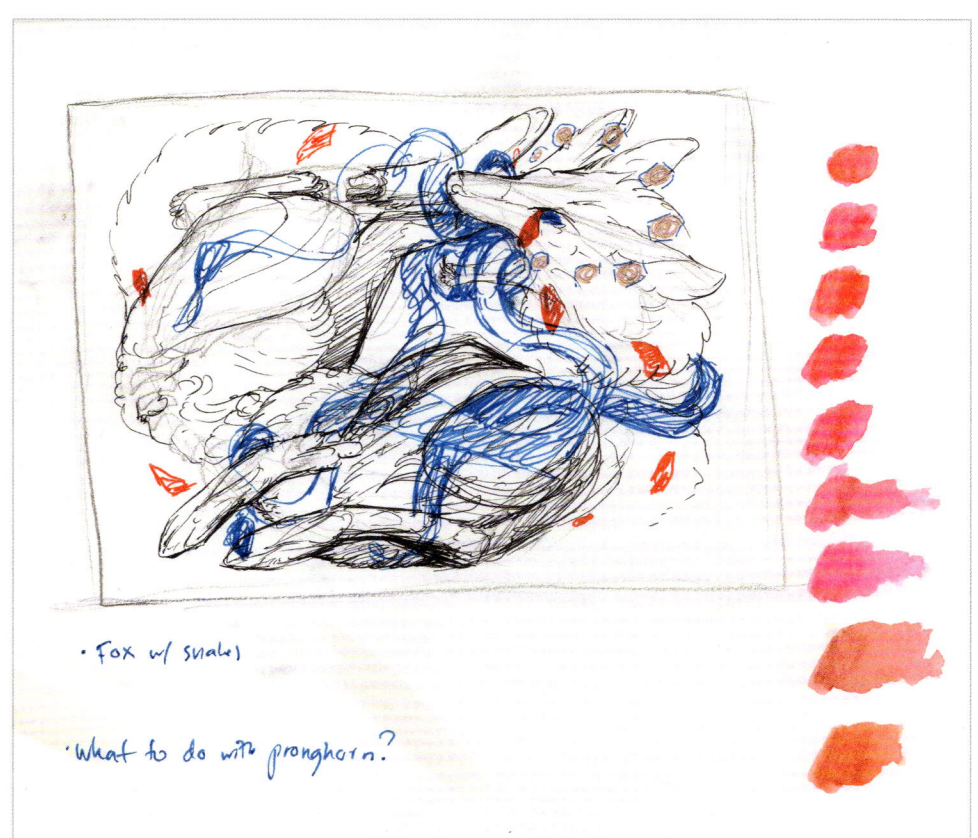

• Fox w/ snakes

• What to do with pronghorn?

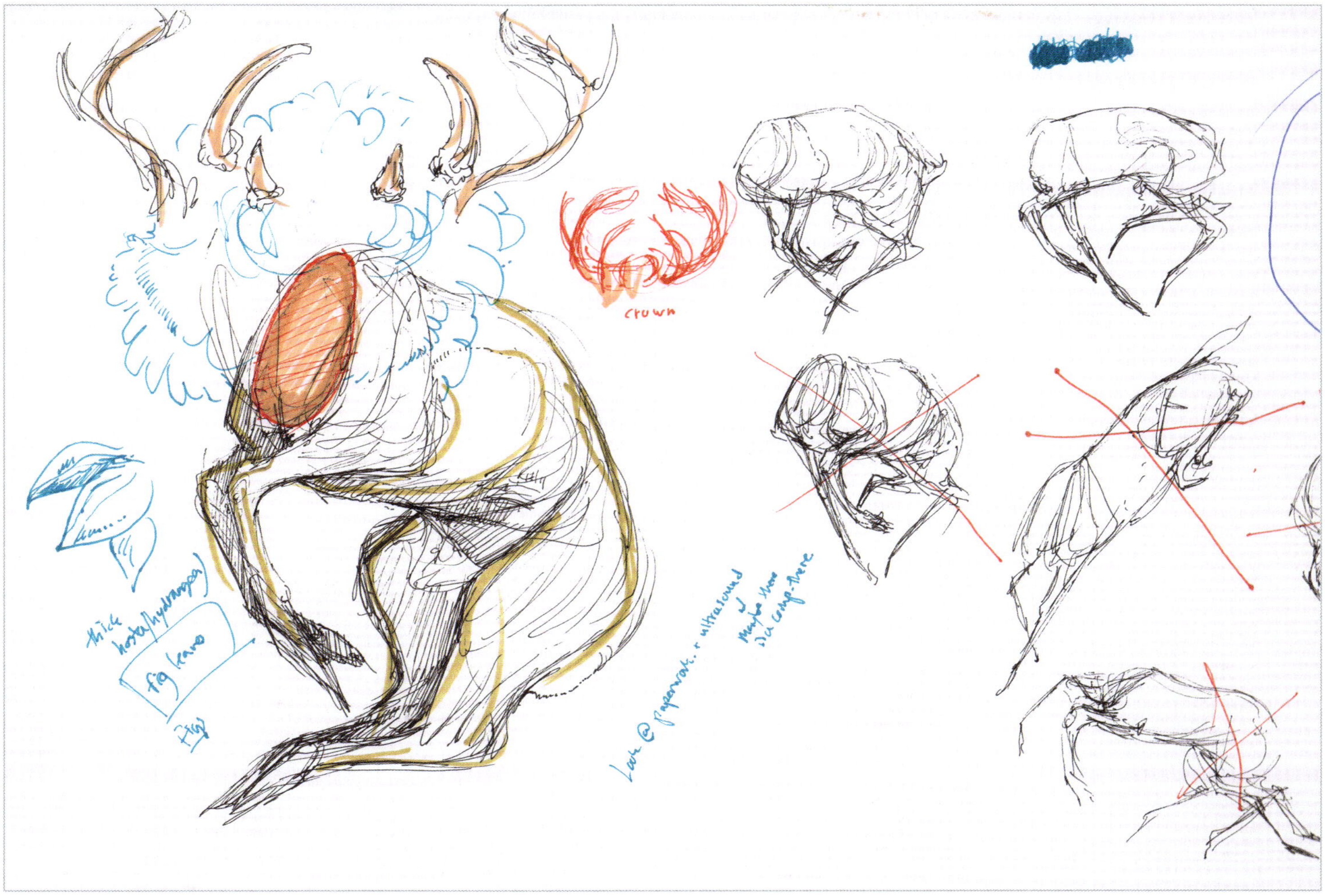

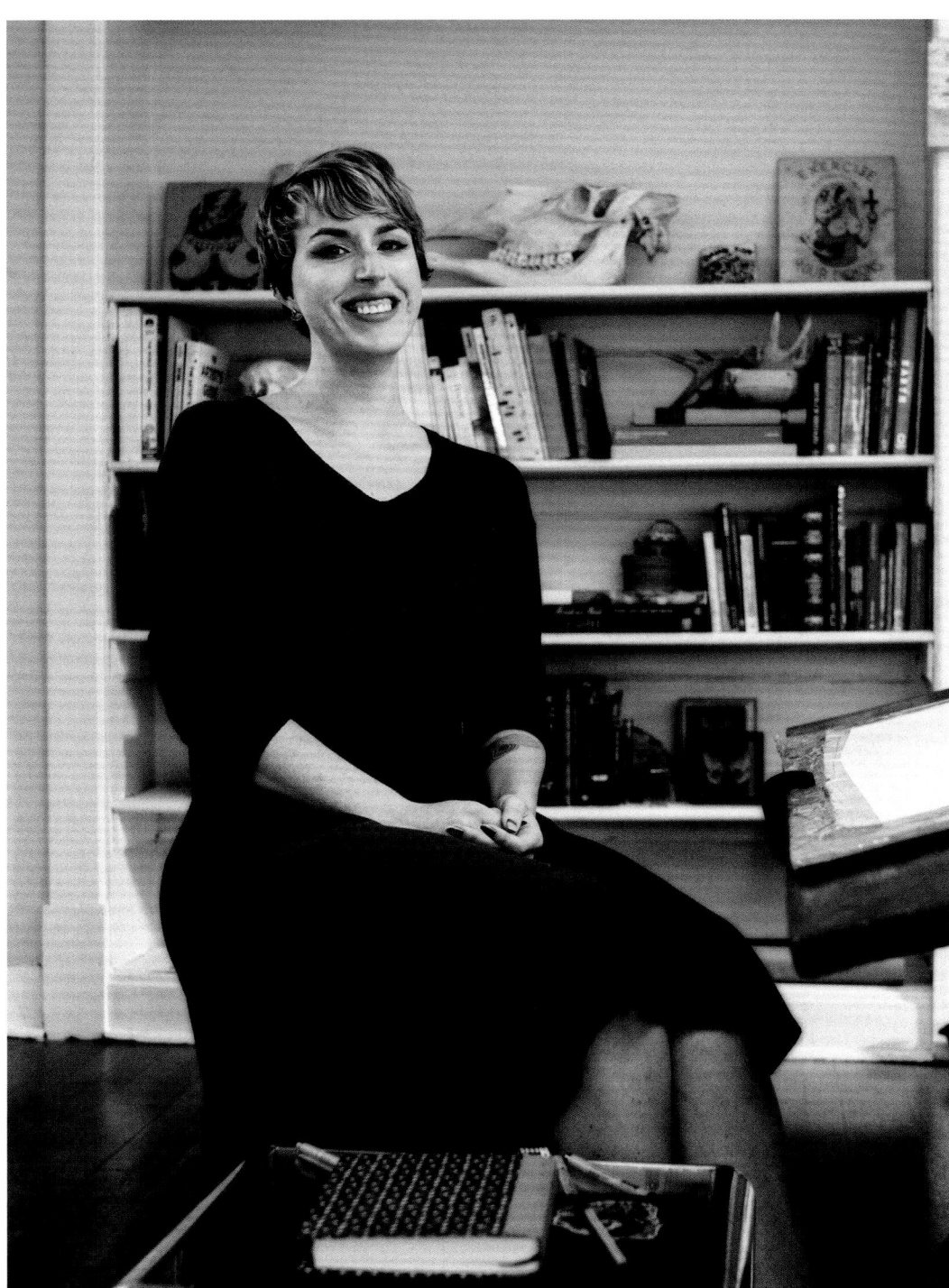

Photo by VIRGINIA HAROLD
www.VirginiaHarold.com

Lauren Marx (b. 1991) was raised and currently resides in Saint Louis, Missouri. She received her Bachelor of Fine Arts, with an emphasis in drawing, in 2014 from Webster University's Leigh Gerdine College of Fine Arts. Since then, Lauren has dedicated her life to pursuing her passion for illustration and furthering her love of the natural as well as the supernatural world. Lauren primarily works in permanent or semi-permanent drawing mediums such as pen, ink, and watercolor. Her work focuses on utilizing the native flora and fauna of North America to explore themes of life and death, historic religious symbolism in art, and her own mental health. Lauren's art is heavily influenced by her love of scientific illustration, medieval marginalia and bestiaries, and Renaissance religious paintings. She continues to create new and engaging work, which you can see and follow at LaurenMarx.com and on Instagram @LaurenMarxArt.

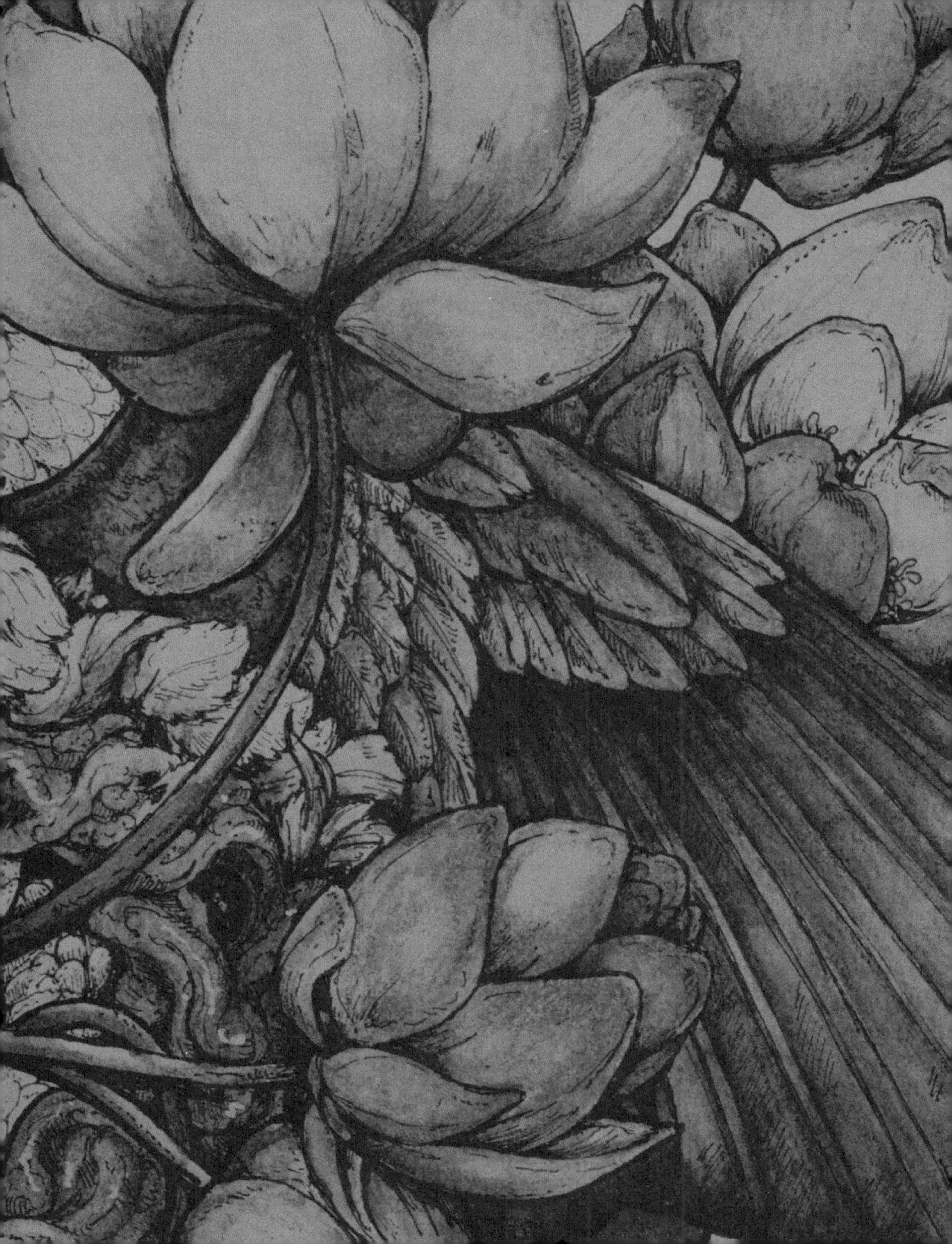

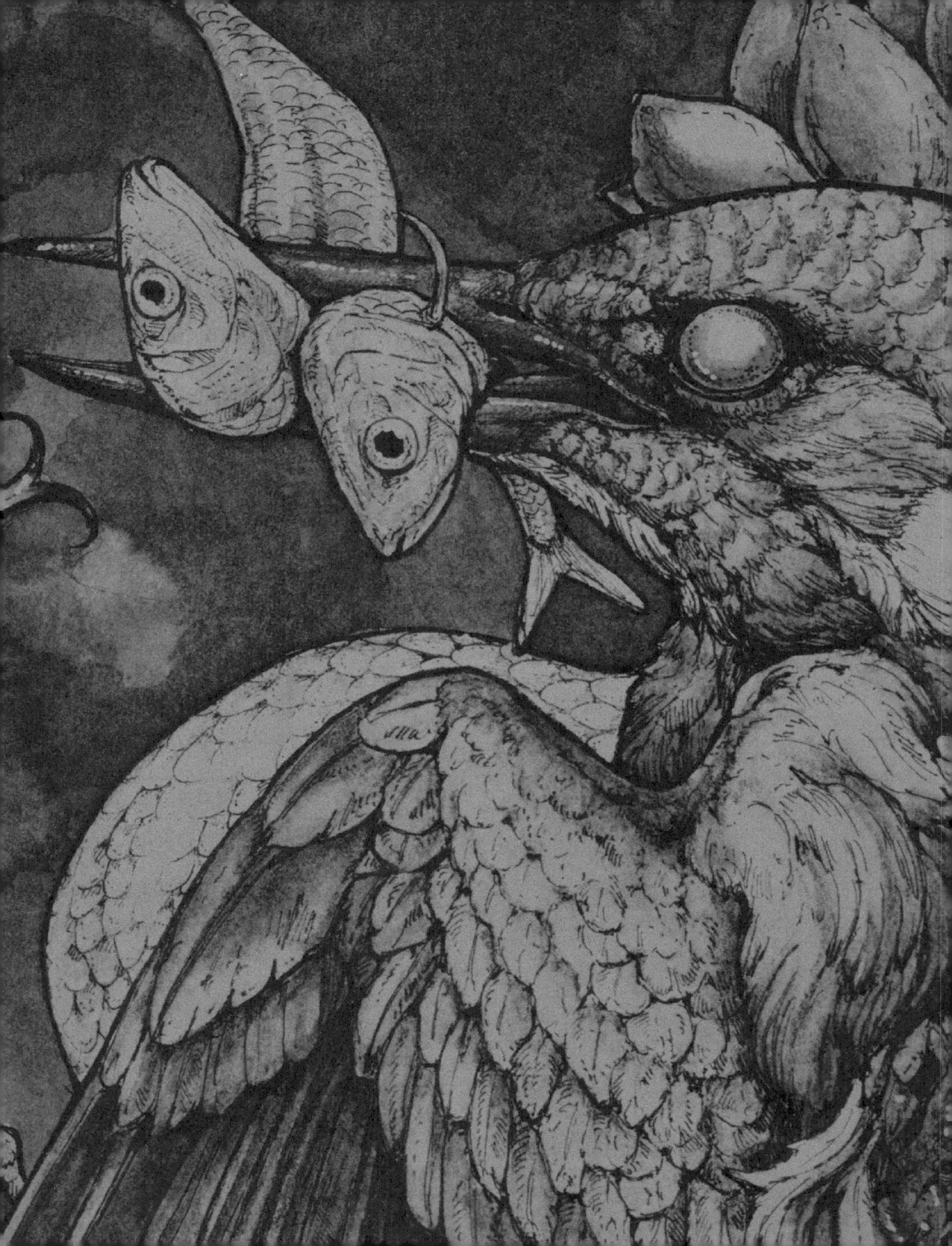